P9-DOG-720

The
Economist

Pocket
World in
Figures

2013 Edition

THE ECONOMIST IN ASSOCIATION WITH
PROFILE BOOKS LTD

Published by Profile Books Ltd,
3A Exmouth House, Pine Street, London EC1R OJH

This edition published by Profile Books in association with
The Economist, 2012

Material researched and compiled by
Andrea Burgess, Mark Doyle, Ian Emery, James Fransham,
Andrew Gilbert, Conrad Heine, Carol Howard, David McKelvey,
Jane Shaw, Roxana Willis, Christopher Wilson

Typeset in Officina by MacGuru Ltd
info@macguru.org.uk

Printed in Italy by
L.E.G.O Spa. Lavis

A CIP catalogue record for this book is available
from the British Library

ISBN 978 1 84668 599 6

Contents

CONTENTS

Notes

This 2013 edition of *The Economist Pocket World in Figures*
includes new rankings on such diverse topics as mobile
banking, a global peace index, art museums, Olympic venues
and athletes, the shadow economy, species under threat and
more city data. The world rankings consider 194 countries, all
those with a population of at least 1m or a GDP of at least
$1bn, they are listed on pages 250–54. The country profiles
cover 67 major countries. Also included are profiles of the
euro area and the world. The extent and quality of the
statistics available varies from country to country. Every care
has been taken to specify the broad definitions on which the
data are based and to indicate cases where data quality or
technical difficulties are such that interpretation of the
figures is likely to be seriously affected. Nevertheless, figures
from individual countries may differ from standard
international statistical definitions. The term "country" can
also refer to territories or economic entities.

Some country definitions
Macedonia is officially known as the Former Yugoslav Republic
of Macedonia. Data for Cyprus normally refer to Greek Cyprus
only. Data for China do not include Hong Kong or Macau.
Bosnia includes Herzegovina. Data for Sudan are largely for
the country before it became two countries, Sudan and South
Sudan, in July 2011. For countries such as Morocco they
exclude disputed areas. Congo-Kinshasa refers to the
Democratic Republic of Congo, formerly known as Zaire.
Congo-Brazzaville refers to the other Congo. Data for the EU
refer to the 27 members as at January 1 2007, unless
otherwise noted. Euro area data normally refer to the 16
members that had adopted the euro as at December 31 2009:
Austria, Belgium, Cyprus, France, Finland, Germany, Greece,
Ireland, Italy, Luxembourg, Malta, Netherlands, Portugal,
Slovakia, Slovenia and Spain. Some tables include Estonia
which joined in January 2011. For more information about the
EU and the euro area see the glossary on pages 248–9.

Statistical basis
The all-important factor in a book of this kind is to be able to
make reliable comparisons between countries. Although this
is never quite possible for the reasons stated above, the best
route, which this book takes, is to compare data for the same
year or period and to use actual, not estimated, figures
wherever possible. In some cases, only OECD members are

considered. Where a country's data is excessively out of date, it is excluded. The research for this edition of *The Economist Pocket World in Figures* was carried out in 2012 using the latest available sources that present data on an internationally comparable basis.

Data in the country profiles, unless otherwise indicated, refer to the year ending December 31 2010. Life expectancy, crude birth, death and fertility rates are based on 2010–15 projected averages; human development indices for 2011 and energy data are for 2009; marriage and divorce, employment, health and education, consumer goods and services data refer to the latest year for which figures are available; internet hosts are as at January 2012.

Other definitions

Data shown in country profiles may not always be consistent with those shown in the world rankings because the definitions or years covered can differ.

Statistics for principal exports and principal imports are normally based on customs statistics. These are generally compiled on different definitions to the visible exports and imports figures shown in the balance of payments section.

Definitions of the statistics shown are given on the relevant page or in the glossary on pages 248–9. Figures may not add exactly to totals, or percentages to 100, because of rounding or, in the case of GDP, statistical adjustment. Sums of money have generally been converted to US dollars at the official exchange rate ruling at the time to which the figures refer.

Energy consumption data are not always reliable, particularly for the major oil producing countries; consumption per head data may therefore be higher than in reality. Energy exports can exceed production and imports can exceed consumption if transit operations distort trade data or oil is imported for refining and re-exported.

Abbreviations

bn	billion (one thousand million)	ha	hectare
EU	European Union	m	million
g	kilogram	PPP	Purchasing power parity
km	kilometre	TOE	tonnes of oil equivalent
GDP	Gross domestic product	trn	trillion (one thousand billion)
GNI	Gross national income	...	not available

World rankings

Countries: natural facts

Countries: *the largest*[a]

'000 sq km

1	Russia	17,075	31	Tanzania	945
2	Canada	9,971	32	Nigeria	924
3	China	9,561	33	Venezuela	912
4	United States	9,373	34	Namibia	824
5	Brazil	8,512	35	Pakistan	804
6	Australia	7,682	36	Mozambique	799
7	India	3,287	37	Turkey	779
8	Argentina	2,767	38	Chile	757
9	Kazakhstan	2,717	39	Zambia	753
10	Algeria	2,382	40	Myanmar	677
11	Congo-Kinshasa	2,345	41	Afghanistan	652
12	Saudi Arabia	2,200	42	South Sudan	644
13	Greenland	2,176	43	Somalia	638
14	Mexico	1,973	44	Central African Rep.	622
15	Indonesia	1,904	45	Ukraine	604
16	Sudan	1,862	46	Madagascar	587
17	Libya	1,760	47	Kenya	583
18	Iran	1,648	48	Botswana	581
19	Mongolia	1,565	49	France	544
20	Peru	1,285	50	Yemen	528
21	Chad	1,284	51	Thailand	513
22	Niger	1,267	52	Spain	505
23	Angola	1,247	53	Turkmenistan	488
24	Mali	1,240	54	Cameroon	475
25	South Africa	1,226	55	Papua New Guinea	463
26	Colombia	1,142	56	Sweden	450
27	Ethiopia	1,134	57	Morocco	447
28	Bolivia	1,099		Uzbekistan	447
29	Mauritania	1,031	59	Iraq	438
30	Egypt	1,000	60	Paraguay	407

Mountains: *the highest*[b]

	Name	Location	Height (m)
1	Everest	China-Nepal	8,848
2	K2 (Godwin Austen)	China-Jammu and Kashmir	8,611
3	Kangchenjunga	India-Nepal	8,586
4	Lhotse	China-Nepal	8,516
5	Makalu	China-Nepal	8,463
6	Cho Oyu	China-Nepal	8,201
7	Dhaulagiri	Nepal	8,167
8	Manaslu	Nepal	8,163
9	Nanga Parbat	Jammu and Kashmir	8,126
10	Annapurna I	Nepal	8,091
11	Gasherbrum I	China-Jammu and Kashmir	8,068
12	Broad Peak	China-Jammu and Kashmir	8,047
13	Gasherbrum II	China-Jammu and Kashmir	8,035
14	Xixabangma Feng	China	8,012

a Includes freshwater.
b Includes separate peaks which are part of the same massif.

Rivers: *the longest*

Name	Location	Length (km)
1 Nile	Africa	6,695
2 Amazon	South America	6,516
3 Yangtze	Asia	6,380
4 Mississippi-Missouri system	North America	5,959
5 Ob'-Irtysh	Asia	5,568
6 Yenisey-Angara-Selanga	Asia	5,550
7 Huang He (Yellow)	Asia	5,464
8 Congo	Africa	4,667
9 Río de la Plata-Paraná	South America	4,500
10 Irtysh	Asia	4,440

Deserts: *the largest*

Name	Location	Area ('000 sq km)
1 Sahara	Northern Africa	8,600
2 Arabian	South-western Asia	2,300
3 Gobi	Mongolia/China	1,166
4 Patagonian	Argentina	673
5 Great Victoria	Western and Southern Australia	647
6 Great Basin	South-western United States	492
7 Chihuahuan	Northern Mexico	450
8 Great Sandy	Western Australia	400

Lakes: *the largest*

Name	Location	Area ('000 sq km)
1 Caspian Sea	Central Asia	371
2 Superior	Canadat/United States	82
3 Victoria	East Africa	69
4 Huron	Canada/United States	60
5 Michigan	United States	58
6 Tanganyika	East Africa	33
7 Baikal	Russia	31
Great Bear	Canada	31

Islands: *the largest*

Name	Location	Area ('000 sq km)
1 Greenland	North Atlantic Ocean	2,176
2 New Guinea	South-west Pacific Ocean	809
3 Borneo	Western Pacific Ocean	746
4 Madagascar	Indian Ocean	587
5 Baffin	North Atlantic Ocean	507
6 Sumatra	North-east Indian Ocean	474
7 Honshu	Sea of Japan-Pacific Ocean	227
8 Great Britain	Off coast of north-west Europe	218

Notes: Estimates of the lengths of rivers vary widely depending on eg, the path to take through a delta. The definition of a desert is normally a mean annual precipitation value equal to 250ml or less. Australia is defined as a continent rather than an island.

Population: size and growth

Largest populations
Million, 2010

1	China	1,354.1	34	Poland	38.0
2	India	1,214.5	35	Algeria	35.4
3	United States	317.6	36	Canada	33.9
4	Indonesia	232.5	37	Uganda	33.8
5	Brazil	195.4	38	Morocco	32.4
6	Pakistan	184.8	39	Iraq	31.5
7	Bangladesh	164.4	40	Nepal	29.9
8	Nigeria	158.3	41	Peru	29.5
9	Russia	140.4	42	Afghanistan	29.1
10	Japan	127.0	43	Venezuela	29.0
11	Mexico	110.6	44	Malaysia	27.9
12	Philippines	93.6	45	Uzbekistan	27.8
13	Vietnam	89.0	46	Saudi Arabia	26.2
14	Ethiopia	85.0	47	Ghana	24.3
15	Egypt	84.5		Yemen	24.3
16	Germany	82.1	49	North Korea	24.0
17	Turkey	75.7	50	Mozambique	23.4
18	Iran	75.1	51	Taiwan	23.0
19	Thailand	68.1	52	Syria	22.5
20	Congo-Kinshasa	67.8	53	Côte d'Ivoire	21.6
21	France	62.6	54	Australia	21.5
22	United Kingdom	61.9	55	Romania	21.2
23	Italy	60.1	56	Sri Lanka	20.4
24	Myanmar	50.5	57	Madagascar	20.1
	South Africa	50.5	58	Cameroon	20.0
26	South Korea	48.5	59	Angola	19.0
27	Colombia	46.3	60	Chile	17.1
28	Ukraine	45.4	61	Netherlands	16.7
29	Spain	45.3	62	Burkina Faso	16.3
30	Tanzania	45.0	63	Niger	15.9
31	Sudan	43.2	64	Kazakhstan	15.8
32	Kenya	40.9	65	Malawi	15.7
33	Argentina	40.7	66	Cambodia	15.1

Largest populations
Million, 2025

1	India	1,459.0	15	Vietnam	99.3
2	China	1,395.3	16	Congo-Kinshasa	95.4
3	United States	349.8	17	Turkey	84.0
4	Indonesia	271.9	18	Iran	83.1
5	Nigeria	229.8	19	Germany	80.3
6	Pakistan	220.6	20	Thailand	72.9
7	Brazil	216.2	21	Tanzania	70.9
8	Bangladesh	175.2	22	United Kingdom	67.6
9	Russia	139.0	23	France	67.2
10	Mexico	131.0	24	Italy	61.1
11	Japan	122.8	25	Sudan	60.8
12	Philippines	118.1	26	Kenya	59.1
13	Ethiopia	110.0	27	Colombia	54.7
14	Egypt	100.9	28	South Africa	53.8

Fastest growing populations
Average annual % change, 2010–15

1	Niger	3.52	25	Chad		2.59
2	Malawi	3.24	26	Somalia		2.56
3	Uganda	3.14	27	Nigeria		2.53
4	Afghanistan	3.13	28	French Guiana		2.52
5	Iraq	3.10		Guatemala		2.52
6	Tanzania	3.08	30	Guinea		2.51
7	Zambia	3.05	31	Kuwait		2.41
8	Yemen	3.02	32	Sudan		2.39
9	Burkina Faso	2.98	33	Ghana		2.26
10	Mali	2.96	34	Mauritania		2.24
11	Rwanda	2.92		Mozambique		2.24
	Timor-Leste	2.92	36	Congo-Brazzaville		2.18
13	Eritrea	2.91		Côte d'Ivoire		2.18
14	Qatar	2.90	38	Papua New Guinea		2.17
15	Madagascar	2.82		United Arab Emirates		2.17
16	West Bank & Gaza	2.81	40	Zimbabwe		2.15
17	Equatorial Guinea	2.72	41	Cameroon		2.14
18	Angola	2.70	42	Bahrain		2.13
	Benin	2.70		Saudi Arabia		2.13
20	Gambia, The	2.68	44	Sierra Leone		2.09
	Kenya	2.68	45	Guinea-Bissau		2.08
22	Liberia	2.64	46	Ethiopia		2.07
23	Congo-Kinshasa	2.62	47	Togo		2.04
24	Senegal	2.60	48	Macau		2.01

Slowest growing populations
Average annual % change, 2010–15

1	Moldova	-0.68	24	Macedonia	0.12
2	Bulgaria	-0.66	25	Haiti	0.13
3	Georgia	-0.59	26	Taiwan	0.15
4	Ukraine	-0.55	27	Austria	0.16
5	Lithuania	-0.44		Slovakia	0.16
6	Latvia	-0.38	29	Bermuda	0.19
7	Belarus	-0.32		Channel Islands	0.19
8	Virgin Islands (US)	-0.25	31	Barbados	0.22
9	Bosnia	-0.24		Guyana	0.22
10	Romania	-0.23	33	Greece	0.23
11	Germany	-0.20		Italy	0.23
12	Croatia	-0.19		Slovenia	0.23
13	Hungary	-0.16	36	Armenia	0.26
14	Russia	-0.10		Martinique	0.26
	Serbia	-0.10	38	Czech Republic	0.27
16	Estonia	-0.07	39	Netherlands	0.28
	Japan	-0.07	40	Belgium	0.29
18	Cuba	-0.05	41	Malta	0.31
19	Puerto Rico	-0.04	42	Finland	0.32
20	Greenland	-0.01		Trinidad & Tobago	0.32
21	Poland	0.04	44	Albania	0.33
22	Portugal	0.05	45	Aruba	0.34
23	Montenegro	0.08			

Population: matters of breeding and sex

Crude birth rates
Births per 1,000 population, 2010–15

Highest			Lowest		
1	Niger	47.7	1	Bosnia	8.2
2	Zambia	46.5	2	Japan	8.5
3	Mali	45.0	3	Austria	8.6
4	Malawi	44.5	4	Germany	8.7
5	Uganda	43.9	5	Hong Kong	8.8
6	Chad	43.4		Portugal	8.8
7	Somalia	43.0	7	Taiwan	9.0
8	Burkina Faso	42.4	8	Italy	9.1
9	Afghanistan	42.3		Malta	9.1
10	Congo-Kinshasa	42.1	10	Channel Islands	9.3
11	Tanzania	41.0	11	Singapore	9.5
12	Rwanda	40.6	12	Cuba	9.6
13	Angola	39.9	13	Croatia	9.8
14	Nigeria	39.3	14	Slovenia	9.9
15	Benin	38.3		South Korea	9.9
16	Guinea	37.6	16	Andorra	10.0
	Liberia	37.6		British Virgin Is	10.0
	Timor-Leste	37.6		Bulgaria	10.0
19	Guinea-Bissau	37.4		Switzerland	10.0
20	Yemen	37.2	20	Greece	10.1
21	Gambia, The	36.9		Hungary	10.1
	Kenya	36.9	22	Macau	10.2
23	Sierra Leone	36.5	23	Romania	10.3
24	Mozambique	36.3	24	Macedonia	10.5
25	Equatorial Guinea	35.9	25	Spain	10.6
	Senegal	35.9	26	Slovakia	10.7
27	Cameroon	34.9			

Births to women aged 15–19, 000s, 2005–10

Highest

1	India	24,388.2	21	Colombia	779.5
2	Nigeria	4,541.2	22	Niger	761.3
3	Congo-Kinshasa	3,389.0	23	Russia	752.2
4	Brazil	3,147.3	24	Iraq	745.1
5	Bangladesh	2,968.7	25	South Africa	739.8
6	Indonesia	2,418.9	26	Mali	703.0
7	China	2,242.2	27	Madagascar	693.5
8	United States	2,142.3	28	Côte d'Ivoire	663.7
9	Mexico	1,878.0	29	Sudan	655.6
10	Ethiopia	1,604.0	30	Cameroon	651.8
11	Pakistan	1,466.8	31	Turkey	622.9
12	Tanzania	1,460.3	32	Venezuela	597.5
13	Uganda	1,280.5	33	Vietnam	594.1
14	Philippines	1,244.3	34	Iran	591.1
15	Kenya	1,067.4	35	Thailand	560.4
16	Afghanistan	923.4	36	Yemen	520.1
17	Egypt	921.1	37	Burkina Faso	517.6
18	Mozambique	870.8	38	Zambia	485.3
19	Angola	820.2	39	Argentina	474.5
20	Nepal	785.0	40	Chad	460.5

Fertility rates, 2010–15

Average number of children per woman

Highest			Lowest		
1	Niger	6.9	1	Bosnia	1.1
2	Somalia	6.3		Hong Kong	1.1
	Zambia	6.3		Macau	1.1
4	Mali	6.1		Taiwan	1.1
5	Afghanistan	6.0	5	Andorra	1.3
	Malawi	6.0		Malta	1.3
7	Timor-Leste	5.9		Portugal	1.3
	Uganda	5.9	8	Austria	1.4
9	Burkina Faso	5.8		Hungary	1.4
10	Chad	5.7		Japan	1.4
11	Congo-Kinshasa	5.5		Macedonia	1.4
	Tanzania	5.5		Poland	1.4
13	Nigeria	5.4		Romania	1.4
14	Rwanda	5.3		Singapore	1.4
15	Angola	5.1		Slovakia	1.4
	Benin	5.1		South Korea	1.4
17	Equatorial Guinea	5.0			
	Guinea	5.0			
	Liberia	5.0			

Women[a] who use modern methods of contraception

Highest, 2010 or latest, %			Lowest, 2010 or latest, %		
1	China	84.0	1	Somalia	1.2
	United Kingdom	84.0	2	Chad	1.7
3	Portugal	82.5	3	Guinea	4.0
4	Norway	82.2	4	Angola	4.5
5	Thailand	79.8	5	Niger	5.0
6	Switzerland	77.5	6	Eritrea	5.1
7	Brazil	77.1	7	Sudan	5.7
8	Hong Kong	75.4	8	Congo-Kinshasa	5.8
9	Finland	75.4	9	Benin	5.9
10	France	74.8	10	Sierra Leone	6.0
	Uruguay	74.8	11	Equatorial Guinea	6.1
12	United States	73.0		Guinea-Bissau	6.1
13	Belgium	72.9	13	Mali	6.3
14	Virgin Islands (US)	72.6	14	Burundi	7.5
15	New Zealand	72.3	15	Côte d'Ivoire	8.0
16	Puerto Rico	72.2		Mauritania	8.0
17	Canada	72.0	17	Nigeria	8.1
	Denmark	72.0	18	Central African Rep.	8.6
19	Cuba	71.6	19	Macedonia	9.8
20	Costa Rica	71.5	20	Senegal	10.0
21	Hungary	71.3	21	Albania	10.2
22	Australia	70.8	22	Liberia	10.3
23	Paraguay	70.1	23	Togo	11.1
	South Korea	70.1	24	Bosnia	11.2

a Married women aged 15–49; excludes traditional methods of contraception, such as the rhythm method.

Population: age

Median age[a]

Highest, 2011		Lowest, 2011	
1 Japan	44.7	1 Niger	15.5
2 Germany	44.3	2 Uganda	15.7
3 Italy	43.2	3 Mali	16.3
4 Channel Islands	42.6	4 Afghanistan	16.6
5 Bermuda	42.4	Angola	16.6
6 Finland	42.0	Timor-Leste	16.6
7 Austria	41.8	7 Congo-Kinshasa	16.7
Hong Kong	41.8	Zambia	16.7
9 Slovenia	41.7	9 Malawi	16.9
10 Bulgaria	41.6	10 Burkina Faso	17.1
11 Croatia	41.5	Chad	17.1
12 Greece	41.4	12 Yemen	17.4
Switzerland	41.4	13 Somalia	17.5
14 Belgium	41.2	Tanzania	17.5
15 Portugal	41.0	15 Gambia, The	17.8
16 Netherlands	40.7	Mozambique	17.8
Sweden	40.7	Senegal	17.8
18 Denmark	40.6	18 Benin	17.9
19 Latvia	40.2	19 West Bank & Gaza	18.1
20 Spain	40.1	20 Liberia	18.2
21 Andorra	40.0	Madagascar	18.2
22 Canada	39.9	22 Guinea	18.3
France	39.9	Iraq	18.3
24 Hungary	39.8	24 Sierra Leone	18.4
United Kingdom	39.8	25 Kenya	18.5
26 Estonia	39.7	Nigeria	18.5
27 Malta	39.5	27 Ethiopia	18.7
28 Bosnia	39.4	Rwanda	18.7
Czech Republic	39.4	29 Guatemala	18.9
Martinique	39.4	30 Eritrea	19.0
31 Lithuania	39.3	Guinea-Bissau	19.0
Ukraine	39.3	32 Côte d'Ivoire	19.2
33 Luxembourg	38.9	33 Cameroon	19.3
34 Virgin Islands (US)	38.8	Zimbabwe	19.3

Highest, 2050		Lowest, 2050	
1 Bosnia	53.2	1 Zambia	17.9
2 Japan	52.3	2 Malawi	19.6
3 Portugal	52.1	Niger	19.6
4 Cuba	52.0	4 Somalia	19.7
5 South Korea	51.8	5 Tanzania	20.9
6 Macau	51.6	6 Uganda	22.0
7 Singapore	51.4	7 Mali	22.1
8 Netherlands Antilles	51.3	8 Burkina Faso	22.2
9 Hong Kong	50.7	9 Nigeria	23.1
10 Malta	50.6	10 Chad	23.9

a Age at which there are an equal number of people above and below.

Population: density

Highest population density
People per sq km, 2010

Highest			Lowest		
1	Macau	20,909.8	1	Greenland	0.0
2	Singapore	7,447.2	2	Mongolia	1.8
3	Hong Kong	6,417.8	3	French Guiana	2.6
4	Bahrain	1,818.2	4	Namibia	2.8
5	Malta	1,318.1	5	Australia	2.9
6	Bermuda	1,225.3	6	Iceland	3.1
7	Maldives	1,060.0	7	Suriname	3.2
8	Bangladesh	1,032.6	8	Mauritania	3.4
9	Channel Islands	786.4	9	Canada	3.4
10	West Bank & Gaza	671.0	10	Botswana	3.5
11	Mauritius	636.8		Guyana	3.5
12	Taiwan	635.7	12	Libya	3.6
13	Barbados	635.7	13	Gabon	5.6
14	Aruba	597.2	14	Kazakhstan	5.9
15	South Korea	484.1	15	Central African Rep.	7.1
16	Puerto Rico	422.4	16	Russia	8.4
17	Lebanon	406.5	17	Chad	8.7
18	Rwanda	403.4	18	Bolivia	9.0
19	Netherlands	400.0		Oman	9.0
20	India	372.5	20	Turkmenistan	10.3
21	Martinique	368.3	21	Congo-Brazzaville	11.8
22	Haiti	360.1	22	Niger	12.2
23	Belgium	350.9	23	Mali	12.4
24	Réunion	337.1	24	Norway	12.7
25	Israel	335.0	25	Saudi Arabia	12.8
26	Japan	334.9	26	New Caledonia	13.5
27	Guam	327.7	27	Belize	13.6
28	St Lucia	323.3	28	Argentina	14.5
29	Sri Lanka	317.9	29	Somalia	14.6
30	Virgin Islands (US)	314.3	30	Papua New Guinea	14.8
31	Philippines	310.9	31	Algeria	14.9
32	Burundi	301.2	32	Angola	15.3
33	El Salvador	294.3	33	Bhutan	15.4
34	Guadeloupe	270.2	34	Finland	15.9
35	Vietnam	264.9		Paraguay	15.9
36	Trinidad & Tobago	261.5	36	New Zealand	16.1
37	United Kingdom	255.4	37	Sudan	17.4
38	Netherlands Antilles	250.9		Zambia	17.4
39	Jamaica	249.4	39	Uruguay	19.2
40	Germany	230.5	40	Sweden	20.8
41	Pakistan	218.1	41	Chile	22.6
42	Cayman Islands	213.0		Peru	22.6
43	Dominican Republic	204.6	43	Brazil	22.9
44	Nepal	203.6	44	Bahamas	24.7
45	North Korea	202.0	45	Equatorial Guinea	25.0
46	Italy	201.0	46	Laos	26.2
47	Antigua & Barbuda	200.7	47	Kyrgyzstan	26.7
48	Luxembourg	196.2	48	Congo-Kinshasa	28.1
49	Seychelles	190.1	49	Mozambique	29.2
50	Switzerland	185.6	50	Estonia	29.7

City living

Biggest cities[a]
Population m, 2015

1	Tokyo, Japan	38.2		Nanjing, China	6.7
2	Delhi, India	25.6	50	Hangzhou, China	6.5
3	Shanghai, China	23.0		Harbin, China	6.5
4	Mexico City, Mexico	21.7	52	Miami, US	6.4
5	New York, US	21.3		Santiago, Chile	6.4
6	Mumbai, India	21.2	54	Philadelphia, US	6.3
7	São Paulo, Brazil	21.0		Riyadh, Saudi Arabia	6.3
8	Beijing, China	18.1	56	Luanda, Angola	6.2
9	Dhaka, Bangladesh	17.4	57	Chittagong, Bangladesh	6.0
10	Karachi, Pakistan	15.6		Shenyang, China	6.0
11	Kolkata, India	15.1		Toronto, Canada	6.0
12	Buenos Aires, Argentina	14.2	60	Barcelona, Spain	5.9
13	Los Angeles, US	14.1	61	Belo Horizonte, Brazil	5.8
14	Lagos, Nigeria	13.1	62	Pune, India	5.7
15	Manila, Philippines	12.9	63	Surat, India	5.6
16	Istanbul, Turkey	12.5	64	Dallas, US	5.5
17	Guangzhou, China	12.4		Xi'an, China	5.5
	Rio de Janeiro, Brazil	12.4	66	Singapore	5.4
19	Shenzhen, China	12.3	67	Atlanta, US	5.3
20	Moscow, Russia	12.1	68	Boston, US	5.2
21	Cairo, Egypt	11.9		Houston, US	5.2
22	Osaka, Japan	11.8	70	St Petersburg, Russia	5.0
23	Chongqing, China	11.1		Washington, DC, US	5.0
	Paris, France	11.1	72	Abidjan, Côte d'Ivoire	4.9
25	Jakarta, Indonesia	10.5		Alexandria, Egypt	4.9
26	Khartoum, Sudan	10.3		Guadalajara, Mexico	4.9
	Kinshasa, Congo-Kins.	10.3		Yangon, Myanmar	4.9
	Wuhan, China	10.3	76	Sydney, Australia	4.8
29	Chicago, US	10.2	77	Ankara, Turkey	4.7
30	Bangalore, India	10.0		Detroit, US	4.7
31	Chennai, India	9.9		Monterrey, Mexico	4.7
32	Lima, Peru	9.8		Shantou, China	4.7
33	Seoul, South Korea	9.7		Zhengzhou, China	4.7
	Tianjin, China	9.7	82	Salvador, Brazil	4.5
35	Bogotá, Colombia	9.6	83	Dar es Salaam, Tanzania	4.4
36	London, UK	9.4		Suzhou, China	4.4
37	Bangkok, Thailand	9.3	85	Qingdao, China	4.3
38	Hyderabad, India	8.9	86	Brasília, Brazil	4.2
39	Lahore, Pakistan	8.5		Jinan, China	4.2
40	Dongguan, China	7.9		Melbourne, Australia	4.2
41	Chengdu, China	7.8	89	Changchun, China	4.1
42	Foshan, China	7.6		Jeddah, Saudi Arabia	4.1
	Tehran, Iran	7.6		Johannesburg, S. Africa	4.1
44	Ho Chi Minh City, Vietnam	7.4		Medellín, Colombia	4.1
	Hong Kong	7.4		Montreal, Canada	4.1
46	Ahmedabad, India	7.3		Phoenix, US	4.1
47	Madrid, Spain	7.2		Pôrto Alegre, Brazil	4.1
48	Baghdad, Iraq	6.7			

a Urban agglomerations. Data may change from year-to-year based on reassessments of agglomeration boundaries.

Urban population

Urban population, highest % residing in a single city, 2010

1	Hong Kong	100.0		21	Athens, Greece	48.6
	Singapore	100.0		22	Kigali, Rwanda	48.1
3	Kuwait City, Kuwait	86.2		23	Ouagadougou,BurkinaFaso	45.2
4	Khartoum, Sudan	81.2		24	Niamey, Niger	44.7
5	San Juan, Puerto Rico	66.9		25	Bishkek, Kyrgyzstan	44.1
6	Lomé, Togo	64.2		26	Lisbon, Portugal	43.7
7	Ulan Bator, Mongolia	61.1		27	Luanda, Angola	43.0
8	Brazzaville,Congo-Brazza.	60.9		28	Monrovia, Liberia	42.5
9	Yerevan, Armenia	56.2			N'Djaména, Chad	42.5
10	Dakar, Senegal	55.7		30	Baku, Azerbaijan	42.0
11	Phnom Penh, Cambodia	53.9		31	Kabul, Afghanistan	41.8
12	Beirut, Lebanon	53.8		32	Abidjan, Côte d'Ivoire	41.6
13	Montevideo, Uruguay	53.3		33	Port-au-Prince, Haiti	41.3
14	Nouakchott, Mauritania	53.2		34	Mogadishu, Somalia	41.0
15	Panama City, Panama	53.0		35	Lima, Peru	40.0
16	Asunción, Paraguay	52.3		36	Freetown, Sierra Leone	39.9
17	Conakry, Guinea	49.1		37	Dublin, Ireland	39.8
18	San José, Costa Rica	49.0		38	San Salvador, ElSalvador	39.5
19	Tbilisi, Georgia	48.7		39	Santiago, Chile	39.1
	Tel Aviv, Israel	48.7		40	Kinshasa, Congo-Kinsha	37.8

City liveability[a]

January 2012

	Best				Worst	
1	Melbourne, Australia	97.5		1	Dhaka, Bangladesh	38.7
2	Vienna, Austria	97.4		2	Port Moresby, Papua NG	38.9
3	Vancouver, Canada	97.3		3	Lagos, Nigeria	39.0
4	Toronto, Canada	97.2		4	Harare, Zimbabwe	39.4
5	Adelaide, Australia	96.6		5	Algiers, Algeria	40.9
	Calgary, Canada	96.6			Karachi, Pakistan	40.9
7	Sydney, Australia	96.1		7	Tripoli, Libya	42.9
8	Helsinki, Finland	96.0		8	Douala, Cameroon	44.0
9	Perth, Australia	95.9		9	Abidjan, Cote d'Ivoire	44.7
10	Auckland, NZ	95.7		10	Tehran, Iran	45.8
11	Zurich, Switzerland	95.6		11	Dakar, Senegal	48.3
12	Geneva, Switzerland	95.2		12	Colombo, Sri Lanka	48.5
	Osaka, Japan	95.2		13	Kathmandu, Nepal	50.6
14	Hamburg, Germany	95.0		14	Lusaka, Zambia	51.1
	Stockholm, Sweden	95.0		15	Phnom Penh, Cambodia	51.4
16	Montreal, Canada	94.8		16	Nairobi, Kenya	51.9
	Paris, France	94.8		17	HoChiMinhCity, Vietnam	52.4
18	Frankfurt, Germany	94.7		18	Damascus, Syria	52.5
	Tokyo, Japan	94.7		19	Cairo, Egypt	53.9
20	Brisbane, Australia	94.2		20	Al Khobar, Saudi Arabia	54.2
21	Berlin, Germany	94.0			Hanoi, Vietnam	54.2
22	Copenhagen, Denmark	93.8				
	Wellington, NZ	93.8				
24	Oslo, Norway	93.4				

a Based on a range of factors including stability, health care, culture, education, infrastructure.

Urban population

Highest, %, 2010			*Lowest, %, 2010*		
1	Bermuda	100.0	1	Burundi	12.1
	Cayman Islands	100.0	2	Papua New Guinea	12.8
	Hong Kong	100.0	3	Trinidad & Tobago	14.8
	Macau	100.0	4	St Lucia	14.9
	Singapore	100.0	5	Sri Lanka	15.5
6	Puerto Rico	99.2	6	Malawi	16.3
	Qatar	99.2	7	Uganda	17.3
8	Guadeloupe	98.4	8	Ethiopia	18.1
9	Kuwait	98.3	9	Nepal	18.4
10	Belgium	97.6	10	South Sudan	18.8
11	Virgin Islands (US)	96.0	11	Niger	18.9
12	Malta	95.4	12	Rwanda	20.4
13	Réunion	95.1	13	Cambodia	20.8
14	Venezuela	94.3	14	Swaziland	21.1
15	Iceland	94.2	15	Chad	22.2
16	Netherlands Antilles	94.1	16	Eritrea	23.2
17	Japan	93.5	17	Afghanistan	24.8
18	Guam	93.3	18	Kenya	25.6
19	Argentina	93.1	19	Tajikistan	26.8
20	Uruguay	92.9	20	Guyana	28.6

Urban growth

Highest, %, 2010–15			*Lowest, %, 2010–15*		
1	Burkina Faso	6.02	1	St Lucia	-3.13
2	Uganda	5.74	2	Latvia	-0.38
3	Eritrea	5.01	3	Georgia	-0.37
4	Niger	4.91	4	Lithuania	-0.27
5	Yemen	4.78	5	Ukraine	-0.26
6	Mali	4.77	6	Romania	-0.18
	Tanzania	4.77	7	Virgin Islands (US)	-0.10
8	Madagascar	4.73	8	Cuba	-0.08
9	Rwanda	4.50	9	Poland	-0.04
10	Burundi	4.45	10	Germany	-0.03
11	Afghanistan	4.41	11	Estonia	0.02
	Laos	4.41	12	Puerto Rico	0.06
13	Kenya	4.36		Slovakia	0.06
14	Timor-Leste	4.25	14	Bulgaria	0.10
15	South Sudan	4.23	15	Russia	0.13
16	Malawi	4.20	16	Slovenia	0.17
17	Congo-Kinshasa	4.19	17	Dominica	0.18
18	Zambia	4.15	18	Bermuda	0.19
19	Benin	4.12	19	Belarus	0.21
20	Angola	3.97	20	Czech Republic	0.24
21	Maldives	3.91	21	Martinique	0.25
22	Guinea	3.86	22	Croatia	0.30
23	Somalia	3.79	23	Belgium	0.32
24	Nigeria	3.75		Greenland	0.32
25	Haiti	3.68	25	Macedonia	0.33
26	Bhutan	3.65	26	Armenia	0.34
27	Gambia	3.63	27	Montenegro	0.38

Refugees[a] and asylum seekers

Refugees[a], country of origin
'000, 2010

1	Afghanistan	3,054.7	11	Serbia[b]	183.3
2	Iraq	1,683.6	12	Central African Rep.	164.9
3	Somalia	770.2	13	Turkey	146.8
4	Congo-Kinshasa	476.7	14	Sri Lanka	141.1
5	Myanmar	415.7	15	Angola	134.9
6	Colombia	395.6	16	Rwanda	114.8
7	Sudan	387.3	17	Russia	111.9
8	Vietnam	338.7	18	West Bank & Gaza	93.3
9	Eritrea	222.5	19	Burundi	84.1
10	China	184.6	20	Bhutan	75.1

Countries with largest refugee[a] populations
'000, 2010

1	Pakistan	1,900.6	11	Bangladesh	229.3
2	Iran	1,073.4	12	Venezuela	201.6
3	Syria	1,005.5	13	France	200.7
4	Germany	594.3	14	Yemen	190.1
5	Jordan	450.9	15	India	184.8
6	Kenya	402.9	16	Sudan	178.3
7	Chad	347.9	17	Congo-Kinshasa	166.3
8	China	301.0	18	Canada	165.6
9	United States	264.6	19	Ethiopia	154.3
10	United Kingdom	238.2	20	Uganda	135.8

Origin of asylum applications to industrialised countries
'000, 2010

1	Serbia[b]	28.9	11	Eritrea	8.5
2	Afghanistan	24.8	12	Georgia	7.4
3	China	24.6	13	Macedonia	6.4
4	Iraq	20.1		Turkey	6.4
5	Russia	18.9	15	Bangladesh	6.2
6	Somalia	17.0	16	Congo-Kinshasa	5.8
7	Iran	14.4	17	Mexico	5.5
8	Pakistan	10.8	18	Guinea	5.3
9	Nigeria	9.5	19	Syria	5.1
10	Sri Lanka	8.9	20	Armenia	5.0

Asylum applications in industrialised countries
'000, 2010

1	United States	55.5	9	Netherlands	13.3
2	France	47.8	10	Austria	11.0
3	Germany	41.3	11	Greece	10.3
4	Sweden	31.8	12	Norway	10.1
5	Canada	23.2	13	Turkey	9.2
6	United Kingdom	22.1	14	Australia	8.3
7	Belgium	19.9	15	Italy	8.2
8	Switzerland	13.5	16	Poland	6.5

a According to UNHCR. Includes people in "refugee-like situations".
b Including Kosovo.

The world economy

Biggest economies
GDP, $bn, 2010

1	United States	14,587	24	Taiwan	430
2	China	5,927	25	Norway	417
3	Japan	5,459	26	Venezuela	392
4	Germany	3,281	27	Iran	387
5	France[a]	2,560	28	Austria	379
6	United Kingdom	2,262	29	Argentina	369
7	Brazil	2,088	30	South Africa	364
8	Italy	2,061	31	Thailand	319
9	India	1,727	32	Denmark	312
10	Canada	1,577	33	Greece	301
11	Russia	1,480	34	United Arab Emirates	298
12	Spain	1,407	35	Colombia	289
13	Australia	1,132	36	Finland	238
14	Mexico	1,036		Malaysia	238
15	South Korea	1,014	38	Portugal	229
16	Netherlands	779	39	Hong Kong	224
17	Turkey	734	40	Egypt	219
18	Indonesia	707	40	Israel	217
19	Switzerland	528	42	Chile	213
20	Belgium	469	43	Singapore	209
	Poland	469	44	Ireland	207
22	Sweden	459	45	Nigeria	203
23	Saudi Arabia	435	46	Philippines	200

Biggest economies by purchasing power
GDP PPP, $bn, 2010

1	United States	14,587	23	Saudi Arabia	623
2	China	10,170	24	Thailand	591
3	Japan	4,299	25	South Africa	528
4	India	4,195	26	Egypt	501
5	Germany	3,059	27	Pakistan	467
6	Russia	2,820	28	Colombia	438
7	United Kingdom	2,221	29	Malaysia	418
8	France	2,214	30	Belgium	410
9	Brazil	2,185	31	Nigeria	380
10	Italy	1,933	32	Philippines	370
11	Mexico	1,652	33	Sweden	366
12	Spain	1,485	34	Switzerland	363
13	South Korea	1,422	35	United Arab Emirates	355
14	Canada	1,333	36	Venezuela	353
15	Turkey	1,141	37	Austria	336
16	Indonesia	1,037	38	Hong Kong	329
17	Australia	851	39	Greece	321
18	Iran[b]	846	40	Romania	311
19	Taiwan	824	41	Ukraine	308
20	Poland	759	42	Algeria	299
21	Netherlands	701	43	Singapore	294
22	Argentina	647	44	Norway	280

Note: For a list of 195 countries with their GDPs, see pages 250–254.
a Includes overseas departments. b 2009

Regional GDP

$bn, 2011		*% annual growth 2006–11*	
World	69,660	World	3.3
Advanced economies	44,420	Advanced economies	0.8
G7	33,670	G7	0.4
Euro area (17)	13,120	Euro area (17)	0.4
Asia[a]	11,320	Asia[a]	8.7
Latin America	5,610	Latin America	3.8
Central & Eastern Europe[b]	4,340	Central & Eastern Europe[b]	3.2
Middle East & N. Africa	2,770	Middle East & N. Africa	4.3
Sub-Saharan Africa	1,200	Sub-Saharan Africa	5.2

Regional purchasing power

GDP, % of total, 2011		*$ per head, 2011*	
World	100.0	World	11,480
Advanced economies	51.1	Advanced economies	39,320
G7	38.5	G7	40,890
Euro area (17)	14.3	Euro area (17)	33,790
Asia[a]	25.1	Asia[a]	5,510
Latin America	8.7	Latin America	11,860
Central & Eastern Europe[b]	7.8	Central & Eastern Europe[b]	13,280
Middle East & N. Africa	4.9	Middle East & N. Africa	9,900
Sub-Saharan Africa	2.5	Sub-Saharan Africa	2,380

Regional population

% of total (7.1bn), 2011		*No. of countries[c], 2011*	
World	100.0	World	184
Advanced economies	14.9	Advanced economies	34
G7	10.8	G7	7
Euro area (17)	4.8	Euro area (17)	17
Asia[a]	52.3	Asia[a]	27
Latin America	8.4	Latin America	32
Central & Eastern Europe[b]	6.8	Central & Eastern Europe[b]	27
Middle East & N. Africa	5.7	Middle East & N. Africa	20
Sub-Saharan Africa	11.9	Sub-Saharan Africa	44

Regional international trade

Exports of goods & services *% of total, 2011*		*Current account balances* *$bn, 2011*	
World	100.0	World	374
Advanced economies	62.4	Advanced economies	-103
G7	34.2	G7	-375
Euro area (17)	25.9	Euro area (17)	41
Asia[a]	16.0	Asia[a]	201
Latin America	5.5	Latin America	-68
Central & Eastern Europe[b]	7.4	Central & Eastern Europe[b]	-2
Middle East & N. Africa	6.5	Middle East & N. Africa	366
Sub-Saharan Africa	2.1	Sub-Saharan Africa	-21

a Excludes Hong Kong, Japan, Singapore, South Korea and Taiwan.
b Includes Turkey.
c IMF definition.

Living standards

Highest GDP per head

$, 2010

1	Luxembourg	105,190	31	Italy	34,080
2	Bermuda	89,240	32	New Zealand	32,370
3	Norway	85,390	33	Hong Kong	31,760
4	Switzerland	67,460	34	Spain	30,550
5	Qatar[a]	61,530	35	Cyprus	28,780
6	Cayman Islands	57,050	36	Israel	28,510
7	Denmark	56,240	37	Brunei[a]	27,390
8	Macau	51,400	38	Martinique[a]	26,980
9	Australia	50,750	39	Greece	26,610
10	Channel Islands	48,920	40	Réunion[a]	25,170
11	Sweden	48,900	41	Guadeloupe[a]	24,760
12	United States	47,150	42	French Polynesia	24,670
13	Netherlands	46,900	43	Puerto Rico	24,200
14	Canada	46,210	44	Slovenia	22,890
15	Ireland	46,170	45	Aruba	22,850
16	Faroe Islands[a]	45,210	46	Greenland[a]	22,510
17	Austria	45,180	47	Bahamas	22,450
18	Finland	44,380	48	Portugal	21,490
19	Belgium	43,080	49	South Korea	20,760
20	Japan	42,830	50	Equatorial Guinea	20,010
21	Kuwait[a]	41,360	51	French Guiana[a]	19,890
22	Andorra	41,140	52	Malta	19,850
23	Singapore	41,120	53	Czech Republic	18,250
24	Germany	40,120	54	Bahrain[a]	17,610
25	United Arab Emirates	39,620	55	Oman[a]	17,280
26	Iceland	39,540	56	Slovakia	16,070
27	France	39,450	57	Saudi Arabia	15,840
28	United Kingdom	36,340	58	Trinidad & Tobago	15,360
29	Taiwan	35,600	59	Barbados	15,000
30	New Caledonia	35,320		Guam[b]	15,000

Lowest GDP per head

$, 2010

1	Somalia	110	17	Uganda	510
2	Burundi	190	18	Nepal	520
3	Congo-Kinshasa	200		Tanzania	520
4	Liberia	250		Togo	520
5	Sierra Leone	320	21	Rwanda	530
6	Malawi	340	22	Burkina Faso	540
7	Ethiopia	360	23	Guinea-Bissau	580
	Niger	360	24	Zimbabwe	590
9	Eritrea	400	25	Mali	600
10	Mozambique	410	26	Timor-Leste	620
11	Madagascar	420	27	Bangladesh	670
12	Guinea	450		Haiti	670
13	Central African Rep.	460	29	Chad	680
14	Gambia, The	470	30	Benin	750
15	Afghanistan	500	31	Kenya	790
	North Korea	500	32	Cambodia	800

a 2009   b Latest estimate.

Highest purchasing power
GDP per head in PPP (USA = 100), 2010

1	Bermuda[a]	189.3	35	Bahamas	67.3
2	Qatar	187.1	36	Cyprus	65.9
3	Luxembourg	182.6	37	Faroe Islands[a]	64.7
4	Macau	135.1	38	New Zealand	62.6
5	Singapore	122.9	39	South Korea	61.7
6	Norway	121.4	40	Israel	60.6
7	Cayman Islands[a]	121.0	41	Greece	60.2
8	Channel Islands[a]	110.1	42	Bahrain	57.3
9	Brunei[b]	105.9	43	Slovenia	57.1
10	United Arab Emirates	100.1	44	Oman[b]	56.8
11	United States	100.0	45	Malta	56.1
12	Hong Kong	98.6	46	Greenland[a]	55.2
13	Switzerland	98.4	47	Trinidad & Tobago	54.6
14	Netherlands	89.4	48	Portugal	53.9
15	Andorra[a]	88.5	49	Czech Republic	52.0
16	Ireland	85.8	50	Slovakia	49.4
17	Denmark	85.2	51	Saudi Arabia	48.2
18	Austria	84.8	52	Martinique[b]	48.1
19	Canada	82.8	53	Aruba[a]	46.2
20	Sweden	82.8	54	Réunion[b]	44.7
21	Kuwait	82.2	55	Antigua & Barbuda	44.4
22	Australia	80.9	56	Guadeloupe[b]	44.2
23	Belgium	79.8	57	Estonia	43.8
24	Germany	79.3	58	Hungary	43.6
25	Finland	77.3	59	Russia	42.2
26	United Kingdom	75.7	60	Poland	42.2
27	Iceland	75.6	61	Croatia	41.4
28	Taiwan	75.5	62	Barbados[b]	41.2
29	New Caledonia[a]	74.9	63	Lithuania	39.0
30	Equatorial Guinea	73.7	64	French Polynesia[a]	38.2
31	France	72.4	65	Libya[b]	36.0
32	Japan	71.5	66	French Guiana[b]	35.3
33	Spain	68.4	67	Latvia	34.7
34	Italy	67.8	68	Puerto Rico[a]	34.6

Lowest purchasing power
GDP per head in PPP (USA = 100), 2010

1	Congo-Kinshasa	0.74	13	Madagascar	2.05
2	Burundi	0.87	14	Togo	2.12
3	Liberia	0.89	15	Ethiopia	2.21
4	Zimbabwe[a]	0.93	16	Mali	2.26
5	Eritrea	1.16	17	Guinea	2.31
6	Somalia[a]	1.27	18	Haiti	2.36
7	Niger	1.54	19	Rwanda	2.47
8	Central African Rep.	1.67	20	Guinea-Bissau	2.52
9	Sierra Leone	1.75	21	Nepal	2.54
10	Malawi	1.87	22	Afghanistan	2.56
11	Timor-Leste	1.97	23	Burkina Faso	2.66
12	Mozambique	2.00	24	Uganda	2.70

a Latest available estimate.   b 2009

The quality of life

Human development index[a]

Highest, 2011

1	Norway	94.3		31	Andorra	83.8
2	Australia	92.9			Brunei	83.8
3	Netherlands	91.0		33	Estonia	83.5
	United States	91.0		34	Slovakia	83.4
5	Canada	90.8		35	Malta	83.2
	Ireland	90.8		36	Qatar	83.1
	New Zealand	90.8		37	Hungary	81.6
8	Germany	90.5		38	Poland	81.3
9	Sweden	90.4		39	Lithuania	81.0
10	Switzerland	90.3		40	Portugal	80.9
11	Japan	90.1		41	Bahrain	80.6
12	Hong Kong	89.8		42	Chile	80.5
	Iceland	89.8			Latvia	80.5
14	South Korea	89.7		44	Argentina	79.7
15	Denmark	89.5		45	Croatia	79.6
16	Israel	88.8		46	Barbados	79.3
17	Belgium	88.6		47	Uruguay	78.3
18	Austria	88.5		48	Romania	78.1
19	France	88.4		49	Cuba	77.6
	Slovenia	88.4		50	Bahamas	77.1
21	Finland	88.2			Bulgaria	77.1
22	Spain	87.8			Montenegro	77.1
23	Italy	87.4		53	Mexico	77.0
24	Luxembourg	86.7			Saudi Arabia	77.0
25	Singapore	86.6		55	Panama	76.8
26	Czech Republic	86.5		56	Serbia	76.6
27	United Kingdom	86.3		57	Antigua & Barbuda	76.4
28	Greece	86.1		58	Malaysia	76.1
29	United Arab Emirates	84.6		59	Kuwait	76.0
30	Cyprus	84.0				

Human development index[a]

Lowest, 2011

1	Congo-Kinshasa	28.6		13	Mali	35.9
2	Niger	29.5		14	Ethiopia	36.3
3	Burundi	31.6		15	Zimbabwe	37.6
4	Mozambique	32.2		16	Afghanistan	39.8
5	Chad	32.8		17	Côte d'Ivoire	40.0
6	Liberia	32.9			Malawi	40.0
7	Burkina Faso	33.1		19	Sudan	40.8
8	Sierra Leone	33.6		20	Gambia, The	42.0
9	Central African Rep.	34.3		21	Benin	42.7
10	Guinea	34.4		22	Rwanda	42.9
11	Eritrea	34.9		23	Djibouti	43.0
12	Guinea-Bissau	35.3			Zambia	43.0

a GDP or GDP per head is often taken as a measure of how developed a country is, but its usefulness is limited as it refers only to economic welfare. The UN Development Programme combines statistics on average and expected years of schooling and life expectancy with income levels (now GNI per head, valued in PPP US$). The HDI is shown here scaled from 0 to 100; countries scoring over 80 are considered to have very high human development, 67–79 high, 50–66 medium and those under 50 low.

Inequality-adjusted human development index[a]
Highest, 2011

1	Norway	89.0	13	Czech Republic	82.1
2	Australia	85.6	14	Austria	82.0
3	Sweden	85.1	15	Belgium	81.9
4	Netherlands	84.6	16	France	80.4
5	Iceland	84.5	17	Luxembourg	79.9
6	Ireland	84.3		Spain	79.9
7	Denmark	84.2	19	United Kingdom	79.1
	Germany	84.2	20	Slovakia	78.7
9	Switzerland	84.0	21	Israel	77.9
10	Slovenia	83.7		Italy	77.9
11	Finland	83.3	23	United States	77.1
12	Canada	82.9	24	Estonia	76.9

Gini coefficient[b]

Highest 2000–11			*Lowest 2000–11*		
1	Haiti	59.5	1	Sweden	25.0
2	Angola	58.6	2	Norway	25.8
3	Colombia	58.5	3	Finland	26.9
4	South Africa	57.8	4	Belarus	27.2
5	Honduras	57.7	5	Ukraine	27.5
6	Bolivia	57.3	6	Serbia	28.2
7	Brazil	53.9	7	Germany	28.3
8	Guatemala	53.7	8	Austria	29.1
9	Thailand	53.6	9	Tajikistan	29.4
10	Rwanda	53.1	10	Ethiopia	29.8
11	Suriname	52.8	11	Montenegro	30.0
12	Liberia	52.6	12	Armenia	30.9
13	Lesotho	52.5		Kazakhstan	30.9

Economic freedom index[c]
2012

1	Hong Kong	89.9	14	United Kingdom	74.1
2	Singapore	87.5	15	Netherlands	73.3
3	Australia	83.1	16	Estonia	73.2
4	New Zealand	82.1	17	Finland	72.3
5	Switzerland	81.1	18	Taiwan	71.9
6	Canada	79.9	19	Cyprus	71.8
7	Chile	78.3		Macau	71.8
8	Mauritius	77.0	21	Sweden	71.7
9	Ireland	76.9	22	Japan	71.6
10	United States	76.3	23	Lithuania	71.5
11	Denmark	76.2	24	Qatar	71.3
12	Bahrain	75.2		St Lucia	71.3
13	Luxembourg	74.5	26	Germany	71.0

a When there is inequality in the distribution of health, education and income, the IHDI of an average person in society is less than the ordinary HDI.
b The lower its value, the more equally household income is distributed.
c Ranks countries on the basis of indicators of how government intervention can restrict the economic relations between individuals, published by the Heritage Foundation. Scores are from 80–100 (free) to 0–49.9 (repressed) (see Glossary).

Economic growth

Highest economic growth
Average annual % increase in real GDP, 2000–10

1	Equatorial Guinea	17.0	28	Maldives	6.8
2	Azerbaijan	14.2	29	Mongolia	6.5
3	Turkmenistan	13.2	30	Sudan	6.4
4	Qatar	12.9	31	Jordan	6.3
5	Angola	11.3		Panama	6.3
6	China	10.5	33	Georgia	6.2
7	Myanmar	10.3	34	Cape Verde	6.1
8	Sierra Leone	9.5	35	Bahrain	5.9
9	Nigeria	8.9		Bangladesh	5.9
10	Bhutan	8.6		Kosovo	5.9
	Chad	8.6	38	Ghana	5.8
12	Ethiopia	8.3		Suriname	5.8
	Kazakhstan	8.3	40	Burkina Faso	5.7
14	Armenia	8.1		Mali	5.7
15	Cambodia	8.0		Peru	5.7
	Mozambique	8.0		Trinidad & Tobago	5.7
17	Tajikistan	7.9	44	Singapore	5.6
18	Rwanda	7.8		Zambia	5.6
19	Timor-Leste	7.7	46	Albania	5.5
20	India	7.5	47	Kuwait	5.4
21	Belarus	7.4	48	Dominican Republic	5.3
	Uganda	7.4		Iran	5.3
23	Vietnam	7.3		Niger	5.3
24	Afghanistan[a]	7.1		United Arab Emirates	5.3
	Laos	7.1	52	Indonesia	5.2
26	Tanzania	7.0		Lebanon	5.2
27	Uzbekistan	6.9		Sri Lanka	5.2

Lowest economic growth
Average annual % change in real GDP, 2000–10

1	Zimbabwe	-5.1	20	Austria	1.5
2	Haiti	0.1		Fiji	1.5
3	Italy	0.4		Malta	1.5
4	Liberia	0.5		Norway	1.5
5	Bahamas	0.6	24	Mexico	1.6
	Denmark	0.6		United States	1.6
	Portugal	0.6	26	Switzerland	1.7
8	Jamaica	0.7		United Kingdom	1.7
	Japan	0.7	28	Finland	1.8
10	Eritrea	0.9		St Lucia	1.8
	Germany	0.9	30	Canada	1.9
12	Central African Rep.	1.0		El Salvador	1.9
13	Côte d'Ivoire	1.1	32	Greece	2.0
	France	1.1		Hungary	2.0
15	Barbados	1.2	34	Spain	2.1
16	Antigua & Barbuda	1.4		Sweden	2.1
	Belgium	1.4	36	Iceland	2.2
	Brunei	1.4		New Zealand	2.2
	Netherlands	1.4		Togo	2.2

a 2002–10

Highest economic growth
Average annual % increase in real GDP, 1990–2000

1	Equatorial Guinea	31.6	10	Cape Verde	6.8
2	China	10.4	11	Ireland	6.7
3	Vietnam	7.6	12	Mozambique	6.5
4	Maldives	7.5		South Korea	6.5
5	Lebanon	7.1	14	Chile	6.4
	Malaysia	7.1	15	Taiwan	6.2
	Singapore	7.1		Uganda	6.2
8	Cambodia	7.0	17	Dominican Republic	6.1
9	Qatar	6.9		Laos	6.1

Lowest economic growth
Average annual % change in real GDP, 1990–2000

1	Ukraine[a]	-7.7	11	Kyrgyzstan[a]	-1.8
2	Sierra Leone	-7.6	12	Burundi	-1.7
3	Moldova[a]	-6.3	13	Romania	-1.6
4	Congo-Kinshasa	-5.6	14	Djibouti[b]	-1.4
5	Tajikistan[a]	-4.2	15	Belarus[a]	-0.2
6	Bulgaria	-4.0		Zambia	-0.2
7	Azerbaijan[a]	-3.5	17	Mongolia	-0.1
8	Kazakhstan[a]	-2.4	18	Suriname	0.0
9	Russia[a]	-2.3	19	Libya	0.2
10	Turkmenistan[a]	-2.1			

Highest services growth
Average annual % increase in real terms, 2002–10

1	Lesotho	22.5	10	Congo-Kinshasa[c]	11.6
2	Maldives	16.2	11	China	11.3
3	Equatorial Guinea[c]	14.8	12	Kyrgyzstan	10.6
4	Azerbaijan	14.5	13	Bhutan[c]	10.2
5	Afghanistan	14.0	14	Namibia	10.0
6	Nigeria[d]	13.4	15	Moldova	9.9
7	Myanmar	12.9	16	Uzbekistan	9.8
8	Ethiopia	12.1	17	India	9.8
9	Angola	11.7	18	Armenia	9.0

Lowest services growth
Average annual % change in real terms, 2002–10

1	Zimbabwe	-4.1	10	Bahamas[d]	1.4
2	Guinea	-2.4		Côte d'Ivoire	1.4
3	Haiti	0.3		Portugal	1.4
4	Eritrea[c]	0.4	13	France[c]	1.5
5	Italy	0.8	14	Fiji	1.6
6	Denmark	0.9		Germany	1.6
	Japan[c]	0.9		Jamaica	1.6
8	Finland	1.2	17	Austria	1.7
9	Hungary	1.3	18	Switzerland	1.8

a 1992–2000 b 1991–2000 c 2002–09 d 2002–07
Note: Rankings of highest and lowest industrial growth 2002–10 can be found on page 46 and highest and lowest agricultural growth 2002–10 on page 49.

Trading places

Biggest exporters
% of total world exports (goods, services and income), 2010

1	Euro area (16)	15.90	22	Saudi Arabia	1.33
2	United States	11.88		Sweden	1.33
3	China	9.01	24	Malaysia	1.16
4	Germany	8.42	25	Brazil	1.15
5	Japan	4.97	26	Austria	1.14
6	United Kingdom	4.30	27	Hong Kong	1.13
7	France	4.14	28	Thailand	1.11
8	Netherlands	3.20	29	United Arab Emirates	1.09
9	Italy	2.95	30	Luxembourg	1.05
10	South Korea	2.67	31	Poland	0.98
11	Canada	2.48	32	Norway	0.95
12	Russia	2.29	33	Denmark	0.87
13	Switzerland	2.17	34	Indonesia	0.84
14	Belgium	2.07	35	Turkey	0.76
15	Spain	2.05	36	Czech Republic	0.68
16	India	1.67	37	Hungary	0.60
17	Singapore	1.64	38	Iran	0.57
18	Taiwan	1.60	39	Finland	0.55
19	Mexico	1.51	40	South Africa	0.50
20	Australia	1.42	41	Chile	0.42
21	Ireland	1.35			

Most trade dependent
Trade[a] as % of GDP, 2010

1	Zimbabwe	125.0
2	Vietnam	108.9
3	Guyana	101.1
4	Singapore	100.7
5	Malaysia	95.4
6	United Arab Emirates	93.9
7	Lesotho	89.1
8	Slovakia	86.1
9	Qatar	80.8
10	Iraq	79.3
11	Angola	79.2
12	Equatorial Guinea	79.1
13	Bahrain	79.0
14	Suriname	77.7
15	Mongolia	76.3
16	Oman	76.2
17	Paraguay	75.4
18	Papua New Guinea	74.1
19	Mauritania	72.9
20	Congo-Brazzaville	72.6
	New Caledonia	72.6
22	Thailand	72.3

Least trade dependent
Trade[a] as % of GDP, 2010

1	Bermuda	9.2
2	North Korea	9.3
3	United States	11.7
4	Greece	13.2
5	Central African Rep.	14.0
6	Brazil	14.6
7	Japan	15.6
8	Cuba	16.8
9	Euro area (16)	16.8
	United Kingdom	17.6
11	Pakistan	19.0
12	Colombia	19.1
13	Spain	19.8
14	Iceland	20.6
15	Rwanda	20.7
16	Djibouti	21.4
17	France	21.3
18	Sudan	21.9
19	Italy	22.0
20	Cameroon	22.1
21	Cyprus	22.4
22	New Zealand	22.6

Notes: The figures are drawn wherever possible from balance of payment statistics so have differing definitions from statistics taken from customs or similar sources. For Hong Kong and Singapore, only domestic exports and retained imports are used. Euro area data exclude intra-euro area trade.
a Average of imports plus exports of goods.

Biggest traders of goods[a]
% of world, 2011

	Exports				Imports	
1	China	10.4		1	United States	12.3
2	Germany	8.1		2	China	9.5
	United States	8.1		3	Germany	6.8
4	Japan	4.5		4	Japan	4.6
5	Netherlands	3.6		5	France	3.9
6	France	3.3		6	United Kingdom	3.5
7	South Korea	3.0		7	Netherlands	3.2
8	Italy	2.9		8	Italy	3.0
	Russia	2.9		9	South Korea	2.9
10	Belgium	2.6		10	Belgium	2.5
	United Kingdom	2.6			Canada	2.5
12	Canada	2.5			India	2.5
13	Saudi Arabia	2.0		13	Mexico	2.0
14	Mexico	1.9			Spain	2.0
15	Taiwan	1.7		15	Russia	1.8
16	India	1.6		16	Taiwan	1.5
	Spain	1.6		17	Australia	1.3
	United Arab Emirates[b]	1.6			Brazil	1.3
19	Australia	1.5			Turkey	1.3
20	Brazil	1.4		20	Thailand	1.2
21	Switzerland	1.3		21	Poland	1.1
	Thailand	1.3			Switzerland	1.1
					United Arab Emirates[b]	1.1

Biggest earners from services and income
% of world exports of services and income, 2010

1	Euro area (16)	19.21	22	Denmark	1.31
2	United States	18.08	23	Australia	1.30
3	United Kingdom	7.40	24	Russia	1.24
4	Germany	7.01	25	Norway	1.02
5	France	5.29	26	Taiwan	0.95
6	China	4.73	27	Finland	0.69
7	Japan	4.72	28	Malaysia	0.67
8	Hong Kong	3.34	29	Greece	0.63
9	Luxembourg	3.06	30	Poland	0.60
10	Switzerland	2.97		Thailand	0.60
11	Netherlands	2.90	32	Brazil	0.59
12	Spain	2.67		Turkey	0.59
13	Ireland	2.61	34	Portugal	0.55
14	Italy	2.59	35	Hungary	0.53
15	Singapore	2.44	36	Israel	0.45
16	Belgium	2.34		Macau	0.45
17	India	1.97	38	Saudi Arabia	0.43
18	Canada	1.93	39	Czech Republic	0.39
19	Sweden	1.79	40	Egypt	0.36
20	South Korea	1.48	41	Ukraine	0.33
21	Austria	1.37	42	Philippines	0.31

a Individual countries only.
b Estimate.

Balance of payments: current account

Largest surpluses
$m, 2010

1	China	305,374	26	United Arab Emirates	11,263
2	Japan	195,750	27	Philippines	8,924
3	Germany	187,940	28	Angola	7,421
4	Switzerland	76,901	29	Belgium	6,349
5	Russia	70,253	30	Israel	6,342
6	Saudi Arabia	66,751	31	Indonesia	5,643
7	Netherlands	51,635	32	Brunei	5,623
8	Norway	51,444	33	Oman	5,096
9	Singapore	49,558	34	Finland	4,459
10	Taiwan	39,900	35	Trinidad & Tobago	4,146
11	Kuwait	36,822	36	Luxembourg	4,122
12	Qatar	33,528	37	Chile	3,802
13	Sweden	30,408	38	Argentina	3,082
14	South Korea	28,214	39	Kazakhstan	3,013
15	Malaysia	27,290	40	Bangladesh	2,502
16	Iran	25,457	41	Nigeria	2,476
17	Denmark	17,134	42	Uzbekistan	2,397
18	Libya	16,801	43	Timor-Leste	1,717
19	Azerbaijan	15,040	44	Côte d'Ivoire[a]	1,670
20	Thailand	14,754	45	Myanmar	1,527
21	Venezuela	14,378	46	Gabon[b]	1,485
22	Hong Kong	13,936	47	Hungary	1,417
23	Macau	12,233	48	Ireland	954
24	Algeria	11,832	49	Bolivia	874
25	Austria	11,461	50	Bahrain	770

Largest deficits
$m, 2010

1	United States	-470,900	22	New Zealand	-4,994
2	Italy	-72,015	23	Egypt	-4,504
3	United Kingdom	-71,600	24	Dominican Republic	-4,435
4	Spain	-64,342	25	Vietnam	-4,287
5	Euro area (16)	-55,960	26	Morocco	-4,209
6	India	-51,781	27	Equatorial Guinea	-3,490
7	Canada	-49,307	28	Serbia	-3,115
8	Brazil	-47,365	29	Ukraine	-3,018
9	Turkey	-47,099	30	Slovakia	-3,009
10	France	-44,500	31	Panama	-2,953
11	Australia	-31,990	32	Cyprus	-2,803
12	Greece	-30,897	33	Ghana	-2,701
13	Portugal	-22,850	34	Kenya	-2,512
14	Poland	-21,873	35	Turkmenistan	-2,349
15	South Africa	-10,117	36	Peru	-2,315
16	Lebanon	-8,909	37	Cuba[c]	-2,309
17	Colombia	-8,855	38	Tunisia	-2,104
18	Belarus	-8,317	39	Tanzania	-1,978
19	Romania	-6,480	40	Zimbabwe	-1,966
20	Czech Republic	-5,992	41	Haiti	-1,956
21	Mexico	-5,738	42	Ecuador	-1,785

Note: Euro area data exclude intra-euro area trade. a 2009 b 2006 c 2008

Largest surpluses as % of GDP
%, 2010

1	Timor-Leste	245.0	26	Hong Kong	6.2
2	Macau	43.8	27	Uzbekistan	6.1
3	Brunei	43.2	28	Germany	5.7
4	Kuwait	29.6	29	Denmark	5.5
5	Azerbaijan	29.0	30	China	5.2
6	Qatar	26.3	31	Djibouti	4.8
7	Singapore	23.7	32	Russia	4.7
8	Libya	23.4	33	Congo-Brazzaville	4.6
9	Trinidad & Tobago	20.1		Thailand	4.6
10	Suriname	17.7	35	Philippines	4.5
11	Saudi Arabia	15.4	36	Bolivia	4.4
12	Switzerland	14.6	37	United Arab Emirates	3.8
13	Norway	12.3	38	Venezuela	3.7
14	Bermuda	12.2	39	Japan	3.6
15	Malaysia	11.5		Myanmar	3.6
16	Gabon[a]	11.3	41	Estonia	3.5
17	Taiwan	9.3	42	Bahrain	3.4
18	Oman	8.8	43	Austria	3.0
19	Angola	8.7		Latvia	3.0
20	Luxembourg	7.7	45	Israel	2.9
21	Algeria	7.3	46	South Korea	2.8
	Côte d'Ivoire[b]	7.3	47	Bangladesh	2.5
23	Iran	6.6	48	Zambia	2.4
	Netherlands	6.6	49	Gambia, The	2.1
	Sweden	6.6	50	Kazakhstan	2.0

Largest deficits as % of GDP
%, 2010

1	Liberia	-74.8	22	Georgia	-12.6
2	Haiti	-29.1		St Lucia	-12.6
3	Zimbabwe	-26.3	24	Cyprus	-12.1
4	Sierra Leone	-25.3	25	Albania	-11.9
5	Montenegro	-25.1	26	Turkmenistan	-11.7
6	Equatorial Guinea	-24.9	27	Mozambique	-11.6
7	Maldives	-24.3	28	Iceland	-11.3
8	Lebanon	-22.8	29	Cape Verde	-11.2
9	Niger	-20.6	30	Panama	-11.1
10	Burundi	-20.1	31	Bahamas	-10.5
11	Netherlands Antilles[b]	-19.5		Swaziland	-10.5
12	Lesotho	-19.3	33	Greece	-10.3
13	Kosovo	-17.3	34	Moldova	-10.2
14	New Caledonia	-16.5		Uganda	-10.2
15	Aruba	-16.4	36	Kyrgyzstan	-10.1
16	Belarus	-15.2	37	Portugal	-10.0
17	Armenia	-14.7		West Bank & Gaza[b]	-10.0
	Nicaragua	-14.7	39	Central African Rep.	-9.8
19	Mongolia	-14.3	40	Madagascar	-9.7
20	Fiji	-13.0	41	Papua New Guinea	-9.6
21	Mali	-12.9	42	Antigua & Barbuda	-9.3

a 2006   b 2009

Official reserves[a]

$m, end-2011

1	China	3,254,690		16	Thailand	174,891
2	Japan	1,295,835		17	Italy	169,874
3	Euro area (17)	847,744		18	France	168,489
4	Saudi Arabia	556,572		19	Mexico	149,209
5	United States	537,267		20	Malaysia	133,595
6	Russia	497,410		21	Indonesia	110,137
7	Taiwan	386,285		22	Libya	107,133
8	Brazil	352,009		23	Poland	97,713
9	Switzerland	330,587		24	United Kingdom	94,549
10	South Korea	306,934		25	Turkey	87,937
11	India	298,739		26	Denmark	84,956
12	Hong Kong	285,405		27	Philippines	75,124
13	Singapore	243,786		28	Israel	74,874
14	Germany	234,098		29	Canada	65,820
15	Algeria	191,365		30	Iraq	60,960

Official gold reserves

Market prices, $m, end-2011

1	Euro area (17)	531,027		14	Saudi Arabia	15,895
2	United States	400,357		15	United Kingdom	15,279
3	Germany	167,170		16	Lebanon	14,116
4	Italy	120,689		17	Spain	13,856
5	France	119,877		18	Austria	13,779
6	China	51,901		19	Belgium	11,192
7	Switzerland	51,197		20	Turkey	9,615
8	Russia	43,462		21	Algeria	8,543
9	Japan	37,663		22	Philippines	7,834
10	Netherlands	30,145		23	Thailand	7,502
11	India	27,454		24	Libya	7,073
12	Portugal	18,831		25	Sweden	6,188
13	Venezuela	18,005		26	South Africa	6,155

Workers' remittances

Inflows, $m, 2010

1	India	54,035		16	Lebanon	7,558
2	China	53,038		17	United Kingdom	7,532
3	Mexico	22,048		18	Indonesia	6,916
4	Philippines	21,423		19	Italy	6,803
5	France	15,629		20	Morocco	6,423
6	Germany	11,338		21	Ukraine	5,607
7	Bangladesh	10,852		22	United States	5,277
8	Spain	10,507		23	Russia	5,264
9	Belgium	10,178		24	Australia	4,840
10	Nigeria	10,045		25	Guatemala	4,229
11	Pakistan	9,690		26	Sri Lanka	4,155
12	South Korea	8,708		27	Colombia	4,058
13	Vietnam	8,260		28	Brazil	4,000
14	Egypt	7,725		29	Romania	3,883
15	Poland	7,614		30	Netherlands	3,834

a Foreign exchange, SDRs, IMF position and gold at market prices.

Exchange rates

The Economist's Big Mac index

		Big Mac prices in local currency	in $	Implied PPP[a] of the $	Actual $ exchange rate	Under (–)/ over (+) valuation against $, %
Countries with the most under-valued currencies, January 2012						
1	India[b]	84.00	1.62	20.01	51.90	-61
2	Ukraine	17.00	2.11	4.05	8.04	-50
3	Hong Kong	16.50	2.12	3.93	7.77	-49
4	Malaysia	7.35	2.34	1.75	3.14	-44
5	China[c]	15.40	2.44	3.67	6.32	-42
	South Africa	19.95	2.45	4.75	8.13	-42
7	Indonesia	22,534.00	2.46	5,369.00	9,160.00	-41
	Thailand	78.00	2.46	18.58	31.80	-41
9	Taiwan	75.00	2.50	17.87	30.00	-40
10	Egypt	15.50	2.57	3.69	6.04	-39
	Russia	81.00	2.55	19.30	31.80	-39
	Sri Lanka	290.00	2.55	69.09	113.90	-39
13	Poland	9.10	2.58	2.17	3.52	-38
14	Hungary	645.00	2.63	153.67	246.00	-37
15	Mexico	37.00	2.70	8.82	13.68	-36
	Philippines	118.00	2.68	28.11	44.00	-36
	Saudi Arabia	10.00	2.67	2.38	3.75	-36
18	Lithuania	7.80	2.87	1.86	2.72	-32
19	Pakistan	260.00	2.89	61.95	90.10	-31
20	Latvia	1.65	3.00	0.39	0.55	-29
21	South Korea	3,700.00	3.19	882.00	1,159.00	-24
22	United Arab Emir.	12.00	3.27	2.86	3.67	-22
23	Czech Republic	70.22	3.45	16.73	20.40	-18
24	Turkey	6.60	3.54	1.57	1.86	-16
25	Peru	10.00	3.71	2.38	2.69	-12
26	Singapore	4.85	3.75	1.16	1.29	-11
27	United Kingdom	2.49	3.82	1.69[d]	1.54[d]	-9
28	Costa Rica	2,050.00	4.02	488.00	510.00	-4
	New Zealand	5.10	4.05	1.22	1.26	-4
Countries with the most over-valued currencies, January 2012						
1	Norway	41.00	6.79	9.77	6.04	62
	Switzerland	6.50	6.81	1.55	0.96	62
3	Sweden	41.00	5.91	9.77	6.93	41
4	Brazil	10.25	5.68	2.44	1.81	35
5	Denmark	31.50	5.37	7.50	5.86	28
6	Australia	4.80	4.94	1.14	0.97	18
7	Argentina	20.00	4.64	4.77	4.31	10
	Canada	4.73	4.63	1.13	1.02	10
	Uruguay	90.00	4.63	21.44	19.45	10
10	Colombia	8,400.00	4.54	2,001.00	1,852.00	8
11	Euro area[e]	3.49	4.43	1.20[f]	1.27[f]	6

a Purchasing-power parity: local price in the 40 countries listed divided by United States price ($4.20, average of four cities).
b Maharaja Mac.   c Average of five cities.   d Dollars per pound.
e Weighted average of prices in euro area.   f Dollars per euro.

Public finance

Government debt
As % of GDP, 2011

1	Japan	205.5	16	Spain	75.3
2	Greece	170.0	17	Netherlands	75.2
3	Iceland	128.3	18	Israel	74.2
4	Italy	119.7	19	Poland	63.3
5	Portugal	117.6	20	Denmark	61.8
6	Ireland	114.1	21	Finland	57.2
7	United States	102.7	22	Slovenia	56.4
8	Belgium	102.3	23	Sweden	48.7
9	France	100.1	24	Czech Republic	48.3
10	United Kingdom	97.9	25	Slovakia	46.8
11	Euro area (15)	95.1	26	New Zealand	44.3
12	Germany	87.2	27	Switzerland	41.0
13	Hungary	84.7	28	South Korea	34.7
14	Canada	83.8	29	Norway	34.0
15	Austria	79.7	30	Australia	26.6

Government spending
As % of GDP, 2011

1	Denmark	57.9	16	New Zealand	47.2
2	France	56.1	17	Iceland	46.1
3	Finland	54.1	18	Germany	45.7
4	Belgium	53.4	19	Israel	45.0
5	Sweden	51.3	20	Norway	44.6
6	Slovenia	50.9	21	Poland	43.6
7	Austria	50.5		Spain	43.6
8	Greece	50.1	23	Czech Republic	43.4
	Netherlands	50.1	24	Canada	42.9
10	Italy	49.9	25	Japan	42.8
11	Euro area (15)	49.4	26	Luxembourg	42.0
12	United Kingdom	49.1	27	United States	41.7
13	Portugal	48.9	28	Estonia	38.2
14	Ireland	48.7	29	Slovakia	37.4
15	Hungary	48.4	30	Australia	35.2

Tax revenue
As % of GDP, 2010

1	Denmark	48.2		Iceland	36.3
2	Sweden	45.8	15	United Kingdom	35.0
3	Belgium	43.8	16	Czech Republic	34.9
4	Italy	43.0	17	Estonia	34.0
5	France	42.9	18	Israel	32.4
6	Norway	42.8	19	Poland[a]	31.8
7	Finland	42.1	20	Spain	31.7
8	Austria	42.0	21	New Zealand	31.3
9	Netherlands[a]	38.2		Portugal	31.3
10	Slovenia	37.7	23	Canada	31.0
11	Hungary	37.6	24	Greece	30.9
12	Luxembourg	36.7	25	Switzerland	29.8
13	Germany	36.3	26	Slovakia	28.4

Note: Includes only OECD countries.   a 2009

Democracy

Democracy index

Most democratic = 10, 2011

Most			Least		
1	Norway	9.80	1	North Korea	1.08
2	Iceland	9.65	2	Chad	1.62
3	Denmark	9.52	3	Turkmenistan	1.72
4	Sweden	9.50	4	Uzbekistan	1.74
5	New Zealand	9.26	5	Equatorial Guinea	1.77
6	Australia	9.22		Myanmar	1.77
7	Switzerland	9.09		Saudi Arabia	1.77
8	Canada	9.08	8	Central African Rep.	1.82
9	Finland	9.06	9	Iran	1.98
10	Netherlands	8.99	10	Guinea-Bissau	1.99
11	Luxembourg	8.88		Syria	1.99
12	Ireland	8.56	12	Laos	2.10
13	Austria	8.49	13	Congo-Kinshasa	2.15
14	Germany	8.34	14	Eritrea	2.34
15	Malta	8.28	15	Sudan	2.38

Parliamentary seats

Lower chambers, seats per 100,000 population, May 2012

Most			Least		
1	Antigua & Barbuda	21.11	1	India	0.04
2	Bahamas	11.08	2	United States	0.14
3	Barbados	10.99	3	Pakistan	0.20
4	St Lucia	10.34	4	Nigeria	0.23
5	Belize	10.26	5	Brazil	0.26
6	Gabon	7.97	6	Philippines	0.31
7	Bhutan	6.47		Russia	0.31
8	Swaziland	5.56	8	Colombia	0.36
9	Lesotho	5.53	9	Japan	0.38
10	Slovenia	4.43	10	Mexico	0.44
11	Ireland	3.71	11	Uzbekistan	0.55
12	Namibia	3.42	12	Egypt	0.63
13	Congo-Brazzaville	3.39	13	Argentina	0.64

Women in parliament

Lower chambers, women as % of total seats, May 2012

1	Rwanda	56.3	15	Angola	38.2
2	Andorra	50.0	16	Belgium	38.0
3	Cuba	45.2	17	Argentina	37.4
4	Sweden	44.7	18	Spain	36.0
5	Seychelles	43.8		Tanzania	36.0
6	Finland	42.5	20	Uganda	35.0
7	South Africa	42.3	21	Nepal	33.2
8	Netherlands	40.7	22	Germany	32.9
9	Nicaragua	40.2	23	Ecuador	32.3
10	Iceland	39.7		Timor-Leste	32.3
11	Norway	39.6	25	New Zealand	32.2
12	Mozambique	39.2		Slovenia	32.2
13	Denmark	39.1	27	Belarus	31.8
14	Costa Rica	38.6	28	Guyana	31.3

Inflation

Consumer price inflation

Highest, 2011, %		*Lowest, 2011, %*	
1 Belarus	53.2	1 Japan	-0.3
2 Venezuela	27.1	2 Switzerland	0.2
3 Iran	22.7	3 St Lucia[b]	0.6
4 Guinea	21.4	4 Montenegro[b]	0.7
5 Uganda	18.7	5 Belize[b]	0.9
6 Suriname	17.7	Morocco	0.9
7 Congo-Kinshasa[a]	17.3	United Arab Emirates	0.9
8 Kyrgyzstan	16.6	8 Bahamas[b]	1.3
Sierra Leone[b]	16.6	Gabon	1.3
10 Yemen	16.4	Norway	1.3
11 Kenya	14.0	11 Taiwan	1.4
12 Afghanistan	13.8	12 Central African Rep.[b]	1.5
13 Angola	13.5	13 Netherlands Antilles[c]	1.8
14 Sudan[b]	13.0	Slovenia	1.8
15 Tanzania	12.7	15 Czech Republic	1.9
16 Tajikistan	12.4	Qatar	1.9
17 Pakistan	11.9	17 Bahrain[b]	2.0
18 Maldives	11.3	Bhutan[b]	2.0
19 Serbia	11.1	19 France	2.1
20 Nigeria	10.8	20 Benin[b]	2.3
21 Mozambique	10.4	Croatia	2.3
22 Egypt	10.1	Germany	2.3
		Netherlands	2.3

Highest average annual consumer price inflation, 2006–11, %		*Lowest average annual consumer price inflation, 2006–11, %*	
1 Zimbabwe[d]	212.0	1 Japan	-0.2
2 Venezuela	26.9	2 Switzerland	0.7
3 Ethiopia[e]	18.7	3 Ireland	1.2
4 Belarus	18.3	4 Lebanon[e]	1.3
5 Iran	17.7	5 Bhutan[e]	1.4
6 Congo-Kinshasa[f]	17.1	Taiwan	1.4
7 Myanmar[e]	17.0	7 France	1.6
8 Guinea	16.4	8 Germany	1.7
9 Ukraine	14.1	Morocco	1.7
10 Pakistan	13.4	10 Netherlands	1.8
11 Angola	13.3	Sweden	1.8
12 Ghana	13.1	12 Canada	1.9
13 Kyrgyzstan	13.0	Portugal	1.9
14 Kenya	12.4	14 Italy	2.0
15 Egypt	12.1	15 Belize[e]	2.1
Jamaica	12.1	Norway	2.1
17 Liberia[g]	12.0	17 Austria	2.2
18 Yemen	11.9	Finland	2.2
19 Mongolia	11.8	United States	2.2
20 Burundi	11.7	20 Denmark	2.3
Sri Lanka[e]	11.7	Luxembourg	2.3
Tajikistan	11.7	Spain	2.3
Vietnam[e]	11.7	23 Malta	2.4

a 2008 b 2010 c 2009 d Estimates. e 2006–10 f 2006–08 g 2006–09

Commodity prices

2011, % change on a year earlier		*2005–11, % change*	
1 Beef (US)	21.0	1 Gold	254.0
2 Wool (NZ)	16.2	2 Tin	253.7
3 Gold	16.0	3 Corn	226.3
4 Wool (Aus)	15.3	4 Coconut oil	185.0
5 Beef (Aus)	15.2	5 Cotton	177.5
6 Oil[a]	10.9	6 Rubber	170.8
7 Rice	4.6	7 Palm oil	166.5
8 Lamb	2.7	8 Sugar	163.1
9 Corn	1.6	9 Soya oil	145.3
10 Coffee	-5.5	10 Lead	145.0
Hides	-5.5	11 Copper	139.5
12 Tea	-6.3	12 Coffee	135.6
13 Soya oil	-8.8	13 Wheat	123.9
14 Soyabeans	-12.8	14 Soyabeans	116.0
15 Aluminium	-17.1	15 Tea	94.7
16 Coconut oil	-17.3	16 Cocoa	94.0
17 Lead	-18.5	17 Rice	90.3
18 Zinc	-18.7	18 Soya meal	83.6
19 Copper	-19.2	19 Wool (Aus)	81.3
Wheat	-19.2	20 Wool (NZ)	76.7
21 Palm oil	-19.8	21 Oil[a]	68.4
22 Soya meal	-20.4	22 Lamb	67.7
23 Timber	-21.7	23 Zinc	58.7
24 Nickel	-21.9	24 Nickel	54.9
25 Sugar	-24.4	25 Beef (Aus)	48.7
26 Tin	-27.9	26 Aluminium	26.4

The Economist's house-price indicators

Q1 2012[b], % change on a year earlier		*Q1 2007–Q1 2012[b], % change*	
1 Canada	6.8	1 Hong Kong	72.0
2 Singapore	5.9	2 Singapore	34.1
3 Austria	5.1	3 China	23.2
Hong Kong	5.1	4 Canada	19.8
5 France	4.3	5 Switzerland	19.5
6 Belgium	4.0	6 Australia	15.5
7 Switzerland	3.8	7 Belgium	15.2
8 New Zealand	2.5	8 Austria	12.7
9 Germany	2.3	9 Sweden	11.2
10 United Kingdom	0.9	10 South Africa	10.7
11 China	0.3	11 Germany	6.6
12 South Africa	-0.3	12 France	5.8
13 Italy	-2.2	13 New Zealand	-2.3
14 Sweden	-2.8	14 Italy	-5.2
15 Japan	-3.2	15 Netherlands	-6.7
Netherlands	-3.2	16 United Kingdom	-10.3
17 United States	-4.0	17 Japan	-12.1
18 Australia	-4.8	18 Spain	-16.8
19 Denmark	-4.9	19 Denmark	-17.2
20 Spain	-6.9	20 United States	-30.1

a West Texas Intermediate. b Or latest.

Debt

Highest foreign debt[a]

$bn, 2010

1	China	548.6	24	Colombia	63.1
2	Russia	384.7	25	Pakistan	56.8
3	South Korea	362.0	26	Venezuela	55.6
4	Brazil	347.0	27	Hong Kong	55.0
5	Poland	296.0	28	Iraq	53.0
6	Turkey	293.9	29	Bulgaria	48.1
7	India	290.3	30	South Africa	45.2
8	Mexico	200.1	31	Kuwait	45.0
9	Indonesia	179.1	32	Latvia	39.6
10	Hungary	179.0	33	Peru	36.3
11	United Arab Emirates	152.0	34	Vietnam	35.1
12	Argentina	127.8	35	Egypt	34.8
13	Romania	121.5	36	Serbia	32.2
14	Kazakhstan	118.7	37	Slovakia	32.0
15	Ukraine	116.8	38	Lithuania	29.6
16	Qatar	108.0	39	Belarus	25.7
17	Israel	106.0	40	Morocco	25.4
18	Taiwan	102.0	41	Bangladesh	25.0
19	Chile	86.3	42	Lebanon	24.3
20	Czech Republic	86.0	43	Estonia	22.0
21	Malaysia	81.5		Singapore	22.0
22	Philippines	72.4	45	Sudan	21.8
23	Thailand	71.3	46	Tunisia	21.6

Highest foreign debt burden[a]

Present value of foreign debt as % of GDP, 2010

1	Hungary	139.0	22	Papua New Guinea	54.9
2	Latvia	129.1	23	Guinea	53.6
3	Estonia	116.0	24	United Arab Emirates	51.0
4	Zimbabwe	110.3	25	Israel	48.7
5	Jamaica	102.2	26	Côte d'Ivoire	48.0
6	Bulgaria	94.9	27	Chile	47.7
7	Kazakhstan	89.1	28	Tunisia	47.5
8	Qatar	83.6	29	Armenia	46.5
9	Ukraine	75.0		El Salvador	46.5
10	Sudan	70.2	31	Panama	43.7
11	Lithuania	68.7	32	Czech Republic	43.4
12	Mauritania	68.4	33	Tajikistan	42.4
13	Lebanon	67.1	34	Belarus	41.8
	Serbia	67.1	35	Turkey	39.4
15	Bahrain	66.1	36	Kyrgyzstan	37.8
16	Moldova	65.5	37	Argentina	37.5
17	Laos	65.4		Colombia	37.5
18	Georgia	65.0	39	Bosnia	37.3
19	Poland	63.0	40	Nicaragua	36.8
20	Romania	58.1	41	Slovakia	36.7
21	Macedonia	57.0	42	Sri Lanka	36.6

a Foreign debt is debt owed to non-residents and repayable in foreign currency; the
figures shown include liabilities of government, public and private sectors. Developed
countries have been excluded.

Highest foreign debt[a]
As % of exports of goods and services, 2010

1	Eritrea	731.6	22	Angola	150.3
2	Sudan	339.2	23	Brazil	146.0
3	Zimbabwe	275.3	24	Tajikistan	145.9
4	Latvia	260.0	25	Guinea	145.2
5	Jamaica	221.3	26	Ukraine	144.0
6	Colombia	211.9	27	Hungary	140.6
7	Laos	210.8	28	Qatar	139.8
8	Serbia	201.2	29	Poland	138.6
9	Georgia	183.9	30	Moldova	135.9
10	Armenia	182.6	31	Estonia	128.8
11	El Salvador	177.1	32	Mauritania	126.1
12	Romania	170.9	33	Macedonia	118.4
13	Burkina Faso	168.7	34	Israel	117.8
14	Turkey	165.0	35	Guatemala	117.6
15	Bulgaria	159.1	36	Sierra Leone	115.1
16	Pakistan	158.8	37	Lithuania	107.1
17	Sri Lanka	156.1	38	Ethiopia	106.7
18	Kazakhstan	154.7	39	Rwanda	102.7
19	Cuba	152.4	40	Indonesia	102.0
20	Burundi	151.5	41	Iraq	101.6
21	Nepal	150.6		Uruguay	101.6

Highest debt service ratio[b]
Average, %, 2010

1	Latvia	76.4	24	Haiti	15.7
2	Kazakhstan	71.4	25	Chile	15.2
3	Tajikistan	44.8	26	Pakistan	15.2
4	Ukraine	40.7	27	Macedonia	15.1
5	Turkey	36.7	28	Cuba	14.6
6	Lithuania	34.3	29	Estonia	14.3
7	Armenia	33.4		Guatemala	14.3
8	Hungary	32.0		Nicaragua	14.3
9	Romania	31.2	32	Bulgaria	14.2
10	Serbia	30.9	33	Sri Lanka	13.0
11	Jamaica	27.9	34	Papua New Guinea	12.9
12	Poland	24.7	35	Moldova	12.8
13	Kyrgyzstan	21.9		Russia	12.8
14	Colombia	21.0	37	Uruguay	12.4
15	Bosnia	19.9	38	Israel	12.0
16	Lebanon	19.1	39	Albania	11.1
17	Brazil	19.0	40	Czech Republic	11.0
	El Salvador	19.0		Dominican Republic	11.0
19	Philippines	18.4	42	Morocco	10.7
20	Georgia	18.1	43	Nepal	10.5
21	Argentina	16.7	44	Tunisia	10.4
	Peru	16.7	45	South Korea	10.3
23	Indonesia	16.6	46	Tunisia	10.1

b Debt service is the sum of interest and principal repayments (amortisation) due on outstanding foreign debt. The debt service ratio is debt service expressed as a percentage of the country's exports of goods and services.

Aid

Largest recipients of bilateral and multilateral aid[a]
$m, 2010

1	Afghanistan	6,374	24	Rwanda	1,034
2	Ethiopia	3,529	25	South Africa	1,032
3	Congo-Kinshasa	3,413	26	Malawi	1,027
4	Haiti	3,076	27	Morocco	994
5	Pakistan	3,021	28	Jordan	955
6	Tanzania	2,961	29	Senegal	931
7	Vietnam	2,945	30	Zambia	913
8	India	2,807	31	Colombia	910
9	West Bank & Gaza	2,519	32	Côte d'Ivoire	848
10	Iraq	2,192	33	Nepal	821
11	Nigeria	2,069	34	Niger	749
12	Sudan	2,055	35	Zimbabwe	738
13	Mozambique	1,959	36	Cambodia	737
14	Uganda	1,730	37	Benin	691
15	Ghana	1,694	38	Bolivia	676
16	Kenya	1,631	39	Yemen	666
17	Liberia	1,423	40	Brazil	664
18	Bangladesh	1,417	41	Serbia	651
19	Indonesia	1,393	42	China	648
20	Congo-Brazzaville	1,314	43	Burundi	632
21	Mali	1,093	44	Nicaragua	628
22	Burkina Faso	1,065	45	Georgia	626
23	Turkey	1,049	46	Ukraine	624

Largest recipients of bilateral and multilateral aid[a]
$ per head, 2010

1	Cape Verde	658.2	23	Namibia	113.5
2	West Bank & Gaza	607.1	24	Mongolia	110.0
3	Dominican Republic	463.6	25	Armenia	109.9
4	Liberia	356.6	26	Nicaragua	108.5
5	Maldives	346.8	27	Mauritania	107.8
6	Congo-Brazzaville	325.2	28	Lebanon	106.2
7	Kosovo	324.8	29	Albania	105.6
8	Haiti	307.9	30	Mauritius	97.9
9	Timor-Leste	261.1	31	Guinea-Bissau	92.6
10	Antigua & Barbuda	211.9	32	Serbia	89.3
11	Guyana	204.3	33	Fiji	88.8
12	Suriname	199.3	34	Macedonia	86.3
13	Afghanistan	185.3	35	Mozambique	83.8
14	Bhutan	179.9	36	Sierra Leone	80.9
15	Jordan	157.9	37	Botswana	78.2
16	Djibouti	149.4	38	Benin	78.1
17	Georgia	140.8	39	Swaziland	77.3
18	Moldova	131.5	40	Honduras	75.8
19	Bosnia	130.9	41	Burundi	75.4
20	Montenegro	122.9	42	Senegal	74.9
21	Equatorial Guinea	121.6	43	Papua New Guinea	74.7
22	Lesotho	118.5	44	Belize	72.8

a Israel also receives aid, but does not disclose amounts.

Largest bilateral and multilateral donors[a]

$m, 2010

1	United States	30,353	15	Denmark	2,871
2	United Kingdom	13,053	16	Switzerland	2,300
3	Germany	12,985	17	Finland	1,333
4	France	12,915	18	Austria	1,208
5	Japan	11,054	19	South Korea	1,174
6	Netherlands	6,357	20	Turkey	967
7	Spain	5,949	21	Ireland	895
8	Canada	5,202	22	Portugal	649
9	Norway	4,580	23	Greece	508
10	Sweden	4,533	24	Russia	472
11	Australia	3,826	25	United Arab Emirates	412
12	Saudi Arabia	3,480	26	Luxembourg	403
13	Belgium	3,004	27	Taiwan	381
14	Italy	2,996	28	Poland	378

Largest bilateral and multilateral donors[a]

% of GDP, 2010

1	Norway	1.10	15	Canada	0.34
2	Luxembourg	1.05	16	Australia	0.32
3	Sweden	0.97		Austria	0.32
4	Denmark	0.91	18	Portugal	0.29
5	Netherlands	0.81	19	Iceland	0.28
6	Saudi Arabia	0.77	20	New Zealand	0.26
7	Belgium	0.64	21	Cyprus	0.23
8	United Kingdom	0.57	22	United States	0.21
9	Finland	0.55	23	Japan	0.20
10	Ireland	0.52	24	Malta	0.18
11	France	0.50	25	Greece	0.17
12	Spain	0.43		Kuwait	0.17
13	Switzerland	0.40	27	United Arab Emirates	0.16
14	Germany	0.39	28	Italy	0.15

Largest financial resource donors[b]

% of GNI, 2010

1	Switzerland	3.86	13	United Kingdom	1.12
2	Finland	1.78	14	Norway	1.10
3	Belgium	1.68		Sweden	1.10
3	Netherlands	1.67	16	Luxembourg	1.07
5	Ireland	1.57	17	Germany	0.93
6	Denmark	1.52	18	Japan	0.86
7	Canada	1.46	19	Spain	0.74
	United States	1.46	20	Italy	0.47
9	France	1.35	21	New Zealand	0.32
10	Austria	1.29	22	Greece	0.26
11	Australia	1.23	23	Portugal	0.07
12	South Korea	1.17			

a China also provides aid, but does not disclose amounts.
b Including other financial resources to developing countries and multinational organisations.

Industry and services

Largest industrial output
$bn, 2010

1	China	2,771		23	Taiwan	136
2	United States	2,769		24	Switzerland	135
3	Japan[a]	1,338		25	Poland	131
4	Germany	827		26	Iran[b]	126
5	Brazil	478		27	Venezuela[b]	114
6	Russia	467		28	Malaysia	106
7	Italy	465			Sweden	106
8	France[a]	451		30	Argentina	105
9	United Kingdom	437		31	South Africa	101
10	India	421		32	Austria	100
11	Canada[b]	420		33	Colombia	96
12	South Korea	359		34	Algeria	95
13	Mexico	341		35	Belgium	91
14	Indonesia	332		35	Chile	84
15	Spain	331		37	Egypt	78
16	Saudi Arabia	269		38	Libya[c]	68
17	Australia	209		39	Nigeria[b]	67
18	Turkey	171		40	Czech Republic	65
19	Netherlands	166			Philippines	65
20	United Arab Emirates	165		42	Ireland[a]	64
21	Norway	149		43	Finland	60
22	Thailand	142			Kazakhstan	60

Highest growth in industrial output
Average annual % increase in real terms, 2002–10

1	Azerbaijan	20.8		11	Ethiopia	9.5
2	Afghanistan	14.3		12	Cambodia	9.2
	Equatorial Guinea[d]	14.3			Tanzania	9.2
4	Laos	13.5		14	Uganda	9.1
5	Belarus	12.4		15	Malawi	9.0
6	China	12.1		16	Vietnam	8.9
7	Bhutan[d]	11.5		17	Tajikistan	8.8
8	Angola	11.4		18	India	8.7
9	Sudan	11.2		19	Maldives	8.6
10	Zambia	9.8		20	Georgia	8.5

Lowest growth in industrial output
Average annual % change in real terms, 2002–10

1	Namibia	-6.8			Denmark	-1.2
2	Grenada	-2.9			Portugal	-1.2
3	Hong Kong[d]	-2.6		13	Canada	-1.1
4	Malta	-2.5			Norway[d]	-1.1
	Moldova	-2.5		15	Luxembourg	-1.0
	Zimbabwe[d]	-2.5		16	Jamaica	-0.9
7	Cameroon[e]	-1.8			United Kingdom	-0.9
8	Italy	-1.4		18	Japan[d]	-0.6
9	Bermuda[f]	-1.2		19	France[d]	-0.5
	Brunei	-1.2			New Zealand[d]	-0.5

a 2009   b 2007   c 2008   d 2002–09   e 2002–07   f 2002–08

Largest manufacturing output
$bn, 2010

1	United States	1,814	21	Netherlands	92
2	China	1,757	22	Poland	76
3	Japan[a]	906	23	Argentina	69
4	Germany	614	24	Sweden	66
5	Italy	308	25	Austria	65
6	Brazil	281	26	Malaysia	62
7	South Korea	279	27	Belgium[a]	59
8	France[a]	254	28	Ireland[a]	49
9	United Kingdom	231	29	South Africa	48
10	India	227	30	Saudi Arabia	44
11	Russia	209		Singapore	44
12	Mexico	179	32	Philippines	43
13	Canada[b]	178	33	Czech Republic	42
14	Indonesia	175	34	Colombia	40
15	Spain[a]	172	35	Finland	39
16	Turkey	114	36	Norway	34
17	Taiwan	113	37	Denmark	33
	Thailand	113		Egypt	33
19	Australia	98	39	Romania	32
20	Switzerland	96	40	Venezuela[b]	31

Largest services output
$bn, 2010

1	United States	10,649	27	Argentina	200
2	Japan[a]	3,605	28	Hong Kong[a]	185
3	China	2,557	29	South Africa[a]	168
4	Germany	2,083	30	Saudi Arabia	154
5	France[a]	1,876	31	Colombia	150
6	United Kingdom	1,554		Portugal	150
7	Italy	1,337	33	Finland	142
8	Brazil	1,201	34	Singapore	141
9	Spain	923	35	Thailand	137
10	Canada[b]	889	36	Ireland[a]	134
11	India	877	37	United Arab Emirates	130
12	Russia	755	38	Iran[b]	128
13	Australia[c]	625	39	Philippines	110
14	Mexico	613	40	Malaysia	107
15	South Korea	532	41	Chile	106
16	Netherlands	517	42	Czech Republic	103
17	Turkey	410	43	Egypt	101
18	Switzerland	357	44	Romania	99
19	Belgium	324	45	Pakistan	90
20	Taiwan	290	46	Venezuela[b]	87
21	Sweden	286	47	Peru	82
22	Poland	268	48	Kazakhstan	75
23	Indonesia	266	49	Ukraine	74
24	Austria	238	50	Hungary	71
25	Norway	212	51	Bangladesh	51
26	Denmark	204	52	Slovakia	49

a 2009   b 2007   c 2008

Agriculture

Largest agricultural output
$bn, 2010

1	China	599	16	Argentina	34
2	India	304	17	Egypt	29
3	United States	156		Iran[b]	29
4	Indonesia	108	19	Germany	26
5	Brazil	103	20	Malaysia	25
6	Japan[a]	71		Philippines	25
7	Turkey	62	22	Australia	24
8	Nigeria[b]	54	23	South Korea	23
9	Russia	51	24	Canada[b]	22
10	France[a]	42		Vietnam	22
11	Mexico	39	26	Colombia	19
	Thailand	39	27	Bangladesh	18
13	Pakistan	36	28	Poland	15
14	Italy	35		United Kingdom	15
	Spain	35			

Most economically dependent on agriculture
% of GDP from agriculture, 2010

1	Liberia[c]	61.3	14	Mozambique	31.9
2	Central African Rep.[a]	56.5	15	Malawi[a]	30.5
3	Sierra Leone	49.0	16	Afghanistan	29.9
4	Ethiopia	47.7		Ghana	29.9
5	Congo-Kinshasa[a]	42.9	18	Madagascar[a]	29.1
6	Mali[b]	36.5	19	Tanzania	28.1
7	Myanmar	36.4	20	Gambia, The	26.9
8	Nepal	36.1	21	Kenya	25.2
9	Cambodia	36.0	22	Uganda	24.2
10	Papua New Guinea	35.8	23	Sudan	23.6
11	Rwanda[a]	33.9	24	Côte d'Ivoire	22.9
12	Laos	33.0		Syria[a]	22.9
13	Nigeria[b]	32.7	26	Paraguay	22.3

Least economically dependent on agriculture
% of GDP from agriculture, 2010

1	Antigua & Barbuda	0.0		Trinidad & Tobago	0.1
	Djibouti[b]	0.0	15	Bhutan[a]	0.2
	Macau[a]	0.0		Gambia	0.2
	St Lucia	0.0		Lesotho	0.2
5	Bahamas[a]	0.1		Suriname[a]	0.2
	Barbados[a]	0.1		Swaziland	0.2
	Belize[c]	0.1	20	Botswana	0.3
	Brunei[c]	0.1		Eritrea[a]	0.3
	Hong Kong[a]	0.1		Fiji	0.3
	Luxembourg	0.1		Mauritius	0.3
	Maldives	0.1		Montenegro	0.3
	Malta[a]	0.1	25	Equatorial Guinea[a]	0.4
	Singapore	0.1		Guyana	0.4

a 2009 b 2007 c 2008

Highest growth in agriculture
Average annual % increase in real terms, 2002–10

1	Angola	14.4		Tajikistan	6.5
2	Myanmar	9.1		Uzbekistan	6.5
3	Mozambique	8.2	12	Gambia, The	6.4
4	Jordan	7.5	13	Cambodia	6.3
5	Ethiopia	7.2	14	Morocco	6.2
6	Afghanistan[a]	7.0	15	Paraguay	6.1
	Nigeria	7.0	16	Iran[a]	5.9
8	Romania	6.9	17	Belarus	5.5
9	Senegal	6.5		Mali[a]	5.5

Lowest growth in agriculture
Average annual % change in real terms, 2002–10

1	Trinidad & Tobago	-11.7	9	Malta[b]	-4.3
2	Namibia	-7.3	10	Ireland[b]	-3.6
3	Zimbabwe	-7.2	11	Bahamas	-3.5
4	Luxembourg	-5.1	12	Estonia[c]	-3.4
5	Hong Kong[b]	-5.0	13	Slovenia	-2.5
6	St Lucia	-4.8	14	Guyana	-2.3
7	Cyprus[c]	-4.7	15	Bulgaria	-2.2
8	United Arab Emirates[b]	-4.5	16	Japan[b]	-2.0

Biggest producers
'000 tonnes, 2010

Cereals

1	China	497,566	6	France	65,676
2	United States	401,704	7	Russia	59,624
3	India	234,910	8	Bangladesh	51,169
4	Indonesia	84,776	9	Argentina	46,204
5	Brazil	75,731	10	Canada	45,412

Meat

1	China	80,743	6	India	6,270
2	United States	42,170	7	France	5,839
3	Brazil	21,333	8	Mexico	5,828
4	Germany	8,220	9	Spain	5,338
5	Russia	6,905	10	Argentina	4,697

Fruit

1	China	122,185	6	Philippines	16,182
2	India	84,791	7	Mexico	15,256
3	Brazil	39,287	8	Spain	15,184
4	United States	25,384	9	Indonesia	14,868
5	Italy	16,908	10	Turkey	13,946

Vegetables

1	China	473,063	5	Egypt	19,516
2	India	99,680	6	Iran	18,678
3	United States	35,294	7	Russia	13,499
4	Turkey	25,831	8	Italy	13,233

a 2002–07 b 2002–09 c 2002–08

Commodities

Wheat

Top 10 producers, 2010–11
'000 tonnes

1	EU27	136,800
2	China	115,200
3	India	80,800
4	United States	60,100
5	Russia	41,500
6	Australia	27,900
7	Pakistan	23,900
8	Canada	23,200
9	Turkey	17,500
10	Ukraine	16,800

Top 10 consumers, 2010–11
'000 tonnes

1	EU27	123,200
2	China	112,600
3	India	82,100
4	Russia	38,600
5	United States	30,700
6	Pakistan	22,900
7	Turkey	18,200
8	Egypt	17,700
9	Iran	15,100
10	Ukraine	11,400

Rice[a]

Top 10 producers, 2010–11
'000 tonnes

1	China	137,000
2	India	95,980
3	Indonesia	35,500
4	Bangladesh	33,200
5	Vietnam	26,300
6	Thailand	20,262
7	Myanmar	11,862
8	Philippines	10,539
9	Brazil	9,300
10	Japan	7,720

Top 10 consumers, 2010–11
'000 tonnes

1	China	135,000
2	India	90,180
3	Indonesia	39,000
4	Bangladesh	34,000
5	Vietnam	19,400
6	Philippines	12,900
7	Myanmar	11,012
8	Thailand	10,500
9	Brazil	8,400
10	Japan	8,125

Sugar[b]

Top 10 producers, 2010
'000 tonnes

1	Brazil	39,450
2	India	21,150
3	EU27	16,760
4	China	11,600
5	United States	7,640
6	Thailand	6,770
7	Mexico	5,080
8	Pakistan	3,860
9	Australia	3,630
10	Russia	2,970

Top 10 consumers, 2010
'000 tonnes

1	India	22,830
2	EU27	19,150
3	China	14,850
4	Brazil	13,230
5	United States	10,150
6	Russia	5,760
7	Indonesia	5,280
8	Pakistan	4,710
9	Mexico	4,540
10	Egypt	2,890

Coarse grains[c]

Top 5 producers, 2010–11
'000 tonnes

1	United States	330,500
2	China	185,100
3	EU27	139,200
4	Brazil	60,200
5	India	43,700

Top 5 consumers, 2010–11
'000 tonnes

1	United States	298,200
2	China	184,100
3	EU27	148,300
4	Brazil	52,900
5	India	40,200

Tea

Top 10 producers, 2010
'000 tonnes

1	China	1,467
2	India	991
3	Kenya	399
4	Sri Lanka	282
5	Turkey	235
6	Vietnam	198
7	Iran	166
8	Indonesia	150
9	Argentina	89
10	Japan	85

Top 10 consumers, 2010
'000 tonnes

1	China	1,061
2	India	829
3	Russia	176
4	Turkey	139
5	Pakistan	131
6	Japan	125
7	United States	124
8	United Kingdom	119
9	Egypt	92
10	Iran	90

Coffee

Top 10 producers, 2010–11
'000 tonnes

1	Brazil	2,886
2	Vietnam	1,168
3	Indonesia	548
4	Colombia	511
5	Ethiopia	450
6	India	302
7	Mexico	291
8	Honduras	260
9	Peru	239
10	Guatemala	237

Top 10 consumers, 2010–11
'000 tonnes

1	United States	1,307
2	Brazil	1,137
3	Germany	558
4	Japan	432
5	Italy	347
6	France	343
7	Canada	215
8	Indonesia	200
9	Ethiopia	195
10	Spain	194

Cocoa

Top 10 producers, 2010–11
'000 tonnes

1	Côte d'Ivoire	1,511
2	Ghana	1,025
3	Indonesia	450
4	Nigeria	240
5	Cameroon	230
6	Brazil	200
7	Ecuador	145
8	Dominican Republic	54
	Peru	54
10	Papua New Guinea	47

Top 10 consumers, 2009–10
'000 tonnes

1	United States	752
2	Germany	315
3	United Kingdom	230
4	France	227
5	Russia	192
6	Brazil	170
7	Japan	159
8	Spain	100
9	Italy	89
10	Canada	85

a Milled.
b Raw.
c Includes: maize (corn), barley, sorghum, oats, rye, millet, triticale and other.

Copper

Top 10 producers[a], 2010		*Top 10 consumers[b], 2010*	
'000 tonnes		*'000 tonnes*	
1 Chile	5,419	1 China	7,419
2 Peru	1,247	2 United States	1,751
3 China	1,156	3 Germany	1,312
4 United States	1,109	4 Japan	1,060
5 Indonesia	871	5 South Korea	856
6 Australia	870	6 Italy	619
7 Zambia	732	7 Taiwan	532
8 Russia	728	8 India	514
9 Canada	525	9 Brazil	470
10 Poland	425	10 Russia	467

Lead

Top 10 producers[a], 2010		*Top 10 consumers[b], 2010*	
'000 tonnes		*'000 tonnes*	
1 China	1,851	1 China	4,213
2 Australia	712	2 United States	1,500
3 United States	368	3 South Korea	382
4 Peru	262	4 Germany	343
5 Mexico	192	5 Spain	262
6 Russia	97	6 Italy	245
7 India	91	7 Japan	224
8 Bolivia	73	8 United Kingdom	208
9 Sweden	68	9 Brazil	201
10 Canada	65	10 India	191

Zinc

Top 10 producers[a], 2010		*Top 10 consumers[c], 2010*	
'000 tonnes		*'000 tonnes*	
1 China	3,700	1 China	5,306
2 Australia	1,480	2 United States	907
3 Peru	1,470	3 India	538
4 United States	748	4 Japan	516
5 India	740	5 South Korea	501
6 Canada	649	6 Germany	494
7 Mexico	570	7 Italy	339
8 Bolivia	411	8 Belgium	321
9 Kazakhstan	404	9 Brazil	246
10 Ireland	354	10 Taiwan	232

Tin

Top 5 producers[a], 2010		*Top 5 consumers[b], 2010*	
'000 tonnes		*'000 tonnes*	
1 China	129.6	1 China	152.8
2 Indonesia	84.0	2 Japan	35.7
3 Peru	33.8	3 United States	34.7
4 Bolivia	20.2	4 Germany	17.4
5 Australia	18.6	South Korea	17.4

Nickel

Top 10 producers[a], 2010
'000 tonnes

1	Russia	274.1
2	Indonesia	203.3
3	Philippines	173.0
4	Australia	170.0
5	Canada	158.4
6	New Caledonia	129.9
7	China	79.6
8	Cuba	65.4
9	Brazil	52.5
10	Colombia	49.4

Top 10 consumers[b], 2010
'000 tonnes

1	China	561.5
2	Japan	177.0
3	United States	118.8
4	South Korea	101.2
5	Germany	100.3
6	Taiwan	72.7
7	Italy	62.3
8	South Africa	40.8
9	Finland	38.8
10	United Kingdom	32.4

Aluminium

Top 10 producers[d], 2010
'000 tonnes

1	China	16,194
2	Russia	3,947
3	Canada	2,963
4	Australia	1,928
5	United States	1,727
6	India	1,610
7	Brazil	1,536
8	Norway	1,090
9	United Arab Emirates	1,002
10	Bahrain	851

Top 10 consumers[e], 2010
'000 tonnes

1	China	15,805
2	United States	4,242
3	Japan	2,025
4	Germany	1,912
5	India	1,475
6	South Korea	1,255
7	Brazil	985
8	Italy	867
9	Turkey	703
10	Russia	685

Precious metals

Gold [a]
Top 10 producers, 2010
tonnes

1	China	340.9
2	Australia	260.0
3	United States	231.2
4	South Africa	191.4
5	Russia	173.1
6	Peru	164.1
7	Indonesia	126.8
8	Ghana	92.9
9	Canada	91.3
10	Uzbekistan	73.2

Silver [a]
Top 10 producers, 2010
tonnes

1	Mexico	3,999
2	Peru	3,640
3	China	3,500
4	Australia	1,880
5	United States	1,280
6	Chile	1,276
7	Bolivia	1,259
8	Russia	1,145
9	Poland	1,130
10	Argentina	723

Platinum
Top 3 producers, 2010
tonnes

1	South Africa	144.2
2	Russia	25.7
3	United States/Canada	6.2

Palladium
Top 3 producers, 2010
tonnes

1	Russia	84.0
2	South Africa	81.2
3	United States/Canada	29.4

a Mine production. b Refined consumption. c Slab consumption.
d Primary refined production. e Primary refined consumption.

Rubber (natural and synthetic)

Top 10 producers, 2010		*Top 10 consumers, 2010*	
'000 tonnes		*'000 tonnes*	
1 China	3,765	1 China	8,088
2 Thailand	3,452	2 EU27	3,407
3 Indonesia	2,781	3 United States	2,657
4 EU27	2,481	4 Japan	1,738
5 United States	2,322	5 India	1,350
6 Japan	1,595	6 Brazil	910
7 Russia	1,379	7 Germany	854
8 South Korea	1,219	8 Thailand	817
9 Malaysia	1,038	9 Russia	746
10 India	960	10 South Korea	714

Raw wool

Top 10 producers[a], 2010–11		*Top 10 consumers[a], 2010–11*	
'000 tonnes		*'000 tonnes*	
1 Australia	246	1 China	402
2 China	159	2 India	82
3 New Zealand	136	3 Italy	65
4 India	38	4 Turkey	46
5 Iran	33	5 Iran	35
6 South Africa	30	6 New Zealand	17
7 Argentina	29	7 Russia	16
8 Uruguay	27	Uzbekistan	16
9 United Kingdom	26	9 Morocco	15
10 Russia	25	South Korea	15

Cotton

Top 10 producers, 2010–11		*Top 10 consumers, 2010–11*	
'000 tonnes		*'000 tonnes*	
1 China	6,400	1 China	9,594
2 India	5,763	2 India	4,483
3 United States	3,942	3 Pakistan	2,200
4 Brazil	1,960	4 Turkey	1,250
5 Pakistan	1,907	5 Brazil	964
6 Uzbekistan	910	6 United States	849
7 Australia	898	7 Bangladesh	843
8 Turkey	450	8 Indonesia	431
9 Turkmenistan	380	9 Mexico	390
10 Argentina	295	10 Thailand	387

Major oil seeds[b]

Top 5 producers, 2010–11		*Top 5 consumers, 2010–11*	
'000 tonnes		*'000 tonnes*	
1 United States	99,900	1 China	104,775
2 Brazil	78,835	2 USA	57,880
3 Argentina	54,300	3 EU27	45,140
4 China	49,440	4 Argentina	43,617
5 EU27	29,795	5 Brazil	42,380

Oil[c]

Top 10 producers, 2011 '000 barrels per day		Top 10 consumers, 2011 '000 barrels per day	
1 Saudi Arabia[d]	11,161	1 United States	18,835
2 Russia	10,280	2 China	9,758
3 United States	7,841	3 Japan	4,418
4 Iran[d]	4,321	4 India	3,473
5 China	4,090	5 Russia	2,961
6 Canada	3,522	6 Saudi Arabia[d]	2,856
7 United Arab Emirates[d]	3,322	7 Brazil	2,653
8 Mexico	2,938	8 South Korea	2,397
9 Kuwait[d]	2,865	9 Germany	2,362
10 Iraq[d]	2,798	10 Canada	2,293

Natural gas

Top 10 producers, 2011 Billion cubic metres		Top 10 consumers, 2011 Billion cubic metres	
1 United States	651.3	1 United States	690.1
2 Russia	607.0	2 Russia	424.6
3 Canada	160.5	3 Iran[d]	153.3
4 Iran[d]	151.8	4 China	130.7
5 Qatar[d]	146.8	5 Japan	105.5
6 China	102.5	6 Canada	104.8
7 Norway	101.4	7 Saudi Arabia[d]	99.2
8 Saudi Arabia[d]	99.2	8 United Kingdom	80.2
9 Algeria[d]	78.0	9 Germany	72.5
10 Indonesia	75.6	10 Italy	71.3

Coal

Top 10 producers, 2011 Million tonnes oil equivalent		Top 10 consumers, 2011 Million tonnes oil equivalent	
1 China	1,956.0	1 China	1,839.4
2 United States	556.8	2 United States	501.9
3 Australia	230.8	3 India	295.6
4 India	222.4	4 Japan	117.7
5 Indonesia	199.8	5 South Africa	92.9
6 Russia	157.3	6 Russia	90.9
7 South Africa	143.8	7 South Korea	79.4
8 Kazakhstan	58.8	8 Germany	77.6
9 Poland	56.6	9 Poland	59.8
10 Colombia	55.8	10 Australia	49.8

Oil reserves[c]

Top proved reserves, end 2011 % of world total			
1 Venezuela[d]	17.9	5 Iraq[d]	8.7
2 Saudi Arabia[d]	16.1	6 Kuwait[d]	6.1
3 Canada	10.6	7 United Arab Emirates[d]	5.9
4 Iran[d]	9.1	8 Russia	5.3

a Clean basis.   b Soybeans, sunflower seed, cottonseed, groundnuts and rapeseed.
c Includes crude oil, shale oil, oil sands and natural gas liquids.   d Opec members.

Energy

Largest producers
Million tonnes of oil equivalent, 2009

1	China	2,085	16	South Africa	161
2	United States	1,686	17	United Kingdom	159
3	Russia	1,182	18	Algeria	152
4	Saudi Arabia	528	19	Kazakhstan	146
5	India	502	20	Qatar	140
6	Canada	390	21	France	130
7	Indonesia	352		Kuwait	130
8	Iran	350	23	Germany	127
9	Australia	311	24	Iraq	120
10	Brazil	230	25	Angola	101
11	Nigeria	229	26	Colombia	99
12	Mexico	220	27	Japan	94
13	Norway	214	28	Malaysia	90
14	Venezuela	204	29	Egypt	88
15	United Arab Emirates	169	30	Libya	87

Largest consumers
Million tonnes of oil equivalent, 2009

1	China	2,257	16	Saudi Arabia	158
2	United States	2,163	17	South Africa	144
3	India	676	18	Australia	131
4	Russia	647	19	Spain	127
5	Japan	472	20	Ukraine	115
6	Germany	319	21	Nigeria	108
7	France	256	22	Thailand	103
8	Canada	254	23	Turkey	98
9	Brazil	240	24	Poland	94
10	South Korea	229	25	Pakistan	86
11	Iran	216	26	Netherlands	78
12	Indonesia	202	27	Argentina	74
13	United Kingdom	197	28	Egypt	72
14	Mexico	175	29	Malaysia	67
15	Italy	165		Venezuela	67

Energy efficiency[a]

Most efficient
GDP per unit of energy use, 2009

1	Hong Kong	18.4
2	Peru	14.4
3	Albania	13.8
4	Panama	13.2
5	Singapore	12.5
6	Colombia	11.9
7	Malta	11.5
8	Botswana	11.4
9	Ireland	11.3
10	Gabon	10.7
11	Switzerland	10.6

Least efficient
GDP per unit of energy use, 2009

1	Congo-Kinshasa	0.8
2	Trinidad & Tobago	1.5
	Uzbekistan	1.5
4	Turkmenistan	1.7
5	Mozambique	1.9
6	Togo	2.0
7	Iceland	2.1
	Zambia	2.1
9	Ethiopia	2.2
10	Ukraine	2.3
11	Kazakhstan	2.5

a 2005 PPP $ per kg of oil equivalent.

Net energy importers

% of commercial energy use, 2009

Highest			Lowest		
1	Gibraltar	100	1	Congo-Brazzaville	-989
	Hong Kong	100	2	Angola	-749
	Malta	100	3	Gabon	-657
	Singapore	100	4	Norway	-656
5	Cyprus	97	5	Brunei	-506
	Lebanon	97	6	Qatar	-487
	Luxembourg	97	7	Azerbaijan	-439
8	Jordan	96	8	Oman	-346
	Moldova	96	9	Kuwait	-332
10	Morocco	95	10	Libya	-327
11	Ireland	89	11	Algeria	-283
12	Belarus	85	12	Iraq	-272

Largest consumption per head

Kg of oil equivalent, 2009

1	Iceland	16,405	12	Australia	5,971
2	Trinidad & Tobago	15,158	13	Saudi Arabia	5,888
3	Qatar	14,911	14	Norway	5,849
4	Kuwait	11,402	15	Gibraltar	5,597
5	United Arab Emirates	8,588	16	Oman	5,554
6	Bahrain	8,096	17	Belgium	5,300
7	Brunei	7,971	18	Sweden	4,883
8	Luxembourg	7,934	19	Netherlands	4,729
9	Canada	7,534	20	South Korea	4,701
10	United States	7,051	21	Russia	4,561
11	Finland	6,213	22	Kazakhstan	4,091

Sources of electricity

% of total, 2009

Oil			Gas		
1	Benin	100.0	1	Bahrain	100.0
	Gibraltar	100.0		Qatar	100.0
	Malta	100.0		Turkmenistan	100.0
	Yemen	100.0	4	Trinidad & Tobago	99.4
5	Eritrea	99.3	5	Brunei	99.0

Hydropower			Nuclear power		
1	Paraguay	100.0	1	France	76.2
2	Mozambique	99.9	2	Lithuania	74.1
3	Zambia	99.7	3	Slovakia	54.3
4	Nepal	99.6	4	Belgium	52.6
5	Congo-Kinshasa	99.6	5	Ukraine	48.0

Coal		
1	Botswana	100.0
2	Mongolia	96.4
3	South Africa	94.1
4	Estonia	91.4
5	Poland	89.1

Workers of the world

Population in labour force
%, 2010 or latest

Highest			Lowest		
1	Qatar	74.7	1	West Bank & Gaza	23.4
2	Cayman Islands	68.4	2	Iraq	23.5
3	United Arab Emirates	65.6	3	Jordan	25.7
4	Macau	62.0	4	Afghanistan	26.3
5	North Korea	59.9	5	Syria	26.7
6	China	59.8	6	Yemen	26.9
7	Iceland	59.0	7	Mali	28.0
8	Vietnam	58.8	8	Timor-Leste	30.5
9	Myanmar	58.3	9	Somalia	31.4
10	Barbados	58.2	10	Algeria	31.6
11	Bahamas	57.5	11	Nigeria	31.7
	Switzerland	57.5	12	Sudan	32.1
13	Thailand	57.0	13	Mauritania	32.3
14	Bahrain	56.4	14	Djibouti	32.9
	Cambodia	56.4	15	Niger	33.0
16	Canada	55.6	16	Egypt	33.4
17	Singapore	55.2	17	Iran	34.1
18	Kazakhstan	53.8	18	Moldova	34.2
	New Zealand	53.8	19	Lebanon	34.4
20	Nepal	53.5		Liberia	34.4
	Norway	53.5		Pakistan	34.4
22	Georgia	53.4	22	Saudi Arabia	34.8
23	Netherlands	53.3	23	Swaziland	34.9
	Russia	53.3	24	Puerto Rico	35.0
25	Peru	53.2	25	Morocco	35.6
	Sweden	53.2	26	South Africa	36.3
27	Australia	53.1		Tunisia	36.3
28	Denmark	53.0	28	Turkey	36.5
29	Cyprus	52.9	29	Angola	37.3
30	Equatorial Guinea	52.7	30	Libya	37.5

Most male workforce
Highest % men in workforce, 2010 or latest

1	Qatar	87.6
2	United Arab Emirates	85.2
3	Saudi Arabia	85.2
4	Afghanistan	84.8
	Syria	84.8
6	Algeria	83.1
7	Iraq	82.4
8	Iran	82.1
	Oman	82.1
	West Bank & Gaza	82.1
11	Jordan	81.9
12	Bahrain	80.7
13	Pakistan	79.3
14	Kuwait	76.1
15	Egypt	75.8

Most female workforce
Highest % women in workforce, 2010 or latest

1	Mozambique	53.5
2	Burundi	52.1
3	Rwanda	51.8
4	Malawi	51.5
5	Martinique	51.1
6	Sierra Leone	50.7
7	Togo	50.5
8	Estonia	50.4
9	Lithuania	50.3
10	Latvia	50.0
11	Congo-Kinshasa	49.9
12	Cambodia	49.8
	Laos	49.8
	Tanzania	49.8
15	Netherlands Antilles	49.7

Public sector employment

General gov. and public corporations, % of labour force, 2008 or latest

1	Norway	34.5	16	Luxembourg	17.6
2	Denmark	31.5	17	Ireland	16.7
3	Russia	30.6	18	Israel	16.5
4	France	24.3	19	Australia	15.6
5	Finland	22.9	20	United States	14.6
6	Slovenia	22.7	21	Switzerland	14.5
7	Estonia	22.4	22	Italy	14.3
8	Poland	21.5	23	Germany	13.6
9	Netherlands	21.4	24	Spain	12.9
10	Greece	20.7	25	Turkey	12.0
11	Hungary	19.5	26	New Zealand	11.7
12	Czech Republic	19.4	27	Mexico	10.0
13	Slovakia	19.3	28	Brazil	9.9
14	Canada	18.8	29	Chile	9.1
15	United Kingdom	18.6	30	Japan	7.9

Highest rate of unemployment

% of labour force[a], 2010 or latest

1	Namibia	37.6	16	Estonia	16.9
2	Macedonia	32.0	17	Serbia	16.6
3	Armenia	28.6	18	Georgia	16.5
4	Martinique	28.1	19	Zambia	15.9
5	Bosnia	27.2	20	Iraq	15.3
6	Lesotho	25.3	21	Yemen	14.6
7	Réunion	24.5	22	Maldives	14.4
	West Bank & Gaza	24.5		Slovakia	14.4
9	South Africa	23.8	24	Dominican Republic	14.3
10	Botswana	23.4	25	Bahamas	14.2
11	Guadeloupe	22.7		Tunisia	14.2
12	Ethiopia	20.5	27	Albania	13.8
13	Spain	20.1	28	Ireland	13.5
14	Latvia	18.7	29	Puerto Rico	13.4
15	Lithuania	17.8	30	Jordan	12.9

Shadow economy[b]

% of official GDP, 2011

1	Bulgaria	32.3	12	Hungary	22.8
2	Romania	29.6	13	Italy	21.2
3	Croatia	29.5	14	Portugal	19.4
4	Lithuania	29.0	15	Spain	19.2
5	Estonia	28.6	16	Belgium	17.1
6	Turkey	27.7	17	Czech Republic	16.4
7	Latvia	26.5	18	Slovakia	16.0
8	Cyprus	26.0		Slovenia	16.0
9	Malta	25.8	20	Norway	14.8
10	Poland	25.0	21	Sweden	14.7
11	Greece	24.3	22	Denmark	13.8

a ILO definition.
b Transactions taking place outside the taxable and observable realm of the official
   economy captured by GDP numbers.

The business world

Global competitiveness

2012

Overall	Government	Business
1 Hong Kong	Hong Kong	Hong Kong
2 United States	Singapore	Singapore
3 Switzerland	United Arab Emirates	Qatar
4 Singapore	Switzerland	Taiwan
5 Sweden	Taiwan	Sweden
6 Canada	Norway	Malaysia
7 Taiwan	Qatar	Switzerland
8 Norway	Sweden	Norway
9 Germany	Canada	Canada
10 Qatar	New Zealand	Ireland
11 Netherlands	Denmark	United States
12 Luxembourg	Finland	Luxembourg
13 Denmark	Malaysia	Australia
14 Malaysia	Australia	Netherlands
15 Australia	Netherlands	Denmark
16 United Arab Emirates	Luxembourg	Finland
17 Finland	Chile	Germany
18 United Kingdom	Kazakhstan	Israel
19 Israel	Germany	United Arab Emirates
20 Ireland	Ireland	Austria
21 Austria	Israel	Chile
22 South Korea	United States	United Kingdom
23 China	United Kingdom	Thailand
24 New Zealand	Estonia	India
25 Belgium	South Korea	Korea
26 Iceland	Thailand	Philippines
27 Japan	Peru	Brazil
28 Chile	Indonesia	New Zealand
29 France	South Africa	Belgium
30 Thailand	Czech Republic	Turkey
31 Estonia	Jordan	Iceland
32 Kazakhstan	Philippines	China
33 Czech Republic	Austria	Japan
34 Poland	China	Kazakhstan
35 India	Mexico	Indonesia
36 Lithuania	Poland	Lithuania
37 Mexico	Lithuania	South Africa
38 Turkey	Iceland	Estonia
39 Spain	Turkey	Poland
40 Italy	Spain	Peru
41 Portugal	Belgium	Czech Republic
42 Indonesia	India	Mexico
43 Philippines	Slovakia	Slovakia
44 Peru	Bulgaria	Italy

Notes: Overall competitiveness of 59 economies is calculated by combining four factors: economic performance, government efficiency, business efficiency and infrastructure. Column 1 is based on 329 criteria, using hard data and survey data. Column 2 looks at public finance, fiscal policy, institutional and societal frameworks and business legislation. Column 3 includes productivity, the labour market, finance, management practices and attitudes and values.

The business environment

		2012–16 score	2007–2011 score	2007–2011 ranking
1	Singapore	8.68	8.60	1
2	Switzerland	8.48	8.47	2
3	Hong Kong	8.47	8.40	3
4	Australia	8.39	8.26	6
5	Canada	8.38	8.36	4
6	Sweden	8.29	8.28	5
7	New Zealand	8.23	7.98	12
8	Denmark	8.14	8.06	8
9	United States	8.09	8.05	9
10	Norway	8.04	7.92	13
11	Finland	8.03	8.22	7
12	Chile	7.97	7.83	14
13	Taiwan	7.95	7.69	17
14	Netherlands	7.89	8.04	10
15	Germany	7.86	8.01	11
16	Ireland	7.72	7.76	16
17	Austria	7.71	7.66	18
18	Belgium	7.67	7.78	15
19	Qatar	7.53	7.27	22
20	Malaysia	7.47	7.17	23
21	Israel	7.43	7.27	21
22	France	7.41	7.50	19
23	Czech Republic	7.36	7.06	25
	United Arab Emirates	7.36	6.97	28
25	South Korea	7.31	6.96	29
26	Japan	7.30	6.97	27
27	United Kingdom	7.29	7.28	20
28	Estonia	7.27	7.05	26
29	Poland	7.23	6.91	32
	Spain	7.23	7.14	24
31	Slovakia	7.11	6.93	31
32	Mexico	6.92	6.71	35
33	Bahrain	6.88	6.93	30
	Cyprus	6.88	6.81	33
35	Thailand	6.80	6.43	40
36	Slovenia	6.79	6.67	36
37	Brazil	6.71	6.51	38
38	Costa Rica	6.69	6.29	42
39	Kuwait	6.67	6.45	39
40	Portugal	6.62	6.71	34
41	Lithuania	6.55	6.21	43
42	Saudi Arabia	6.53	6.08	45
43	China	6.46	5.99	49
	Latvia	6.46	6.04	47
45	Hungary	6.43	6.60	37
46	Turkey	6.41	5.95	50

Note: Scores reflect the opportunities for, and hindrances to, the conduct of business, measured by countries' rankings in ten categories including market potential, tax and labour-market policies, infrastructure, skills and the political environment. Scores reflect average and forecast average over given date range.

Business creativity and research

Innovation index[a]
2011

1	Switzerland	5.77	13	United Kingdom	4.94
2	Sweden	5.76	14	South Korea	4.89
3	Finland	5.72	15	Belgium	4.83
4	Japan	5.59	16	Austria	4.79
5	United States	5.57	17	France	4.72
6	Israel	5.53	18	Qatar	4.69
7	Germany	5.39	19	Iceland	4.65
8	Singapore	5.33	20	Norway	4.53
9	Taiwan	5.27	21	Luxembourg	4.52
10	Denmark	5.10	22	Australia	4.48
11	Canada	5.07	23	Ireland	4.37
12	Netherlands	5.03	24	Malaysia	4.32

Technological readiness index[b]
2011

1	Switzerland	6.30	13	France	5.63
2	Sweden	6.29	14	Germany	5.61
3	Iceland	6.21	15	Austria	5.40
4	Denmark	6.20		Canada	5.40
5	Netherlands	6.13	17	Ireland	5.34
6	Hong Kong	6.11	18	South Korea	5.33
7	Norway	6.08	19	Portugal	5.31
	United Kingdom	6.08	20	United States	5.23
9	Luxembourg	6.00	21	Israel	5.12
10	Singapore	5.90	22	Australia	5.11
11	Belgium	5.80	23	New Zealand	5.10
12	Finland	5.75	24	Taiwan	5.08

Brain drain[c]

Highest, 2011

1	Algeria	1.7
	Haiti	1.7
3	Burundi	1.8
	Serbia	1.8
5	Kyrgyzstan	2.0
	Lesotho	2.0
	Venezuela	2.0
	Yemen	2.0
9	Macedonia	2.1
	Swaziland	2.1

Lowest, 2011

1	Switzerland	6.3
2	Singapore	5.8
3	United States	5.7
4	Qatar	5.6
	United Kingdom	5.6
6	Canada	5.4
	Sweden	5.4
8	Hong Kong	5.3
9	Saudi Arabia	5.2
	United Arab Emirates	5.2

a The innovation index is a measure of the adoption of new technology, and the interaction between the business and science sectors. It includes measures of the investment into research institutions and protection of intellectual property rights.

b The technological readiness index measures the ability of the economy to adopt new technologies. It includes measures of information and communication technology (ICT) usage, the regulatory framework with regard to ICT, and the availability of new technology to business.

c Scores: 1=talented people leave for other countries, 7=they always remain in home country.

Total expenditure on R&D

% of GDP, 2010 or latest			$bn, 2010 or latest		
1	Israel	4.41	1	United States	401.6
2	Finland	3.88	2	Japan	169.0
3	South Korea	3.74	3	China	104.3
4	Sweden	3.40	4	Germany	92.5
5	Japan	3.36	5	France	57.8
6	Denmark	3.06	6	United Kingdom	39.9
7	Switzerland	2.99	7	South Korea	37.9
8	Taiwan	2.90	8	Canada	28.4
9	United States	2.88	9	Italy	25.9
10	Germany	2.82	10	Brazil	24.9
11	Austria	2.76	11	Australia	24.0
12	Iceland	2.64	12	Spain	19.3
13	Venezuela	2.37	13	Russia	17.2
14	Australia	2.28	14	Sweden	15.7
15	France	2.26	15	Switzerland	15.1
16	Slovenia	2.11	16	Netherlands	14.3
17	Singapore	2.09	17	India	14.0
18	Belgium	1.99	18	Taiwan	12.5
19	Netherlands	1.82	19	Austria	10.5
20	Canada	1.80	20	Israel	9.6
21	Ireland	1.79	21	Denmark	9.5
22	China	1.77	22	Belgium	9.3
23	United Kingdom	1.76	23	Finland	9.2
24	Norway	1.69	24	Venezuela	7.8
25	Estonia	1.63	25	Norway	7.1
	Luxembourg	1.63			

Patents

No. of patents granted to residents Total, average 2008–10 or latest			No. of patents in force Per 100,000 people, 2010		
1	Japan	167,820	1	Luxembourg	4,252
2	United States	89,225	2	United Arab Emirates	2,021
3	China	63,916	3	Ireland	1,768
4	South Korea	51,549	4	Switzerland	1,564
5	Taiwan	33,626	5	Taiwan	1,403
6	Russia	23,394	6	South Korea	1,296
7	Germany	10,851	7	Japan	1,112
8	Italy	9,295	8	Singapore	970
9	France	9,081	9	Sweden	855
10	India	2,480	10	France	694
11	Spain	2,296	11	United Kingdom	683
12	Ukraine	2,276	12	United States	651
13	United Kingdom	2,170	13	Germany	629
14	Canada	1,940	14	Iceland	595
15	Netherlands	1,727	15	Hong Kong	473
16	Poland	1,457	16	Australia	429
17	Sweden	1,054	17	Canada	391
18	Australia	1,010	18	Israel	344
19	Austria	948	19	Greece	284
20	Kazakhstan	934	20	New Zealand	267

Business costs and FDI

Office rents
Central business district, $ per sq. foot, Q4 2011

1	Hong Kong	150.09	13	St Petersburg, Russia	71.53
2	London (West End), UK	142.94	14	Mumbai, India	67.79
			15	Brisbane, Australia	64.75
3	Tokyo, Japan	118.89	16	Manhattan, USA	64.36
4	Moscow, Russia	111.48	17	Milan, Italy	63.15
5	Paris, France	99.84	18	Stockhom, Sweden	60.62
6	Singapore	87.65	19	Beijing, China	56.05
7	Perth, Australia	86.49	20	Delhi (NCR), India	55.03
8	London (City), UK	84.99	21	Melbourne, Australia	54.44
9	Geneva, Switzerland	84.01	22	Oslo, Norway	54.20
10	Sydney, Australia	82.61	23	Washington DC, USA	52.88
11	Lagos, Nigeria	78.04	24	Frankfurt, Germany	51.97
12	Dubai, UAE	76.22	25	Abu Dhabi, UAE	50.58

Minimum wage
Minimum wage as a ratio of the median wage of full-time workers, 2010

1	Turkey	0.67	11	Netherlands	0.47
2	France	0.60		Hungary	0.47
3	New Zealand	0.59	13	Slovakia	0.46
4	Slovenia	0.58		United Kingdom	0.46
5	Portugal	0.56	15	Lithuania	0.45
6	Australia	0.54		Poland	0.45
	Latvia	0.54	17	Canada	0.44
8	Belgium	0.52		Romania	0.44
	Ireland	0.52		Spain	0.44
10	Greece	0.49	20	Luxembourg	0.42

Foreign direct investment[a]

Inflows, $m, 2010

1	United States	228,249
2	China	105,735
3	Hong Kong	68,904
4	Belgium	61,714
5	Brazil	48,438
6	Germany	46,134
7	United Kingdom	45,908
8	Russia	41,194
9	Singapore	38,638
10	France	33,905
11	Australia	32,472
12	British Virgin Islands	30,526
13	Saudi Arabia	28,105
14	Ireland	26,330
15	India	24,640
16	Spain	24,547
17	Canada	23,413

Outflows, $m, 2010

1	United States	328,905
2	Germany	104,857
3	France	84,112
4	Hong Kong	76,077
5	China	68,000
6	Switzerland	58,253
7	Japan	56,263
8	Russia	51,697
9	Canada	38,585
10	Belgium	37,735
11	Netherlands	31,904
12	Sweden	30,399
13	Australia	26,431
14	Spain	21,598
15	Italy	21,005
16	British Virgin Islands	20,598
17	Singapore	19,739

Note: NCR is National Capital Region.
a Investment in companies in a foreign country.

Business red tape, corruption and piracy

Number of days taken to register a new company

Lowest, 2012		Highest, 2012	
1 New Zealand	1	1 Suriname	694
2 Australia	2	2 Congo-Kinshasa	160
Georgia	2	3 Venezuela	141
4 Hong Kong	3	4 Equatorial Guinea	137
Macedonia	3	5 Brazil	119
Rwanda	3	6 Haiti	105
Singapore	3	7 Timor-Leste	103
8 Belgium	4	8 Brunei	101
Hungary	4	9 Laos	93
10 Albania	5	10 Zimbabwe	90
Belarus	5	11 Cambodia	85
Canada	5	12 Eritrea	84
Iceland	5	Togo	84
Portugal	5	14 Iraq	77
Saudi Arabia	5	15 Angola	68
Senegal	5		

Corruption perceptions index[a]

2011, 10 = least corrupt

Lowest		Highest	
1 New Zealand	9.5	1 North Korea	1.0
2 Denmark	9.4	2 Somalia	1.0
Finland	9.4	3 Afghanistan	1.5
4 Sweden	9.3	Myanmar	1.5
5 Singapore	9.2	5 Sudan	1.6
6 Norway	9.0	Turkmenistan	1.6
7 Netherlands	8.9	Uzbekistan	1.6
8 Australia	8.8	8 Haiti	1.8
Switzerland	8.8	Iraq	1.8
10 Canada	8.7	10 Burundi	1.9
11 Luxembourg	8.5	Equatorial Guinea	1.9
12 Hong Kong	8.4	Venezuela	1.9
13 Iceland	8.3	13 Angola	2.0
14 Germany	8.0	Chad	2.0
Japan	8.0	Congo-Kinshasa	2.0
		Libya	2.0

Business software piracy

% of software that is pirated, 2010

1 Georgia	93		Venezuela	88
2 Zimbabwe	91	11	Indonesia	87
3 Bangladesh	90	12	Sri Lanka	86
Moldova	90		Ukraine	86
Yemen	90	14	Iraq	85
6 Armenia	89	15	Pakistan	84
7 Azerbaijan	88	16	Algeria	83
Belarus	88		Paraguay	83
Libya	88		Vietnam	83

a This index ranks countries based on how much corruption is perceived by business people, academics and risk analysts to exist among politicians and public officials.

Businesses and banks

Largest non-bank businesses
By market capitalisation, $bn
End December 2009

1	PetroChina	China	353.2
2	Exxon Mobil	United States	323.7
3	Microsoft	United States	270.6
4	Wal-Mart Stores	United States	203.7
5	BHP Billiton	Australia/United Kingdom	201.1
6	Petrobras	Brazil	199.2
7	Google	United States	196.7
8	Apple	United States	189.6
9	China Mobile	China	188.5
10	Royal Dutch Shell	United Kingdom/Netherlands	186.6
11	BP	United Kingdom	181.8
12	Johnson & Johnson	United States	177.7
13	Nestlé	Switzerland	177.1
	Procter & Gamble	United States	177.1
15	IBM	United States	172.0
16	AT&T	United States	165.4
17	General Electric	United States	161.1
18	China Petroleum & Chemical Corp	China	159.3
19	Chevron	United States	154.5
20	Berkshire Hathaway	United States	153.6
21	Total	France	151.4
22	Roche	Switzerland	147.4
23	Pfizer	United States	146.8
24	Gazprom	Russia	144.4

End March 2012

1	Apple	United States	559.0
2	Exxon Mobil	United States	408.8
3	PetroChina	China	279.1
4	Microsoft	United States	270.6
5	IBM	United States	241.8
6	Royal Dutch Shell	United Kingdom/Netherlands	222.7
7	China Mobile	China	221.0
8	General Electric	United States	212.4
9	Chevron	United States	212.0
10	Wal-Mart Stores	United States	208.4
11	Google	United States	207.7
12	Nestlé	Switzerland	207.6
13	Berkshire Hathaway	United States	201.1
14	AT&T	United States	185.2
15	Procter & Gamble	United States	185.1
16	Johnson & Johnson	United States	181.1
17	BHP Billiton	Australia/London	180.6
18	Petrobras	Brazil	171.0
19	Pfizer	United States	170.7
20	Coca-Cola	United States	167.5
21	Samsung	South Korea	165.9
22	Philip Morris International	United States	152.6
23	Novartis	Switzerland	151.9
24	Roche	Switzerland	151.7

Largest banks

By market capitalisation, $bn
End December 2009

1	Industrial and Commercial Bank of China	China	269.0
2	China Construction Bank	China	201.5
3	HSBC Holdings	United Kingdom	199.2
4	JPMorgan Chase	United States	171.1
5	Bank of China	China	154.0
6	Bank of America	United States	149.6
7	Wells Fargo	United States	138.0
8	Banco Santander	Spain	136.2
9	BNP Paribas	France	94.9
10	Citigroup	United States	93.5
11	Itaú Unibanco	Brazil	90.1
12	Royal Bank of Canada	Canada	75.7
13	Commonwealth Bank of Australia	Australia	75.6
14	Mitsubishi UFJ Financial Group	Japan	68.7
15	BBVA	Spain	68.4

End March 2012

1	Industrial & Commercial Bank of China	China	236.4
2	China Construction Bank	China	193.2
3	Wells Fargo	United States	180.0
4	JPMorgan Chase	United States	175.5
5	HSBC	United Kingdom	160.8
6	Agricultural Bank of China	China	138.3
7	Bank of China	China	126.3
8	Citigroup	United States	107.0
9	Bank of America	United States	102.7
10	Royal Bank of Canada	Canada	83.4
11	Commonwealth Bank of Australia	Australia	82.2
12	Itaú Bank	Brazil	81.8
13	Toronto-Dominion Bank	Canada	76.8
14	Mitsubishi UFJ Financial	Japan	70.6
15	Banco Santander	Spain	69.8

Central bank staff

Per 100,000 population, 2011

Highest			Lowest		
1	Cayman Islands	303.6	1	Ethiopia	0.6
2	San Marino	292.3		Somalia	0.6
3	Bermuda	227.1	3	Pakistan	0.8
4	Seychelles	146.9	4	India	1.6
5	Curaçao & St Maarten	119.2	5	Myanmar	2.1
6	Barbados	86.9	6	Brazil	2.2
7	Aruba	80.1		Indonesia	2.2
8	Panama	78.0	8	North Korea	2.3
9	Bahamas	74.1	9	Eritrea	2.4
10	Tonga	73.6	10	Congo-Kinshasa	2.5
11	Suriname	67.7	11	Mexico	2.6
12	Qatar	57.2		Uganda	2.6

Stockmarkets

Largest market capitalisation

$bn, end 2011

1	United States	15,641		23	Indonesia	390
2	Japan	3,541		24	Saudi Arabia	339
3	China	3,389		25	Singapore	308
4	United Kingdom	2,903		26	Chile	270
5	Canada	1,907		27	Thailand	268
6	France	1,569		28	Belgium	230
7	Brazil	1,229		29	Norway	219
8	Australia	1,198		30	Turkey	202
9	Germany	1,184		31	Colombia	201
10	Spain	1,031		32	Denmark	180
11	India	1,015		33	Philippines	165
12	South Korea	994		34	Israel	145
13	Switzerland	932		35	Finland	143
14	Hong Kong	890		36	Poland	138
15	South Africa	856		37	Qatar	125
16	Russia	796		38	Iran	107
17	Taiwan	623		39	Kuwait	101
18	Netherlands	595		40	United Arab Emirates	94
19	Sweden	470		41	Austria	82
20	Italy	431		42	Peru	79
21	Mexico	409		43	New Zealand	72
22	Malaysia	395		44	Luxembourg	68

Largest gains in global stockmarkets

$ terms, % increase December 31 2010 to January 4th 2012

1	United States (DJIA)	7.3		24	Spain (Madrid SE)	-17.7
2	Indonesia (JSX)	3.9		25	Euro area (FTSE Euro 100)	-18.2
3	United States (S&P 500)	1.6		26	Denmark (OMXCB)	-18.5
4	United States (NAScomp)	-0.2		27	Hong Kong (Hang Seng)	-18.6
5	Malaysia (KLSE)	-2.6		28	Euro area (DJ STOXX 50)	-19.0
6	Saudi Arabia (Tadawul)	-3.2			Russia (RTS, $ terms)	-19.0
7	Thailand (SET)	-3.9		30	China (SSEA)	-19.1
8	United Kingdom (FTSE)	-4.2		31	France (CAC 40)	-19.2
9	Switzerland (SMI)	-7.0		32	Chile (IGPA)	-19.5
10	Norway (OSEAX)	-9.9		33	Belgium (BEL 20)	-20.8
11	South Korea (KOSPI)	-10.1		34	Brazil (BVSP)	-22.1
12	Pakistan (KSE)	-10.3		35	Taiwan (TWI)	-24.0
13	Canada (S&P TSX)	-10.9		36	Israel (TA-100)	-24.7
14	Australia (All Ord)	-11.4		37	Italy (FTSE/MIB)	-26.9
15	Japan (Nikkei 225)	-11.6		38	Argentina (MERV)	-28.9
16	Japan (Topix)	-12.6		39	Czech Republic (PX)	-29.4
17	Mexico (IPC)	-12.9		40	China (SSEB, $ terms)	-30.3
18	Netherlands (AEX)	-14.6		41	Poland (WIG)	-31.9
19	Sweden (OMXS30)	-14.8		42	India (BSE)	-34.6
20	Germany (DAX)	-14.9		43	Hungary (BUX)	-35.1
21	Singapore (STI)	-15.5		44	Austria (ATX)	-35.8
22	Colombia (IGBC)	-15.7		45	Turkey (ISE)	-36.3
23	South Africa (JSE AS)	-17.0		46	Egypt (Case 30)	-50.4

a Total return index.

Largest value traded, $bn
$bn, 2011

1	United States	30,751		23	Singapore	254
2	China	7,671		24	Thailand	232
3	Japan	4,161		25	Norway	208
4	United Kingdom	2,972		26	Finland	174
5	South Korea	2,033		27	Denmark	150
6	Germany	1,758		28	Indonesia	140
7	Hong Kong	1,552		29	Malaysia	129
8	Canada	1,520		30	Israel	117
9	France	1,474		31	Mexico	112
10	Spain	1,419		32	Belgium	107
11	Australia	1,246		33	Poland	96
12	Russia	1,146		34	Chile	57
13	Brazil	961		35	Austria	39
14	Switzerland	928		36	Portugal	36
15	Italy	887		37	Philippines	33
16	Taiwan	867		38	Colombia	27
17	India	740		39	Greece	25
18	Netherlands	554		40	Qatar	23
19	Sweden	506		41	Egypt	22
20	Turkey	414		42	Kuwait	21
21	South Africa	372			New Zealand	21
22	Saudi Arabia	293		44	Iran	20

Number of listed domestic companies
2011

1	India	5,112		25	Turkey	362
2	United States	4,171		26	South Africa	355
3	Japan	3,961		27	Iran	347
4	Canada	3,932		28	Sweden	340
5	Spain	3,241		29	Mongolia	332
6	China	2,342		30	Russia	327
7	United Kingdom	2,001		31	Vietnam	301
8	Australia	1,922		32	Italy	287
9	South Korea	1,792		33	Greece	275
10	Hong Kong	1,472		34	Sri Lanka	253
11	Serbia	1,322		35	Philippines	251
12	Romania	1,267		36	Jordan	247
13	Malaysia	941		37	Switzerland	246
14	France	893		38	Egypt	231
15	Taiwan	772		39	Chile	229
16	Poland	757		40	Bangladesh	216
17	Germany	670		41	Croatia	209
18	Pakistan	638		42	Kuwait	206
19	Israel	576		43	Peru	202
20	Thailand	545		44	Nigeria	196
21	Singapore	462		45	Ukraine	195
22	Indonesia	440		46	Norway	192
23	Bulgaria	393		47	Denmark	186
24	Brazil	366		48	Nepal	181

Transport: roads and cars

Longest road networks
Km, 2010 or latest

#	Country	Km		#	Country	Km
1	United States	6,515,892		21	Saudi Arabia	246,951
2	India	4,379,224		22	Bangladesh	239,226
3	China	3,904,690		23	Argentina	230,516
4	Brazil	1,642,069		24	Romania	211,250
5	Canada	1,409,014		25	Philippines	206,326
6	Japan	1,208,882		26	Hungary	200,564
7	France	1,045,798		27	Nigeria	196,106
8	Russia	993,667		28	Thailand	190,214
9	South Africa	866,168		29	Iran	176,763
10	Australia	820,131		30	Vietnam	174,256
11	Spain	662,364		31	Ukraine	169,520
12	Germany	644,126		32	Colombia	164,183
13	Sweden	582,950		33	Belgium	154,547
14	Italy	490,361		34	Congo-Kinshasa	153,497
15	Indonesia	461,471		35	Netherlands	140,560
16	Turkey	427,390		36	Czech Republic	131,204
17	United Kingdom	419,706		37	Malaysia	116,644
18	Poland	385,347		38	Greece	116,493
19	Mexico	368,144		39	Peru	115,338
20	Pakistan	264,330		40	Austria	112,634

Densest road networks
Km of road per km² land area, 2010 or latest

#	Country	Value		#	Country	Value
1	Macau	21.3			Trinidad & Tobago	1.6
2	Malta	9.8		24	Sri Lanka	1.5
3	Singapore	5.3		25	Ireland	1.4
4	Bahrain	5.1		26	Austria	1.3
	Belgium	5.1			Cyprus	1.3
6	Barbados	3.7			Estonia	1.3
7	Netherlands	3.4			India	1.3
8	Japan	3.2			Lithuania	1.3
9	Puerto Rico	2.8			Spain	1.3
10	Hungary	2.2			Sweden	1.3
11	Jamaica	2.0		33	Poland	1.2
	Luxembourg	2.0			Taiwan	1.2
13	France	1.9		35	Latvia	1.1
	Hong Kong	1.9			Netherlands Antilles	1.1
	Slovenia	1.9			South Korea	1.1
16	Germany	1.8		38	Mauritius	1.0
17	Bangladesh	1.7			Portugal	1.0
	Czech Republic	1.7		40	Greece	0.9
	Denmark	1.7			Israel	0.9
	Switzerland	1.7			Romania	0.9
	United Kingdom	1.7			Slovakia	0.9
22	Italy	1.6			West Bank & Gaza	0.9

Most crowded road networks

Number of vehicles per km of road network, 2010 or latest

1	Hong Kong	286.7	26	Luxembourg	69.8
2	Kuwait	267.7	27	Germany	67.8
3	Macau	246.1	28	Bulgaria	66.2
4	Lebanon	241.9	29	Netherlands	65.9
5	Singapore	239.9	30	Trinidad & Tobago	65.0
6	Guatemala	176.3	31	Tunisia	63.3
7	South Korea	165.0	32	Honduras	61.2
8	Taiwan	162.5	33	Switzerland	61.1
9	Netherlands Antilles	161.5	34	Greece	59.8
10	Israel	131.8	35	Croatia	59.2
11	Jordan	116.6	36	Iran	58.8
12	Bahrain	109.5	37	Armenia	58.1
13	Dominican Republic	107.8	38	Poland	51.7
14	Puerto Rico	103.8	39	Saudi Arabia	50.2
15	Qatar	103.3	40	El Salvador	49.6
16	Mauritius	100.8	41	Cyprus	49.3
17	Malta	90.8	42	Venezuela	48.7
18	Malaysia	87.3	43	Serbia	48.0
19	Italy	86.0	44	Japan	47.6
20	United Kingdom	84.2	45	Bahamas	46.6
21	Mexico	83.3	46	Indonesia	45.0
22	Brunei	80.6	47	Spain	43.8
23	Barbados	79.1	48	Slovakia	43.6
24	Portugal	70.7	49	Moldova	43.3
25	Iraq	70.6	50	Ukraine	43.0

Most car journeys

Average distance travelled per car per year, km, 2010

1	China	36,020	21	Greece	15,085
2	Chile	29,483	22	Cyprus	14,907
3	Peru	29,088	23	Sweden	14,793
4	Thailand	27,790	24	Belgium	14,734
5	India	23,882	25	Portugal	14,370
6	South Korea	20,409	26	Germany	14,268
7	Ecuador	20,398	27	Hong Kong	14,155
8	Tunisia	19,451	28	Netherlands	14,107
9	United States	18,413	29	South Africa	14,045
10	Singapore	17,809	30	Iceland	13,620
11	Pakistan	17,747	31	Switzerland	13,592
12	Israel	17,094	32	Australia	13,445
13	Croatia	16,822	33	Norway	13,413
14	Ireland	16,409	34	New Zealand	13,159
15	Denmark	16,117	35	Luxembourg	12,791
16	Finland	16,101	36	France	12,538
17	Morocco	16,080	37	Japan	12,153
18	Austria	16,051	38	Czech Republic	11,799
19	Estonia	15,844	39	Canada	10,845
20	United Kingdom	15,266	40	Italy	10,792

Highest car ownership
Number of cars per 1,000 population, 2010 or latest

1	Brunei	691	26	United States	447
2	Puerto Rico	678	27	Ireland	446
3	Iceland	669	28	Cyprus	438
4	Luxembourg	650	29	Czech Republic	433
5	New Zealand	641	30	Portugal	432
6	Italy	614	31	Estonia	428
7	Malta	558	32	Kuwait	423
8	Australia	554	33	Barbados	410
9	Lithuania	547		Canada	410
	Netherlands Antilles	547	35	Latvia	407
11	Finland	530	36	Denmark	392
12	Slovenia	529	37	Lebanon	366
13	Austria	524	38	Croatia	356
14	Switzerland	518	39	Bermuda	349
15	Spain	505	40	Bulgaria	339
16	France	502		Trinidad & Tobago	339
	Germany	502	42	Japan	317
18	United Kingdom	500	43	Hungary	313
19	Greece	497	44	Malaysia	308
20	Netherlands	488	45	Bahamas	306
21	Belgium	483	46	Slovakia	299
22	Saudi Arabia	472	47	Qatar	297
23	Sweden	466	48	Belarus	282
24	Norway	465	49	Bahrain	277
25	Poland	452	50	South Korea	268

Lowest car ownership
Number of cars per 1,000 population, 2010 or latest

1	Central African Rep.	1		Myanmar	6
	Ethiopia	1		Papua New Guinea	6
	Somalia	1	24	Burkina Faso	7
4	Bangladesh	2		Mali	7
	Burundi	2		Togo	7
	Chad	2	27	Angola	8
	Laos	2	28	Philippines	8
	Liberia	2	29	Kenya	9
	Rwanda	2		Madagascar	9
10	Congo-Kinshasa	3		Mozambique	9
	Equatorial Guinea	3		Pakistan	9
	Lesotho	3	33	Cameroon	10
	Mauritania	3		Senegal	10
	Nepal	3	35	Zambia	11
	Uganda	3	36	Bhutan	12
16	Gambia, The	5	37	Benin	13
	Malawi	5		Nigeria	13
	Niger	5		Sierra Leone	13
	Tanzania	5	40	Bolivia	15
20	Eritrea	6		India	15
	Guinea	6			

Car production

Number of cars produced, '000, 2010

1	China	9,705	21	Malaysia	454
2	Japan	6,787	22	Indonesia	380
3	Germany	4,930	23	Thailand	313
4	United States	3,733	24	Romania	303
5	South Korea	3,181	25	Argentina	284
6	Brazil	2,585	26	South Africa	243
7	India	2,328	27	Hungary	212
8	France	1,991		Slovenia	212
9	Spain	1,731	29	Taiwan	178
10	Mexico	1,198	30	Pakistan	175
11	Czech Republic	1,031	31	Australia	169
12	Iran	1,008	32	Venezuela	121
13	United Kingdom	925	33	Sweden	111
14	Canada	905	34	Vietnam	107
15	Poland	852	35	Ukraine	98
16	Russia	773	36	Portugal	92
17	Italy	671	37	Colombia	61
18	Turkey	537	38	Austria	60
19	Slovakia	493	39	Egypt	56
20	Belgium	480	40	Ecuador	32

Cars sold

New car registrations, '000, 2010

1	China	8,891	21	Saudi Arabia	403
2	United States	7,007	22	Thailand	389
3	Japan	4,267	23	Argentina	350
4	Germany	2,889	24	Austria	335
5	France	2,210	25	Turkey	317
6	United Kingdom	2,180	26	Poland	311
7	Italy	2,057	27	United Arab Emirates	309
8	Russia	2,048	28	Venezuela	289
9	India	1,787	29	Switzerland	288
10	Brazil	1,431	30	South Africa	277
11	Spain	1,050	31	Sweden	276
12	South Korea	997	32	Pakistan	231
13	Canada	915	33	Portugal	215
14	Iran	733	34	Taiwan	183
15	Australia	666	35	Indonesia	169
16	Malaysia	544	36	Greece	164
17	Mexico	532	37	Denmark	146
18	Netherlands	521	38	Chile	137
19	Belgium	492	39	Czech Republic	129
20	Nigeria	460	40	Norway	127

Transport: planes and trains

Most air travel
Million passenger-km[a] per year, 2010

1	United States	1,224,012	16	Spain	75,015
2	China	351,518	17	South Korea	59,013
3	Germany	218,159	18	Turkey	53,734
4	United Kingdom	210,438	19	Thailand	52,474
5	United Arab Emirates	189,448	20	Qatar	50,719
6	France	151,844	21	Malaysia	46,438
7	Japan	120,617	22	Italy	38,674
8	India	115,226	23	Indonesia	32,307
9	Australia	99,598	24	Switzerland	31,115
10	Ireland	94,583	25	Mexico	30,018
11	Netherlands	92,522	26	Saudi Arabia	29,487
12	Hong Kong	90,411	27	South Africa	26,410
13	Brazil	89,464	28	Portugal	26,003
14	Russia	86,216	29	New Zealand	25,678
15	Singapore	83,942	30	Philippines	20,657

Busiest airports

Total passengers, m, 2011

1	Atlanta, Hartsfield	89.3
2	Beijing, Capital	73.9
3	Chicago, O'Hare	66.7
4	London, Heathrow	65.9
5	Tokyo, Haneda	64.1
6	Los Angeles, Intl.	58.9
7	Paris, Charles de Gaulle	58.2
8	Dallas, Ft Worth	56.9
9	Frankfurt, Main	53.0
10	Denver, Intl.	52.2
11	Hong Kong, Intl.	50.4
12	Madrid, Barajas	49.8
13	Dubai Intl.	47.2
14	New York, JFK	46.5
15	Amsterdam, Schiphol	45.2

Total cargo, m tonnes, 2011

1	Hong Kong, Intl.	4.17
2	Memphis, Intl.	3.92
3	Shanghai, Pudong Intl.	3.23
4	Seoul, Incheon	2.68
5	Anchorage, Intl.	2.58
6	Paris, Charles de Gaulle	2.40
7	Frankfurt, Main	2.28
8	Dubai, Intl.	2.27
9	Tokyo, Narita	2.17
10	Louisville, Standiford Field	2.16
11	Singapore, Changi	1.84
12	Miami, Intl.	1.83
13	Los Angeles, Intl.	1.81
14	Taiwan, Taoyuan Intl.	1.77
15	London, Heathrow	1.55

Average daily aircraft movements, take-offs and landings, 2010

1	Atlanta, Hartsfield	2,603	11	Philadelphia, Intl.	1,272
2	Chicago, O'Hare	2,418	12	London, Heathrow	1,262
3	Dallas, Ft Worth	1,787	13	Frankfurt, Main	1,246
4	Los Angeles, Intl.	1,726	14	Phoenix, Skyharbor Intl.	1,240
5	Denver, Intl.	1,578	15	Madrid, Barajas	1,234
6	Houston, George Bush Intercontinental	1,456	16	Detroit, Metro	1,189
7	Paris, Charles de Gaulle	1,450	17	Minneapolis, St Paul	1,188
8	Las Vegas, McCarran Intl.	1,418	18	New York, JFK	1,145
9	Charlotte/Douglas, Intl.	1,385	19	Newark	1,102
10	Beijing, Capital	1,370	20	Toronto, Pearson Intl.	1,101

a Air passenger–km data refer to the distance travelled by aircraft of national origin.

Longest railway networks
'000 km, 2010

1	United States	228.5	21	Turkey	9.6
2	Russia	85.3	22	Czech Republic	9.5
3	China	65.5	23	Australia	8.6
4	India	63.3	24	Hungary	8.0
5	Canada	58.3	25	Pakistan	7.8
6	Germany	33.7	26	Iran	7.6
7	France	33.6	27	Finland	5.9
8	United Kingdom	31.5	28	Belarus	5.5
9	Brazil	29.8	29	Chile	5.4
10	Mexico	26.7	30	Egypt	5.2
11	Argentina	25.0	31	Austria	5.1
12	South Africa	22.1	32	Sudan	4.5
13	Ukraine	21.7	33	Thailand	4.4
14	Japan	20.0	34	Uzbekistan	4.2
15	Poland	19.7	35	Bulgaria	4.1
16	Italy	18.0		Norway	4.1
17	Spain	15.3	37	Serbia	3.8
18	Kazakhstan	14.2	38	Algeria	3.6
19	Romania	10.8		Belgium	3.6
20	Sweden	10.0		Slovakia	3.6

Most rail passengers
Km per person per year, 2010

1	Switzerland	2,258	13	Kazakhstan	879
2	Japan	1,910	14	Belarus	779
3	Slovakia	1,420	15	Italy	735
4	Denmark	1,322	16	Finland	733
5	France	1,320	17	Sweden	721
6	Austria	1,227	18	Luxembourg	690
7	Ukraine	1,097	19	Taiwan	671
8	Russia	1,075	20	South Korea	661
9	Belgium	972	21	India	636
10	Germany	961	22	Czech Republic	624
11	Netherlands	922	23	China	588
12	United Kingdom	887	24	Norway	546

Most rail freight
Million tonnes-km per year, 2010

1	China	2,523,917	13	Poland	34,266
2	United States	2,468,738	14	Austria	23,104
3	Russia	1,865,305	15	France	22,840
4	India	521,371	16	Uzbekistan	22,227
5	Canada	322,741	17	Iran	20,540
6	Brazil	267,700	18	Japan	20,432
7	Ukraine	218,091	19	Latvia	17,164
8	Kazakhstan	197,302	20	Czech Republic	13,592
9	South Africa	113,342	21	Lithuania	13,431
10	Germany	105,794	22	Italy	12,037
11	Australia	64,172	23	Argentina	12,025
12	Belarus	42,742	24	Turkmenistan	11,547

Transport: shipping

Merchant fleets
Number of vessels, by country of domicile, January 2011

1	Germany	3,798	11	Denmark	975
2	Japan	3,795	12	Indonesia	953
3	China	3,651	13	Netherlands	842
4	Greece	3,213	14	Italy	836
5	United States	1,972	15	United Kingdom	778
6	Russia	1,891	16	Hong Kong	712
7	Norway	1,684	17	Taiwan	662
8	Turkey	1,199	18	Vietnam	562
9	South Korea	1,189	19	India	534
10	Singapore	1,021	20	Malaysia	526

By country of domicile, deadweight tonnage, m, January 2011

1	Greece	202.4	11	Singapore	31.6
2	Japan	197.2	12	Bermuda	30.5
3	Germany	114.8	13	Italy	22.3
4	China	108.0		United Kingdom	22.3
5	South Korea	47.5	15	Turkey	19.8
6	United States	46.4	16	Russia	19.5
7	Norway	43.0	17	Canada	19.1
8	Hong Kong	37.2	18	India	18.1
9	Denmark	35.1	19	Malaysia	14.1
10	Taiwan	33.0	20	Belgium	13.0

Shipbuilding
Deliveries[a], 1,000 dwt, 2010

1	China	61,499	11	Turkey	497
2	South Korea	46,924	12	United States	332
3	Japan	32,598	13	Russia	252
4	Philippines	1,859	14	Spain	225
5	Romania	897	15	Indonesia	180
6	Vietnam	840	16	Netherlands	174
7	Denmark	751	17	India	136
8	Taiwan	661	18	Italy	116
9	Croatia	531		Poland	116
10	Germany	524	20	Bulgaria	103

Order books, % of world total by gross tonnage[b], by country of ownership, Jan. 2

1	Greece	13.6	11	Denmark	2.3
2	China	12.7		Hong Kong	2.3
3	Japan	9.3		Singapore	2.3
4	Germany	8.6	14	Israel	2.2
5	South Korea	6.0		United States	2.2
6	Taiwan	4.1	14	India	1.8
7	Norway	3.0	17	France	0.9
8	Turkey	2.8		United Arab Emirates	0.9
9	Brazil	2.4	19	Canada	0.8
	Italy	2.4	20	Netherlands	0.7

a Sea-going propelled merchant ships of 100 gross tons and above.
b Sea-going cargo-carrying vessels.

Tourism

Most tourist arrivals
Number of arrivals, '000, 2010

1	France	77,526	21	Portugal	12,471
2	Indonesia	68,433	22	Poland	12,319
3	United States	58,248	23	Netherlands	10,506
4	China	54,723	24	Hungary	9,818
5	Spain	52,440	25	Croatia	9,615
6	Italy	45,487	26	Morocco	8,904
7	United Kingdom	29,434	27	Japan	8,836
8	Turkey	25,867	28	South Korea	8,801
9	Malaysia	25,111	29	Singapore	8,687
10	Germany	24,808	30	United Arab Emirates	8,632
11	Mexico	22,130	31	Switzerland	8,629
12	Austria	21,941	32	South Africa	7,461
13	Hong Kong	19,973	33	Belgium	6,793
14	Russia	19,885	34	Tunisia	6,651
15	Ukraine	19,621	35	Syria	6,528
16	Canada	15,976	36	Czech Republic	6,183
17	Thailand	15,671	37	Ireland	5,787
18	Saudi Arabia	13,539	38	Bulgaria	5,752
19	Macau	13,099	39	India	5,722
20	Egypt	12,696	40	Taiwan	5,652

Biggest tourist spenders
$m, 2010

1	United States	82,684	11	Hong Kong	19,811
2	Germany	82,027	12	Australia	19,130
3	United Kingdom	64,113	13	South Korea	19,028
4	China	45,953	14	Spain	17,629
5	France	36,403	15	Belgium	16,901
6	Japan	30,808	16	Norway	16,199
7	Canada	27,807	17	Saudi Arabia	15,368
8	Italy	26,081	18	Sweden	15,102
9	Russia	20,488	19	Singapore	14,862
10	Netherlands	20,316	20	Brazil	11,901

Largest tourist receipts
$m, 2010

1	United States	124,711	13	Macau	16,663
2	Spain	53,183	14	Canada	14,279
3	France	48,123	15	Switzerland	13,923
4	China	43,002	16	India	13,549
5	Italy	40,853	17	Sweden	13,188
6	United Kingdom	35,691	18	Greece	13,090
7	Germany	32,595	19	Netherlands	12,620
8	Australia	26,442	20	Mexico	12,042
9	Austria	19,211	21	Poland	11,229
10	Turkey	19,104	22	Singapore	11,060
11	Hong Kong	18,760	23	South Korea	10,563
12	Malaysia	17,278	24	Croatia	10,456

Education

Primary enrolment
Number enrolled as % of relevant age group

Highest			Lowest	
1	Gabon	180	1	Somalia	32
2	Burundi	156	2	Eritrea	45
3	Madagascar	149	3	Djibouti	59
4	Rwanda	143	4	Papua New Guinea	60
5	Togo	140	5	Niger	71
6	Malawi	135	6	Sudan	73
7	Brazil	127	7	Burkina Faso	79
Cambodia	127	8	Mali	82
9	Benin	126	9	Gambia, The	83
Myanmar	126		Nigeria	83
11	Sierra Leone	125	11	Andorra	84
12	Angola	124	12	Guyana	85
13	Guinea-Bissau	123		

Highest secondary enrolment
Number enrolled as % of relevant age group

| | | | | |
---|---|---|---|---|---
1 | Australia | 129 | 12 | Iceland | 107
2 | Netherlands | 120 | | Portugal | 107
3 | New Zealand | 119 | 14 | Uzbekistan | 106
| Spain | 119 | 15 | Antigua & Barbuda | 105
5 | Denmark | 117 | | Malta | 105
| Ireland | 117 | 17 | Estonia | 104
7 | France | 113 | | Montenegro | 104
8 | Belgium | 111 | 19 | Germany | 103
9 | Brunei | 110 | 20 | Japan | 102
| Norway | 110 | | United Kingdom | 102
11 | Finland | 108 | | |

Highest tertiary enrolment[a]
Number enrolled as % of relevant age group

| | | | | |
---|---|---|---|---|---
1 | South Korea | 104 | 12 | Lithuania | 77
2 | Cuba | 95 | 13 | Australia | 76
| United States | 95 | | Russia | 76
4 | Finland | 92 | 15 | Denmark | 74
5 | Greece | 89 | | Iceland | 74
6 | Slovenia | 87 | | Norway | 74
7 | Puerto Rico | 86 | 18 | Spain | 73
8 | Belarus | 83 | 19 | Argentina | 71
| New Zealand | 83 | | Poland | 71
10 | Ukraine | 79 | | Sweden | 71
11 | Venezuela | 78 | | |

Notes: Latest available year 2006–11. The gross enrolment ratios shown are the actual number enrolled as a percentage of the number of children in the official primary age group. They may exceed 100 when children outside the primary age group are receiving primary education.

a Tertiary education includes all levels of post-secondary education including courses leading to awards not equivalent to a university degree, courses leading to a first university degree and postgraduate courses.

Least literate
% adult population

1	Mali	26.2		15	Côte d'Ivoire	55.3
2	Burkina Faso	28.7		16	Pakistan	55.5
3	Ethiopia	29.8		17	Bangladesh	55.9
4	Chad	33.6		18	Morocco	56.1
5	Guinea	39.5		19	Togo	56.9
6	Sierra Leone	40.9		20	Mauritania	57.5
7	Benin	41.7		21	Liberia	59.1
8	Gambia, The	46.5			Nepal	59.1
9	Haiti	48.7		23	Papua New Guinea	60.1
10	Senegal	49.7		24	Nigeria	60.8
11	Timor-Leste	50.6		25	Yemen	62.4
12	Guinea-Bissau	52.2		26	India	62.8
13	Mozambique	55.1		27	Madagascar	64.5
14	Central African Rep.	55.2		28	Egypt	66.4

Top universities[b]
2011

1	Harvard, US	13	Cornell, US
2	Stanford, US	14	Pennsylvania, US
3	Massachusetts Institute of Technology, US	15	California, San Diego, US
		16	Washington, US
4	California, Berkeley, US	17	California, San Francisco, US
5	Cambridge, UK	18	The Johns Hopkins, Baltimore, US
6	California Institute of Technology, US		
		19	Wisconsin - Madison, US
7	Princeton, US	20	University College London, UK
8	Columbia, US	21	Tokyo, Japan
9	Chicago, US	22	Michigan - Ann Arbor, US
10	Oxford, UK	23	Swiss Federal Institute of Technology Zurich
11	Yale, US		
12	California, Los Angeles, US	24	Imperial College London, UK

Education spending
% of GDP

Highest			Lowest		
1	Timor-Leste	14.0	1	United Arab Emirates	1.0
2	Cuba	13.4	2	Central African Rep.	1.2
3	Lesotho	13.1	3	Zambia	1.3
4	Burundi	9.2	4	Lebanon	1.8
5	Moldova	9.1	5	Brunei	2.0
6	Maldives	8.7	6	Sri Lanka	2.1
7	Djibouti	8.4	7	Bangladesh	2.2
8	Namibia	8.1		Dominican Republic	2.2
9	Botswana	7.8	9	Guinea	2.4
10	Denmark	7.7		Pakistan	2.4
11	Iceland	7.5		Qatar	2.4
12	Cyprus	7.4	12	Antigua & Barbuda	2.5
	Swaziland	7.4		Zimbabwe	2.5

b Based on academic peer review, employer review, faculty/student ratio, research strength and international factors.

Life expectancy

Highest life expectancy
Years, 2010–15

1	Japan	83.7	25	Channel Islands	80.2
2	Hong Kong	83.2		Finland	80.2
3	Andorra[a]	82.5		Luxembourg	80.2
	Switzerland	82.5	28	Greece	80.1
5	Iceland	82.0	29	Belgium	80.0
	Israel	82.0		Faroe Islands[a]	80.0
	Italy	82.0		Malta	80.0
8	Spain	81.8	32	Cyprus	79.9
9	France	81.7		Guadeloupe	79.9
	Sweden	81.7	34	Portugal	79.8
11	Macau	81.3	35	Virgin Islands (US)	79.6
	Norway	81.3	36	Costa Rica	79.5
	Singapore	81.3		Slovenia	79.5
14	Canada	81.2	38	Chile	79.3
15	Austria	81.0		Cuba	79.3
16	Netherlands	80.9		Puerto Rico	79.3
17	Bermuda[a]	80.8	41	Denmark	79.0
	Cayman Islands[a]	80.8	42	United States	78.8
	Ireland	80.8	43	Qatar	78.5
	New Zealand	80.8		Taiwan[a]	78.5
21	South Korea	80.7	45	Brunei	78.2
22	Germany	80.6	46	British Virgin Is[a]	78.0
	Martinique	80.6	47	Czech Republic	77.9
24	United Kingdom	80.4	48	Réunion	77.8

Highest male life expectancy
Years, 2010–15

1	Andorra[a]	80.4	10	Macau	79.1
2	Iceland	80.3		Norway	79.1
3	Hong Kong	80.2	12	Canada	78.9
	Switzerland	80.2		Netherlands	78.9
5	Japan	80.1		New Zealand	78.9
6	Australia	79.9		Singapore	78.9
7	Sweden	79.7	16	Spain	78.8
8	Israel	79.6	17	Qatar	78.7
9	Italy	79.2	18	France	78.5

Highest female life expectancy
Years, 2010–15

1	Denmark	87.4	10	Australia	84.3
2	Japan	87.1	11	Israel	84.2
3	Hong Kong	86.4	12	Bermuda[a]	84.1
4	Canada	85.3	13	South Korea	84.0
5	France	84.9	14	Iceland	83.8
6	Spain	84.8		Macau	83.8
7	Andorra[a]	84.7	16	Martinique	83.7
	Switzerland	84.7		Singapore	83.7
9	Italy	84.6		Sweden	83.7

a 2012 estimate.

Lowest life expectancy
Years, 2010–15

1	Sierra Leone	48.2	27	Côte d'Ivoire	56.4
2	Guinea-Bissau	48.8	28	Benin	56.8
3	Congo-Kinshasa	48.9	29	Liberia	57.5
4	Lesotho	49.1	30	Togo	57.8
5	Swaziland	49.2	31	Congo-Brazzaville	58.0
6	Afghanistan	49.3		Kenya	58.0
7	Central African Rep.	49.5	33	Djibouti	58.5
8	Zambia	49.6	34	Gambia, The	59.0
9	Chad	50.1	35	Mauritania	59.2
10	Mozambique	51.0	36	Tanzania	59.3
11	Burundi	51.1	37	Senegal	59.8
12	Equatorial Guinea	51.5	38	Ethiopia	60.0
13	Angola	51.7	39	Sudan	62.0
	Somalia	51.7	40	Eritrea	62.2
15	Mali	52.1	41	Haiti	62.5
16	Cameroon	52.5	42	Namibia	62.7
	Nigeria	52.5	43	Timor-Leste	63.2
18	Botswana	52.7	44	Gabon	63.3
19	Zimbabwe	53.5		Papua New Guinea	63.3
20	South Africa	53.8	46	Cambodia	63.7
21	Guinea	54.7	47	Ghana	64.7
	Uganda	54.7	48	Turkmenistan	65.2
23	Malawi	55.1	49	Pakistan	65.8
24	Niger	55.3	50	India	66.0
25	Rwanda	55.8		Myanmar	66.0
26	Burkina Faso	56.0			

Lowest male life expectancy
Years, 2010–15

1	Congo-Kinshasa	47.3		Swaziland	49.7
	Guinea-Bissau	47.3	11	Mozambique	50.0
3	Sierra Leone	47.5	12	Somalia	50.1
4	Central African Rep.	47.7	13	Angola	50.2
5	Chad	48.6	14	Equatorial Guinea	50.3
6	Afghanistan	49.2	15	Mali	50.9
	Zambia	49.2	16	Cameroon	51.4
8	Burundi	49.6	17	Nigeria	51.7
9	Lesotho	49.7	18	South Africa	53.1

Lowest female life expectancy
Years, 2010–15

1	Lesotho	48.1	10	Chad	51.6
2	Swaziland	48.5	11	Mozambique	51.8
3	Sierra Leone	48.9	12	Burundi	52.6
4	Afghanistan	49.5	13	Zimbabwe	52.7
5	Zambia	50.0	14	Equatorial Guinea	52.9
6	Guinea-Bissau	50.4	15	Mali	53.1
7	Congo-Kinshasa	50.6	16	Angola	53.2
8	Botswana	51.3	17	Nigeria	53.4
	Central African Rep.	51.3		Somalia	53.4

Death rates and infant mortality

Highest death rates
Number of deaths per 1,000 population, 2010–15

#	Country	Rate		#	Country	Rate
1	Ukraine	16.2			Czech Republic	10.3
2	Guinea-Bissau	15.9			Togo	10.3
3	Congo-Kinshasa	15.7		51	Italy	10.2
4	Chad	15.5			Liberia	10.2
5	Central African Rep.	15.3		53	Denmark	10.1
6	Bulgaria	15.2			North Korea	10.1
7	Afghanistan	15.1			Portugal	10.1
8	Lesotho	15.0		56	Djibouti	9.9
9	Sierra Leone	14.9			Kenya	9.9
	Zambia	14.9			Slovakia	9.9
11	Somalia	14.4		59	Finland	9.8
12	South Africa	14.3			Slovenia	9.8
13	Belarus	14.2		61	Japan	9.6
14	Equatorial Guinea	14.1			Kazakhstan	9.6
	Swaziland	14.1			Sweden	9.6
16	Russia	14.0			Tanzania	9.6
17	Botswana	13.8		65	Macedonia	9.5
	Latvia	13.8			Thailand	9.5
	Mozambique	13.8		67	Austria	9.4
20	Nigeria	13.7			United Kingdom	9.4
21	Angola	13.6		69	Channel Islands	9.3
	Burundi	13.6		70	Mauritania	9.2
	Mali	13.6			Uruguay	9.2
24	Lithuania	13.5		72	Armenia	9.1
25	Cameroon	13.4			Ethiopia	9.1
26	Hungary	13.2		74	France	8.9
27	Moldova	13.1		75	Barbados	8.7
28	Estonia	12.7			Faroe Islands[a]	8.7
29	Guinea	12.4			Gambia, The	8.7
30	Croatia	12.2			Haiti	8.7
	Niger	12.2			Spain	8.7
32	Romania	12.1		80	Gabon	8.6
33	Serbia	12.0			Netherlands	8.6
34	Malawi	11.9			Sudan	8.6
35	Uganda	11.7		83	Malta	8.4
	Zimbabwe	11.7			Norway	8.4
37	Georgia	11.6			Senegal	8.4
38	Rwanda	11.5		86	Myanmar	8.3
39	Burkina Faso	11.2			Switzerland	8.3
	Côte d'Ivoire	11.2			United States	8.3
41	Benin	11.1		89	Greenland[a]	8.2
42	Germany	10.9			Namibia	8.2
43	Congo-Brazzaville	10.7			Trinidad & Tobago	8.2
44	Greece	10.5		92	Luxembourg	8.0
	Poland	10.5			Martinique	8.0
46	Montenegro	10.4			Virgin Islands (US)	8.0
47	Belgium	10.3		95	India	7.9
	Bosnia	10.3				

Note: Both death and, in particular, infant mortality rates can be underestimated in certain countries where not all deaths are officially recorded.   a 2012 estimate.

Highest infant mortality
Number of deaths per 1,000 live births, 2010–15

1	Afghanistan	124.5	23	Uganda	72.3
2	Chad	123.9	24	South Sudan[a]	71.8
3	Guinea-Bissau	109.8	25	Burkina Faso	71.0
4	Congo-Kinshasa	109.5	26	Mauritania	69.9
5	Sierra Leone	103.5	27	Côte d'Ivoire	68.8
6	Somalia	100.0	28	Togo	67.3
7	Angola	96.2	29	Congo-Brazzaville	66.7
8	Central African Rep.	95.8	30	Gambia, The	66.4
9	Burundi	94.1	31	Pakistan	65.7
10	Equatorial Guinea	93.3	32	Swaziland	64.6
11	Rwanda	92.9	33	Ethiopia	62.9
12	Mali	92.2	34	Lesotho	62.1
13	Nigeria	87.6	35	Haiti	58.3
14	Malawi	86.1	36	Kenya	58.1
15	Niger	85.8	37	Sudan	57.3
16	Cameroon	84.9	38	Timor-Leste	56.5
17	Guinea	84.2	39	Tanzania	53.7
18	Zambia	81.0	40	Cambodia	52.8
19	Mozambique	77.9	41	Tajikistan	50.9
20	Liberia	76.9	42	Senegal	49.8
21	Benin	76.7	43	Turkmenistan	48.8
22	Djibouti	75.0	44	India	47.9

Lowest death rates
No. deaths per 1,000 pop., 2010–15

1	United Arab Emirates	1.4
2	Qatar	1.5
3	Bahrain	2.8
4	Kuwait	3.0
5	Brunei	3.4
6	West Bank & Gaza	3.5
7	Maldives	3.6
	Syria	3.6
9	French Guiana	3.7
	Saudi Arabia	3.7
11	Belize	3.8
12	Oman	3.9
13	Jordan	4.0
14	Libya	4.1
15	Costa Rica	4.3
	Macau	4.3
17	Nicaragua	4.6
18	Honduras	4.7
	Malaysia	4.7
20	British Virgin Is[a]	4.8
	Mexico	4.8
22	Algeria	4.9

Lowest infant mortality
No. deaths per 1,000 live births, 2010–15

1	Singapore	1.9
2	Hong Kong	2.0
3	Iceland	2.1
4	Luxembourg	2.3
5	Bermuda[a]	2.5
	Japan	2.5
	Sweden	2.5
8	Finland	2.8
9	Norway	2.9
10	Czech Republic	3.0
11	France	3.3
	Israel	3.3
	Slovenia	3.3
14	Italy	3.4
15	Germany	3.5
	Switzerland	3.5
17	South Korea	3.6
	Spain	3.6
19	Austria	3.7
	Belgium	3.7
21	Andorra[a]	3.8
22	Denmark	3.9
	Ireland	3.9

a 2012 estimate.

Death and disease

Diabetes

*% of population aged 20–79,
2011 age-standardised estimate[a]*

1	Kuwait	21.1
2	Lebanon	20.2
	Qatar	20.2
4	Saudi Arabia	20.0
5	Bahrain	19.9
6	United Arab Emirates	19.2
7	Belize	17.4
8	Guyana	17.0
9	Egypt	16.9
10	Réunion	16.4
11	Jamaica	16.0
12	Mexico	15.9
13	Mauritius	15.1
14	Libya	14.2
15	Puerto Rico	13.3
16	Trinidad & Tobago	13.1
17	Antigua & Barbuda	12.8

Malaria

*Deaths per 100,000 population,
estimate, 2008*

1	Sierra Leone	239
2	Chad	235
3	Burkina Faso	221
4	Guinea-Bissau	203
5	Congo-Kinshasa	193
6	Central African Rep.	192
7	Niger	184
8	Mozambique	171
9	Guinea	165
10	Nigeria	146
11	Mali	131
12	Cameroon	121
	Congo-Brazzaville	121
14	Côte d'Ivoire	116
15	Benin	105
16	Zambia	104
17	Uganda	103

Cancer

*Deaths per 100,000 population,
estimate, 2008*

1	Hungary	318
2	Croatia	301
3	Denmark	290
4	Slovenia	282
5	Italy	277
6	Japan	275
7	Latvia	274
8	Estonia	269
9	Czech Republic	267
10	Germany	266
11	Greece	264
12	United Kingdom	262
13	Poland	261
14	Serbia	260
15	France	259
16	Netherlands	255
17	Lithuania	252
18	Portugal	250
19	Uruguay	247
20	Belgium	244
21	Bulgaria	243
22	Sweden	241
23	Austria	237

Tuberculosis

*Incidence per 100,000 population,
2010*

1	Swaziland	1,287
2	South Africa	981
3	Sierra Leone	682
4	Lesotho	633
	Zimbabwe	633
6	Djibouti	620
7	Namibia	603
8	Gabon	553
9	Mozambique	544
10	Botswana	503
11	Timor-Leste	498
12	Zambia	462
13	Togo	455
14	Cambodia	437
15	Myanmar	384
16	Congo-Brazzaville	372
17	North Korea	345
18	Mauritania	337
19	Guinea	334
20	Congo-Kinshasa	327
21	Central African Rep.	319
22	Angola	304
23	Papua New Guinea	303

a Assumes that every country and region has the same age profile (the age profile of the world population has been used).

Note: Statistics are not available for all countries. The number of cases diagnosed and reported depends on the quality of medical practice and administration and can be under-reported in a number of countries.

Measles immunisation
Lowest % of one-year-old children, 2010

1	Chad	46
	Somalia	46
3	Equatorial Guinea	51
	Guinea	51
5	Lebanon	53
6	Gabon	55
	Papua New Guinea	55
	Uganda	55
9	Haiti	59
10	Senegal	60
11	Guinea-Bissau	61
12	Afghanistan	62
	Central African Rep.	62
14	Mali	63
15	Laos	64
	Liberia	64
17	South Africa	65
18	Timor-Leste	66

DPTª immunisation
Lowest % of one-year-old children, 2010

1	Equatorial Guinea	33
2	Gabon	45
	Somalia	45
4	Central African Rep.	54
5	Papua New Guinea	56
6	Guinea	57
7	Chad	59
	Haiti	59
9	Uganda	60
10	Congo-Kinshasa	63
	South Africa	63
12	Liberia	64
	Mauritania	64
14	Iraq	65
15	Afghanistan	66
16	Nigeria	69
17	Niger	70
	Senegal	70

HIV/AIDS
Prevalence among population aged 15–49, %, 2009

1	Swaziland	25.9
2	Botswana	24.8
3	Lesotho	23.6
4	South Africa	17.8
5	Zimbabwe	14.3
6	Zambia	13.5
7	Namibia	13.1
8	Mozambique	11.5
9	Malawi	11.0
10	Uganda	6.5
11	Kenya	6.3
12	Tanzania	5.6
13	Cameroon	5.3
14	Gabon	5.2
15	Equatorial Guinea	5.0
16	Central African Rep.	4.7
17	Nigeria	3.6
18	Chad	3.4
	Congo-Brazzaville	3.4
	Côte d'Ivoire	3.4
21	Burundi	3.3
22	Togo	3.2
23	Bahamas	3.1
24	Rwanda	2.9
25	Djibouti	2.5
	Guinea-Bissau	2.5

AIDS
Estimated deaths per 100,000 pop., 2009

1	Lesotho	680
2	Zimbabwe	661
3	South Africa	627
4	Swaziland	594
5	Zambia	351
6	Malawi	337
7	Mozambique	325
8	Namibia	306
9	Botswana	296
10	Central African Rep.	248
11	Kenya	201
12	Tanzania	196
	Uganda	196
14	Cameroon	188
15	Burundi	175
16	Côte d'Ivoire	172
17	Gabon	164
18	Equatorial Guinea	141
19	Congo-Brazzaville	139
	Nigeria	139
21	Djibouti	118
22	Togo	117
23	Chad	99
24	Belize	91
	Liberia	91

a Diptheria, pertussis and tetanus

Health

Highest health spending
As % of GDP, 2010

1	United States	17.9
2	Sierra Leone	13.1
3	France	11.9
	Netherlands	11.9
5	Liberia	11.8
6	Moldova	11.7
7	Burundi	11.6
	Germany	11.6
9	Switzerland	11.5
10	Denmark	11.4
11	Canada	11.3
12	Bosnia	11.1
	Lesotho	11.1
14	Austria	11.0
	Portugal	11.0
16	Costa Rica	10.9
17	Belgium	10.7
18	Cuba	10.6
19	Rwanda	10.5
20	Serbia	10.4
21	Greece	10.2
22	Georgia	10.1
	New Zealand	10.1
24	Sweden	9.6
	United Kingdom	9.6
26	Italy	9.5
	Japan	9.5
	Norway	9.5
	Spain	9.5

Lowest health spending
As % of GDP, 2010

1	Qatar	1.8
2	Myanmar	2.0
3	Pakistan	2.2
4	Congo-Kinshasa	2.5
	Turkmenistan	2.5
6	Indonesia	2.6
	Kuwait	2.6
8	Eritrea	2.7
9	Brunei	2.8
	Oman	2.8
11	Angola	2.9
	Sri Lanka	2.9
13	Syria	3.4
14	Bangladesh	3.5
	Gabon	3.5
16	Papua New Guinea	3.6
	Philippines	3.6
18	United Arab Emirates	3.7
19	Madagascar	3.8
20	Libya	3.9
	Thailand	3.9
22	Central African Rep.	4.0
	Singapore	4.0
24	Benin	4.1
	Cape Verde	4.1
	India	4.1
27	Algeria	4.2
28	Kazakhstan	4.3
	Saudi Arabia	4.3

Highest pop. per doctor
2010 or latest[a]

1	Liberia	71,429
2	Malawi	52,632
3	Niger	52,632
4	Ethiopia	45,455
5	Mozambique	38,462
6	Gambia, The	26,316
7	Guinea-Bissau	22,222
8	Mali	20,408
9	Papua New Guinea	18,868
10	Togo	18,868
11	Benin	16,949
12	Senegal	16,949
13	Burkina Faso	15,625
14	Ghana	11,765
15	Congo-Brazzaville	10,526
16	Mauritania	7,692
17	Côte d'Ivoire	6,944

Lowest pop. per doctor
2010 or latest[a]

1	Cuba	149
2	Greece	162
3	Belarus	193
4	Austria	206
5	Georgia	210
6	Norway	240
7	Kazakhstan	244
8	Switzerland	246
9	Spain	253
10	Andorra	256
11	Portugal	259
12	Azerbaijan	264
13	Sweden	265
14	Armenia	266
15	Bulgaria	268
	Iceland	268
	Uruguay	268

a 2007–10

Most hospital beds
Beds per 1,000 pop., 2010 or latest

1	Japan	13.7	21	Finland	6.2
2	Belarus	11.1		Moldova	6.2
3	South Korea	10.3	23	Timor-Leste	5.9
4	Ukraine	8.7	24	Iceland	5.8
5	Germany	8.2		Mongolia	5.8
6	Austria	7.7	26	Luxembourg	5.6
7	Kazakhstan	7.6	27	Croatia	5.4
8	Azerbaijan	7.5		Estonia	5.4
9	Czech Republic	7.1		Serbia	5.4
	Hungary	7.1	30	Switzerland	5.2
11	France	6.9		Tajikistan	5.2
12	Barbados	6.8	32	Kyrgyzstan	5.1
	Lithuania	6.8	33	Ireland	4.9
14	Poland	6.7	34	Greece	4.8
15	Bulgaria	6.6	35	Netherlands	4.7
	Romania	6.6	36	Slovenia	4.6
17	Belgium	6.5		Uzbekistan	4.6
	Slovakia	6.5	38	Argentina	4.5
19	Latvia	6.4		Macedonia	4.5
20	Gabon	6.3		Malta	4.5

Obesity[a]

Men, % of total pop., 2010

1	United States	44.2
2	Argentina	37.4
3	Greece	30.3
4	Mexico	30.1
5	Kuwait	29.6
6	Venezuela	29.5
7	New Zealand	28.9
8	Australia	28.4
9	Malta	28.1
10	Uruguay	25.7
11	Canada	25.5
12	United Arab Emirates	24.5
13	Chile	24.3
14	United Kingdom	23.7
15	Austria	23.1
16	Saudi Arabia	23.0
17	Germany	22.9
18	Barbados	22.0
	Egypt	22.0
20	Bahrain	21.2
21	Finland	20.9
22	Guatemala	20.5
23	Czech Republic	20.2
24	Croatia	20.1
	Cuba	20.1

Women, % of total pop., 2010

1	Barbados	57.2
2	Kuwait	55.2
3	Trinidad & Tobago	52.7
4	Jamaica	48.3
	United States	48.3
6	Egypt	48.0
7	United Arab Emirates	42.0
8	St Lucia	41.7
9	Nicaragua	41.1
10	Mexico	41.0
11	Bolivia	40.2
12	New Zealand	39.9
13	Chile	39.1
14	Dominican Republic	38.7
15	Bahrain	37.9
	Jordan	37.9
17	Argentina	37.8
18	Peru	37.7
19	Fiji	37.1
20	Guatemala	36.8
	South Africa	36.8
22	Mongolia	36.6
23	Malta	36.5
24	Saudi Arabia	36.4
25	Lesotho	36.1

a Defined as body mass index of 30 or more – see page 248.

Marriage and divorce

Highest marriage rates
Number of marriages per 1,000 population, 2010 or latest available year

1	Antigua & Barbuda	21.7		Turkmenistan	6.7
2	Tajikistan	14.6		Ukraine	6.7
3	Mongolia	12.5	28	Channel Islands[a]	6.5
4	Iran	11.4	29	Hong Kong	6.4
5	Bermuda	10.6	30	Malta	6.2
6	Cayman Islands	10.3		Philippines	6.2
	Jordan	10.3		South Korea	6.2
8	Barbados	10.1		Turkey	6.2
9	Lebanon	9.5	34	Egypt	6.1
10	Kyrgyzstan	9.3	35	Poland	6.0
11	Algeria	9.2	36	Kuwait	5.9
12	Azerbaijan	8.8		Trinidad & Tobago	5.9
	West Bank & Gaza	8.8	38	Bahamas	5.8
14	Kazakhstan	8.6		Georgia	5.8
15	Russia	8.5		Montenegro	5.8
16	Mauritius	8.2		Netherlands Antilles	5.8
17	Belarus	8.1	42	China	5.7
18	Cyprus	7.9		Lithuania	5.7
19	Jamaica	7.6		Malaysia	5.7
20	Taiwan	7.3		Tunisia	5.7
21	Indonesia	7.0		Vietnam	5.7
22	Macedonia	6.9	47	Denmark	5.6
	Moldova	6.9		Finland	5.6
24	United States	6.8		Macau	5.6
25	Albania	6.7			

Lowest marriage rates
Number of marriages per 1,000 population, 2010 or latest available year

1	Colombia	1.7		France	3.8
	Qatar	1.7		Guatemala	3.8
3	Venezuela	2.5		New Caledonia	3.8
4	Argentina	2.9	21	Brazil	3.9
5	Peru	3.0		Luxembourg	3.9
6	Chile	3.1		South Africa	3.9
	French Guiana	3.1	24	Dominican Republic	4.1
	Slovenia	3.1		Latvia	4.1
9	Bulgaria	3.2		Netherlands	4.1
10	Andorra	3.4	27	Hungary	4.2
	Martinique	3.4		Suriname	4.2
12	Guadeloupe	3.6	29	Belgium	4.3
13	Réunion	3.7		Italy	4.3
	United Arab Emirates	3.7		Thailand	4.3
	Uruguay	3.7	32	Canada	4.4
16	Aruba	3.8		Czech Republic	4.4
	Estonia	3.8			

a Jersey only
Note: The data are based on latest available figures (no earlier than 2006) and hence will be affected by the population age structure at the time. Marriage rates refer to registered marriages only and, therefore, reflect the customs surrounding registry and efficiency of administration.

Highest divorce rates
Number of divorces per 1,000 population, 2010 or latest available year

1	South Korea	4.6	27	France	2.3
2	Russia	4.5		Germany	2.3
3	Aruba	4.0		Kazakhstan	2.3
4	Belarus	3.9	30	Australia	2.2
5	Puerto Rico	3.8		Cyprus	2.2
6	Taiwan	3.7		Estonia	2.2
7	Moldova	3.2		Jordan	2.2
	United States	3.2		Latvia	2.2
9	Cuba	3.1		Slovakia	2.2
10	Belgium	3.0		Spain	2.2
	Lithuania	3.0	37	Austria	2.1
	United Kingdom	3.0		Canada	2.1
13	Czech Republic	2.9		Kuwait	2.1
	Hong Kong	2.9		Luxembourg	2.1
15	Bermuda	2.7	41	Réunion	2.0
	New Zealand	2.7	42	Japan	1.9
	Switzerland	2.7	43	Cayman Islands	1.8
	Ukraine	2.7		Iceland	1.8
19	Denmark	2.6	45	Barbados	1.7
	Finland	2.6		Dominican Republic	1.7
	Netherlands Antilles	2.6		Iran	1.7
22	Costa Rica	2.5		Mauritius	1.7
	Portugal	2.5		Netherlands	1.7
	Sweden	2.5		Singapore	1.7
25	Hungary	2.4		Trinidad & Tobago	1.7
	Norway	2.4			

Lowest divorce rates
Number of divorces per 1,000 population, 2010 or latest available year

1	Peru	0.1		Jamaica	0.9
2	Guatemala	0.2		Serbia	0.9
	Vietnam	0.2		Venezuela	0.9
4	Bahamas	0.3	24	Albania	1.0
	Bosnia	0.3		Azerbaijan	1.0
6	Chile	0.5		Panama	1.0
7	Egypt	0.6		Saudi Arabia	1.0
8	Georgia	0.7		South Africa	1.0
	Ireland	0.7	29	Croatia	1.1
	Mongolia	0.7		Thailand	1.1
	Qatar	0.7		Tunisia	1.1
	Tajikistan	0.7		United Arab Emirates	1.1
13	Brazil	0.8		West Bank & Gaza	1.1
	Macedonia	0.8	34	Antigua & Barbuda	1.2
	Mexico	0.8		Slovenia	1.2
	Montenegro	0.8	36	Faroe Islands	1.3
17	Armenia	0.9		Greece	1.3
	Ecuador	0.9		Suriname	1.3
	Indonesia	0.9	39	Kyrgyzstan	1.4
	Italy	0.9		Macau	1.4

Households, living costs – and giving

Number of households
Biggest, m, 2010

1	China	393.1	14	Pakistan	25.7
2	India	225.8	15	Italy	24.5
3	United States	119.9	16	Iran	20.5
4	Indonesia	69.1	17	Vietnam	20.1
5	Brazil	55.5	18	Ukraine	20.0
6	Russia	52.7	19	Egypt	19.5
7	Japan	50.8		Philippines	19.5
8	Germany	40.0	21	Ethiopia	18.8
9	Bangladesh	35.5	22	Turkey	18.6
10	Nigeria	32.2	23	Thailand	18.5
11	Mexico	28.3	24	South Korea	18.1
12	United Kingdom	27.4	25	Spain	17.6
13	France	27.2	26	South Africa	13.9

Households with single occupation
% of total, 2010

1	Sweden	47.0	15	Belgium	33.1
2	Norway	39.9	16	Lithuania	32.7
3	Denmark	39.4	17	Hungary	32.4
4	Finland	39.2	18	Japan	31.2
5	Germany	38.6	19	Poland	29.6
6	Switzerland	37.7	20	Italy	28.9
7	Slovakia	36.4	21	Belarus	27.6
8	Netherlands	36.1	22	Canada	27.3
9	Austria	36.0	23	United States	27.2
10	Estonia	35.3	24	Bulgaria	25.4
11	France	34.1	25	Spain	24.8
	United Kingdom	34.1	26	Russia	24.7
13	Czech Republic	33.2	27	Australia	24.5
	Ukraine	33.2		Slovenia	24.5

Households with six or more occupants
% of total, 2010

1	Kuwait	60.5	13	Azerbaijan	28.2
2	Pakistan	58.4	14	Malaysia	27.6
3	United Arab Emirates	54.3	15	Egypt	26.8
4	Saudi Arabia	47.4	16	Bolivia	25.9
5	Algeria	45.6	17	Venezuela	24.1
6	Turkmenistan	42.5	18	Peru	21.2
7	Jordan	41.0	19	Vietnam	19.1
8	Morocco	39.5	20	South Africa	19.0
9	India	37.9		Turkey	19.0
10	Nigeria	37.6	22	Mexico	18.8
11	Tunisia	35.0	23	Singapore	18.1
12	Philippines	32.7	24	Ecuador	17.3

a The cost of living index shown is compiled by the Economist Intelligence Unit for use by companies in determining expatriate compensation: it is a comparison of the cost of maintaining a typical international lifestyle in the country rather than a comparison of the purchasing power of a citizen of the country. The index is based on typical urban prices an international executive and family will face abroad. The prices

Cost of living[a]

December 2011, USA = 100

Highest

1	Japan	166
2	Switzerland	157
3	Norway	156
4	France	150
5	Australia	147
6	Singapore	142
7	Denmark	133
8	Finland	128
9	Austria	120
10	Belgium	117
	New Zealand	117
	United Kingdom	117
13	Spain	116
14	Hong Kong	115
	Sweden	115
16	South Korea	113
17	Israel	112
18	Ireland	111
	New Caledonia	111
20	Italy	110
21	Germany	109
	Venezuela	109
23	Canada	108

Lowest

1	Pakistan	46
2	Iran	54
3	India	56
4	Panama	58
5	Algeria	59
6	Bangladesh	61
7	Oman	63
	Philippines	63
	Qatar	63
10	Saudi Arabia	64
11	Bahrain	65
	Cambodia	65
	Ecuador	65
	Romania	65
	Sri Lanka	65
16	Uzbekistan	67
	Vietnam	67
18	Nigeria	68
19	Egypt	69
	Kenya	69
21	Kuwait	70
	Paraguay	70

World Giving Index[b]

Top givers, % of population, 2011

1	United States	60
2	Ireland	59
3	Australia	58
4	New Zealand	57
	United Kingdom	57
6	Canada	54
	Netherlands	54
8	Sri Lanka	51
	Thailand	51
10	Laos	50
11	Hong Kong	49
12	Morocco	48
13	Iceland	47
	Liberia	47
	Nigeria	47
	Turkmenistan	47

17	Denmark	46
18	Guyana	45
	Malta	45
	Qatar	45
21	Finland	44
	Ghana	44
	Guinea	44
	Luxembourg	44
	Switzerland	44
26	Austria	43
	Cyprus	43
	Germany	43
	Guatemala	43
	Myanmar	43
	Trinidad & Tobago	43

are for products of international comparable quality found in a supermarket or department store. Prices found in local markets and bazaars are not used unless the available merchandise is of the specified quality and the shopping area itself is safe for executive and family members. New York City prices are used as the base, so United States = 100.

b Three criteria are used to assess giving: in the previous month those surveyed either gave money to charity, gave time to those in need or helped a stranger.

Telephones, computers and broadband

Telephone
Telephone lines per 100 people, 2010

1	Bermuda	89.0	16	Sweden	52.5
2	British Virgin Islands	86.5	17	Barbados	50.3
3	Taiwan	78.8	18	Canada	50.0
4	Virgin Islands (US)	69.5	19	United States	48.7
5	Cayman Islands	66.4	20	Denmark	47.4
6	Hong Kong	61.8	21	Ireland	46.5
7	Iceland	60.5	22	Greece	45.8
8	Malta	59.6	23	Andorra	45.0
9	South Korea	59.2	24	Netherlands Antilles	44.9
10	Switzerland	57.1		Slovenia	44.9
11	France	56.2	26	Israel	44.2
12	Germany	55.5	27	Spain	43.9
	Guadeloupe	55.5	28	Netherlands	43.5
14	United Kingdom	53.8	29	Belgium	43.3
15	Luxembourg	53.7	30	Belarus	43.1

Mobile telephone
Subscribers per 100 people, 2010

1	Macau	206.4	18	Singapore	145.2
2	Hong Kong	195.6	19	Croatia	144.5
3	Antigua & Barbuda	189.4	20	Luxembourg	143.3
4	Saudi Arabia	187.9	21	Portugal	142.3
5	Montenegro	185.3	22	Albania	141.9
6	Panama	184.7	23	Argentina	141.8
7	Cayman Islands	177.7	24	Trinidad & Tobago	141.2
8	Vietnam	175.3	25	Czech Republic	137.2
9	Libya	171.5	26	Bulgaria	136.1
10	Suriname	169.6	27	Bermuda	135.8
11	Oman	165.5	28	Israel	133.1
12	Kuwait	160.8	29	Qatar	132.4
13	Finland	156.4	30	Uruguay	131.7
14	Italy	149.6	31	United Kingdom	130.8
15	Lithuania	147.2	32	Serbia	129.2
16	Austria	145.8	33	Barbados	128.1
17	United Arab Emirates	145.5	34	Germany	127.0

Mobile banking[a]
% of population, 2011

1	Kenya	68	11	Tanzania	23
2	Sudan	52	12	Swaziland	20
3	Gabon	50	13	Liberia	19
4	Algeria	44		Mauritania	19
5	Congo-Brazzaville	37	15	Chad	18
6	Somalia	34		Kosovo	18
7	Albania	31	17	Macedonia	16
8	Tajikistan	29	18	Haiti	15
9	Uganda	27		Philippines	15
10	Angola	26	20	Nigeria	13

a Used a mobile phone to either pay a bill, send or receive money in the previous year. Excludes high-income economies.

Computer

Computers per 100 people, 2010

1	Canada	124.8	26	Spain	53.2
2	Netherlands	117.6	27	Slovenia	52.8
3	Switzerland	102.5	28	Belgium	50.2
4	United Kingdom	98.5		Macau	50.2
5	Sweden	98.1	30	Cyprus	49.2
6	Taiwan	92.4	31	Macedonia	47.7
7	United States	91.8	32	Czech Republic	45.1
8	Bahrain	89.0	33	Latvia	44.4
9	Australia	85.7	34	United Arab Emirates	44.3
10	Denmark	84.7	35	Malta	43.0
11	Germany	83.2	36	Israel	36.3
12	Singapore	82.3	37	Costa Rica	33.8
13	France	82.2	38	Malaysia	33.1
14	Austria	79.2	39	Bermuda	30.9
15	Hong Kong	75.4	40	Croatia	30.7
16	Norway	74.7	41	New Caledonia	30.3
17	Luxembourg	73.2	42	Estonia	29.7
18	Slovakia	70.1	43	Mongolia	29.6
19	Iceland	70.0	44	Maldives	29.3
20	Ireland	66.2	45	Lithuania	28.4
21	Finland	64.0	46	Kuwait	28.3
22	New Zealand	63.1	47	Antigua & Barbuda	27.6
23	Japan	61.1	48	Hungary	25.9
24	South Korea	59.9	49	St Lucia	25.5
25	Italy	56.3	50	Namibia	25.1

Broadband

Subscribers per 100 people, 2010

1	Bermuda	61.8	23	New Zealand	24.9
2	Netherlands	38.1		Singapore	24.9
3	Switzerland	37.9	25	Slovenia	24.3
4	Denmark	37.7	26	Australia	24.2
5	South Korea	35.7		Macau	24.2
6	Norway	35.3	28	Israel	24.1
7	Iceland	34.1	29	Austria	23.9
8	France	34.0	30	Spain	22.9
9	Cayman Islands	33.5	31	Taiwan	22.7
10	Faroe Islands	33.4	32	Italy	21.9
11	Luxembourg	33.2	33	Greenland	21.5
12	Sweden	31.9	34	Ireland	21.1
13	Germany	31.7	35	Barbados	20.6
14	United Kingdom	31.6		Lithuania	20.6
15	Belgium	31.5	37	Greece	19.9
16	Hong Kong	29.9	38	Hungary	19.6
17	Canada	29.8	39	Latvia	19.3
18	Andorra	28.9	40	Portugal	19.2
19	Malta	28.0	41	Croatia	18.3
20	United States	27.6	42	Aruba	17.9
21	Japan	26.9	43	Cyprus	17.6
22	Estonia	25.1	44	Belarus	17.4

The internet and music

Internet hosts

By country, January 2012		Per 1,000 pop., January 2012	
1 United States[a]	542,917,145	1 United States[a]	1,709.4
2 Japan	63,660,151	2 Iceland	1,210.1
3 Italy	25,524,865	3 Finland	892.8
4 Brazil	24,304,256	4 Netherlands	832.6
5 Germany	20,638,245	5 Australia	793.5
6 China	20,191,828	6 Denmark	784.5
7 Australia	17,060,964	7 Norway	740.7
8 France	16,946,475	8 New Zealand	715.8
9 Mexico	15,504,559	9 Switzerland	706.5
10 Russia	14,214,334	10 Netherlands Antilles	679.2
11 Netherlands	13,905,139	11 Estonia	656.1
12 Poland	13,030,599	12 Sweden	626.6
13 Argentina	11,124,327	13 Luxembourg	536.3
14 United Kingdom	9,528,006	14 Japan	501.3
15 Canada	8,948,471	15 Belgium	487.5
16 India	6,772,625	16 Cayman Islands	467.8
17 Taiwan	6,225,641	17 Italy	424.7
18 Sweden	5,827,602	18 Austria	415.2
19 Switzerland	5,369,224	19 Czech Republic	401.9
20 Belgium	5,216,655	20 Bermuda	397.3
21 South Africa	4,968,994	21 Aruba	389.5
22 Finland	4,731,588	22 Lithuania	359.4
23 Colombia	4,545,803	23 Poland	342.9
24 Denmark	4,314,548	24 Andorra	331.0
25 Spain	4,268,186	25 Hungary	307.9
26 Czech Republic	4,180,045	26 Israel	305.0
27 Turkey	3,895,483	27 Cyprus	283.9
28 Norway	3,629,637	28 Greece	279.4

Music sales

Total including downloads, $m, 2011		$ per head, 2011	
1 United States	6,493	1 Japan	43.8
2 Japan	5,546	2 Norway	33.4
3 Germany	2,018	3 United Kingdom	31.1
4 United Kingdom	1,951	4 Australia	30.2
5 France	1,392	5 Bulgaria	27.6
6 Australia	659	6 Switzerland	25.5
7 Canada	535	7 Sweden	25.4
8 South Korea	388	8 Germany	24.8
9 Brazil	366	9 Austria	23.9
10 Italy	305	10 Denmark	23.2
11 Netherlands	286	11 France	21.3
12 Sweden	241	12 United States	20.7
13 India	228	13 Belgium	19.2
14 Belgium	209	14 Ireland	19.1
15 Mexico	204	15 Finland	18.7
16 Spain	203	16 New Zealand	17.3
17 Switzerland	199	17 Netherlands	17.0
18 Austria	196	18 Canada	15.7

a   Includes all hosts ending ".com", ".net" and ".org", which exaggerates the numbers.

Facebook users

000s, May 2012		*Per 1,000 pop., May 2012*	
1 United States	157,348	1 Iceland	1,037
2 Brazil	47,011	2 United Arab Emirates	641
3 India	45,826	3 Qatar	639
4 Indonesia	42,272	4 Cayman Islands	617
5 Mexico	33,174	5 Faroe Islands	609
6 United Kingdom	30,945	6 Brunei	570
7 Turkey	30,678	7 Singapore	568
8 Philippines	27,088	8 Norway	567
9 France	24,348	9 Chile	546
10 Germany	23,553	10 Canada	534
11 Italy	21,652	11 Hong Kong	529
12 Argentina	18,346	12 Bahamas	528
13 Canada	18,025	13 Taiwan	516
14 Colombia	16,394	14 Australia	515
15 Spain	16,343	Denmark	515
16 Thailand	14,036	16 New Zealand	514
17 Malaysia	12,130	Sweden	514
18 Taiwan	11,890	18 United States	507
19 Australia	10,946	19 Cyprus	504
20 Egypt	10,669	20 United Kingdom	496
21 Venezuela	9,487	21 Malta	495
22 Chile	9,139	22 Aruba	493
23 Japan	8,700	23 Bahrain	472
24 Peru	8,413	24 Israel	471
25 Poland	8,283	25 Malaysia	464

Internet users

Per 100 population, 2010

1 Iceland	95.6	23 Faroe Islands	75.2
2 Norway	93.3	24 Estonia	74.2
3 Netherlands	90.7	United States	74.2
4 Luxembourg	90.1	26 Belgium	73.7
5 Sweden	90.0	27 Austria	72.7
6 Denmark	88.8	28 Hong Kong	71.8
7 Finland	86.9	29 Latvia	71.5
8 Bermuda	84.7	30 Singapore	71.1
United Kingdom	84.7	31 Barbados	70.0
10 New Zealand	83.0	32 Ireland	69.8
11 Germany	82.5	33 Slovenia	69.3
South Korea	82.5	34 Czech Republic	68.6
13 Switzerland	82.2	35 Cayman Islands	66.0
14 Qatar	81.6	36 Spain	65.8
15 Canada	81.3	37 Israel	65.4
16 Andorra	81.0	38 Hungary	65.2
17 Antigua & Barbuda	80.6	39 Greenland	63.8
18 Slovakia	79.9	40 Malta	63.1
19 United Arab Emirates	78.0	41 Lithuania	62.8
20 Japan	77.6	42 Poland	62.5
21 France	77.5	43 Oman	62.0
22 Australia	75.9	44 Croatia	60.1

Movies and museums

Cinema attendances

Total visits, m, 2010

1	India	4,432.7
2	United States	1,424.4
3	France	204.6
4	United Kingdom	178.6
5	Japan	170.7
6	Russia	152.7
7	Germany	149.3
8	Italy	112.7
9	Spain	106.4
10	Poland	41.4
11	Turkey	37.5
12	Argentina	32.3
13	Netherlands	28.5
14	Belgium	22.1
15	Austria	18.8
16	Egypt	18.3
17	Sweden	18.0
18	Ireland	17.6
19	Portugal	15.5
20	Switzerland	14.9
21	Denmark	13.1
22	Norway	12.9
23	Czech Republic	12.8
24	Greece	12.3
25	Hungary	10.3
26	Finland	6.9
27	Romania	6.0
28	Slovakia	4.4
29	Croatia	3.8
30	Bulgaria	3.4

Visits per head, 2010

1	Iceland	5.6
2	United States	4.6
3	Ireland	3.9
4	India	3.6
5	France	3.3
6	United Kingdom	2.9
7	Norway	2.6
8	Denmark	2.4
9	Spain	2.3
10	Austria	2.2
11	Belgium	2.1
12	Italy	1.9
	Sweden	1.9
	Switzerland	1.9
15	Germany	1.8
16	Netherlands	1.7
17	Portugal	1.5
18	Slovenia	1.4
19	Estonia	1.3
	Finland	1.3
	Japan	1.3
22	Czech Republic	1.2
23	Greece	1.1
	Poland	1.1
	Russia	1.1
26	Hungary	1.0
27	Croatia	0.9
	Latvia	0.9
	Lithuania	0.9

Most popular museums and art galleries

Average daily visits, 2011

1	Louvre, Paris	24,329
2	Metropolitan Museum of Art, New York	16,450
3	British Museum, London	16,023
4	National Gallery, London	14,392
5	Tate Modern, London	13,157
6	National Gallery of Art, Washington, DC	12,034
7	National Palace Museum, Taipei	10,547
8	Centre Pompidou, Paris	9,899
9	National Musuem of Korea, Seoul	8,875
10	Musée d'Orsay, Paris	8,641
11	Museo Nacional del Prado, Madrid	7,977
12	State Museum, St Petersburg	7,890
13	Museum of Modern Art, New York	7,712
14	Victoria & Albert Museum, London	7,642
15	Reina Sofia, Madrid	7,412
16	National Folk Museum of Korea, Seoul	6,455
17	Centro Cultural Banco do Brasil, Rio de Janeiro	6,269
18	National Portait Gallery, London	5,151
19	Galleria degli Uffizi, Florence	4,775
20	Shanghai Museum, Shanghai	4,732

The press

Daily newspapers
Copies per '000 population, 2010

1	Hong Kong	554	16	Germany	242
2	Iceland	540		Malta	242
3	Luxembourg	510	18	Slovenia	207
4	Switzerland	478	19	Ireland	204
5	Sweden	436	20	Estonia	196
6	Norway	412	21	Lithuania	193
7	Finland	403	22	Belarus	188
8	Japan	396	23	Taiwan	176
9	Kuwait	354	24	Canada	166
10	Austria	343		Czech Republic	166
11	Denmark	342	26	France	157
12	South Korea	334	27	Belgium	153
13	Singapore	300		United States	153
14	Netherlands	282	29	Israel	152
15	United Kingdom	261	30	Italy	150

Press freedom[a]
Scores, 2011

Most free			Least free		
1	Finland	-10.00	1	Turkmenistan	144.67
	Norway	-10.00	2	Eritrea	142.00
3	Estonia	-9.00	3	North Korea	141.00
	Netherlands	-9.00	4	Syria	138.00
5	Austria	-8.00	5	Iran	136.60
6	Iceland	-7.00	6	China	136.00
	Luxembourg	-7.00	7	Bahrain	125.00
8	Switzerland	-6.20	8	Vietnam	114.00
9	Cape Verde	-6.00	9	Yemen	101.00
10	Canada	-5.67	10	Sudan	100.75
	Denmark	-5.67	11	Myanmar	100.00
12	Sweden	-5.50	12	Belarus	99.00
13	New Zealand	-5.33	13	Cuba	98.83
14	Czech Republic	-5.00	14	Egypt	97.50
15	Ireland	-4.00	15	Laos	89.00
16	Cyprus	-3.00	16	Somalia	88.33
	Germany	-3.00	17	Sri Lanka	87.50
	Jamaica	-3.00	18	Azerbaijan	87.25
19	Costa Rica	-2.25	19	Equatorial Guinea	86.00
20	Belgium	-2.00	20	Côte d'Ivoire	83.50
	Namibia	-2.00		Djibouti	83.50
22	Japan	-1.00	22	Saudi Arabia	83.25
	Suriname	-1.00	23	Uzbekistan	83.00
24	Poland	-0.67	24	Rwanda	81.00
25	Mali	0.00	25	Kazakhstan	77.50
	Slovakia	0.00		Libya	77.50
27	United Kingdom	2.00	27	Iraq	75.36
28	Niger	2.50	28	Pakistan	75.00
			29	Afghanistan	74.00

a Based on 44 questions on topics such as threats, censorship, monopolies, pressure and new media, answered by journalists and media experts.

Nobel prize winners: 1901–2011

Peace (two or more)

1	United States	19
2	United Kingdom	11
3	France	9
4	Sweden	5
5	Belgium	4
	Germany	4
7	Austria	3
	Norway	3
	South Africa	3
	Switzerland	3
11	Argentina	2
	Egypt	2
	Israel	2
	Russia	2

Economics[a]

1	United States	35
2	United Kingdom	9
3	Norway	2
	Sweden	2
5	Denmark	1
	France	1
	Germany	1
	Israel	1
	Netherlands	1
	Russia	1

Literature (three or more)

1	France	15
2	United States	12
3	United Kingdom	11
4	Germany	8
5	Sweden	7
6	Italy	5
	Spain	5
8	Norway	3
	Poland	3
	Russia	3

Medicine (three or more)

1	United States	53
2	United Kingdom	23
3	Germany	15
4	France	8
5	Sweden	7
6	Switzerland	6
7	Austria	5
	Denmark	5
9	Australia	3
	Belgium	3
	Italy	3

Physics

1	United States	51
2	United Kingdom	20
3	Germany	19
4	France	9
5	Netherlands	6
	Russia	6
7	Japan	5
8	Sweden	4
	Switzerland	4
10	Austria	3
	Italy	3
12	Canada	2
	Denmark	2
14	China	1
	India	1
	Ireland	1
	Pakistan	1
	Poland	1

Chemistry

1	United States	45
2	United Kingdom	23
3	Germany	15
4	France	7
5	Switzerland	6
6	Japan	5
	Sweden	5
8	Canada	4
9	Israel	3
10	Argentina	1
	Austria	1
	Belgium	1
	Czech Republic	1
	Denmark	1
	Finland	1
	Italy	1
	Netherlands	1
	Norway	1
	Russia	1

a Since 1969.
Notes: Prizes by country of residence at time awarded. When prizes have been shared in the same field, one credit given to each country.

Olympics

Summer games, 1896–2012

Year	Host	Sports	Events	Athletes	% women
1896	Athens	9	43	241	0.0%
1900	Paris	17	95	997	2.2%
1904	St. Louis	17	91	651	0.9%
1908	London	22	110	2,008	1.8%
1912	Stockholm	14	102	2,407	2.0%
1920	Antwerp	22	154	2,590	1.1%
1924	Paris	17	126	3,089	4.4%
1928	Amsterdam	15	109	2,883	9.6%
1932	Los Angeles	14	116	1,332	9.5%
1936	Berlin	19	129	3,963	8.4%
1948	London	17	136	4,104	9.5%
1952	Helsinki	17	149	4,955	10.5%
1956	Melbourne	17	145	3,314	11.3%
1960	Rome	17	150	5,338	11.4%
1964	Tokyo	19	163	5,151	13.2%
1968	Mexico	20	172	5,530	14.1%
1972	Munich	23	195	7,134	14.8%
1976	Montreal	21	198	6,084	20.7%
1980	Moscow	21	203	5,179	21.5%
1984	Los Angeles	23	221	6,829	22.9%
1988	Seoul	27	237	8,391	26.1%
1992	Barcelona	32	257	9,356	28.9%
1996	Atlanta	26	271	10,318	34.0%
2000	Sydney	28	300	10,651	38.2%
2004	Athens	28	301	10,625	40.7%
2008	Beijing	28	302	10,942	42.4%
2012	London	26	302	10,500[a]	...

Winter games, 1956–2010[b]

Overall medal winners	Gold	Silver	Bronze
1 Germany	139	130	100
2 Norway	105	117	88
3 United States	87	96	72
4 Austria	54	70	76
5 Canada	52	45	49
6 Sweden	51	34	38
7 Switzerland	43	37	46
8 Finland	42	58	56
9 Russia	38	31	28
10 Italy	37	32	36
11 Netherlands	29	31	26
12 France	27	27	38
13 South Korea	23	14	8
14 China	9	18	17
15 Japan	9	13	15
16 United Kingdom	9	5	15
17 Czech Republic	5	3	7

a Estimate.
b Table excludes Soviet Union medals (1956 to 1988) and as the Unified team in 1992:
Gold 87, Silver 63 and Bronze 67.

Drinking and smoking

Beer drinkers

Retail sales, litres per head of population, 2010

1	Estonia	86.3
2	Czech Republic	79.4
3	Venezuela[a]	75.3
4	Lithuania	71.0
5	Australia[a]	69.9
6	Finland	68.5
7	Germany	67.9
8	Poland	67.3
9	Austria	65.4
10	Russia	62.5
11	United States[a]	60.6
12	Slovenia	58.9
13	Romania	58.3
14	Canada[a]	57.6
15	Latvia	56.8
16	Slovakia	54.2
17	Netherlands	53.2
18	New Zealand[a]	52.7
19	Serbia	52.1
20	Bulgaria	51.6
21	Denmark	50.5
22	South Africa[a]	50.2

Wine drinkers

Retail sales, litres per head of population, 2010

1	Luxembourg	43.4
2	Switzerland	32.0
3	Portugal	31.0
4	Denmark	28.5
5	France	27.1
6	Italy	25.3
7	Slovenia	23.2
8	Belarus	22.1
9	Argentina[a]	21.8
10	Germany	21.4
11	Netherlands	21.3
12	Belgium	21.2
13	Sweden	20.6
14	Hungary	19.4
15	United Kingdom	19.3
16	Austria	17.8
17	New Zealand[a]	17.3
18	Australia[a]	17.1
19	Moldova	14.4
20	Greece	14.0
21	Ireland	13.8
22	Norway	13.4

Alcoholic drink

Retail sales, litres per head of population, 2010

1	Estonia	118.4
2	Finland	99.5
	Germany	99.5
4	Australia[a]	99.4
5	Czech Republic	95.8
6	Luxembourg	91.6
7	Slovenia	89.2
8	Austria	88.8
9	Lithuania	87.4
10	Denmark	83.4
11	Belarus	83.0
12	Russia	82.8
13	Poland	82.5
14	New Zealand[a]	80.2
15	Venezuela[a]	79.7
16	Netherlands	77.9
17	Canada[a]	74.8
18	United States[a]	72.9
19	Latvia	71.9
20	Belgium	71.7
21	Romania	71.2

Cigarettes

Av. ann. consumption of cigarettes per head per day, 2011

1	Moldova	8.9
2	Serbia	7.9
3	Russia	7.4
4	Lebanon	6.5
	Slovenia	6.5
6	Belarus	6.3
	Greece	6.3
8	Bulgaria	6.1
	Ukraine	6.1
10	Czech Republic	5.7
11	Kuwait	5.4
12	Armenia	5.3
13	Bosnia	5.2
14	Macedonia	5.1
	South Korea	5.1
16	China	5.0
17	Austria	4.5
18	Azerbaijan	4.4
	Switzerland	4.4
	Taiwan	4.4
21	Georgia	4.3

a 2009

Crime and punishment

Murders

Homicides per 100,000 pop., 2009 or latest

1	Honduras	82.1
2	El Salvador	66.0
3	Côte d'Ivoire	56.9
4	Jamaica	52.1
5	Venezuela	49.0
6	Belize	41.7
7	Guatemala	41.4
8	Virgin Islands (US)	39.2
9	Zambia	38.0
10	Uganda	36.3
11	Malawi	36.0
12	Trinidad & Tobago	35.2
13	South Africa	33.8
14	Lesotho	33.6
15	Colombia	33.4
16	Congo-Brazzaville	30.8
17	Central African Rep.	29.3
18	Bahamas	28.0
19	Puerto Rico	26.2
20	Ethiopia	25.5

Robberies

Per 100,000 pop., 2009 or latest

1	Belgium	1,762
2	Spain	1,188
3	Argentina	1,003
4	Mexico	607
5	Dominican Republic	573
6	Costa Rica	529
7	Chile	456
8	Trinidad & Tobago	452
9	Nicaragua	443
10	Ecuador	386
11	Uruguay	277
11	Panama	235
13	Colombia	206
14	Portugal	192
15	France	181
16	Belize	178
17	Peru	170
18	Guyana	163
19	Botswana	152
20	Russia	144

Prisoners

Total prison pop., latest available year

1	United States	2,266,832
2	China	1,640,000
3	Russia	741,600
4	Brazil	513,802
5	India	368,998
6	Iran	250,000
7	Thailand	231,066
8	Mexico	230,943
9	South Africa	157,375
10	Ukraine	153,774
11	Indonesia	141,689
12	Turkey	132,369
13	Ethiopia	112,361
14	Vietnam	108,557
15	Philippines	104,710
16	United Kingdom	97,158
17	Poland	85,245
18	Colombia	84,444
19	France	76,428
20	Pakistan	75,586
21	Spain	70,675
22	Japan	69,876
23	Bangladesh	69,650
24	Germany	68,099
25	Italy	66,695

Per 100,000 pop., latest available year

1	United States	730
2	Virgin Islands (US)	539
3	Georgia	531
4	Russia	519
5	Rwanda	450
6	Belarus	438
7	Bermuda	428
8	Belize	415
9	Azerbaijan	407
10	El Salvador	391
11	Bahamas	382
12	Barbados	354
13	Panama	349
14	Greenland	340
15	Ukraine	339
16	Iran	333
17	Thailand	332
18	Antigua & Barbuda	330
19	Guam	328
20	Kazakhstan	323
	St Lucia	323
22	Maldives	311
23	South Africa	310
24	Latvia	304
25	Puerto Rico	303

War and peace

Defence spending
As % of GDP, 2010

1	Saudi Arabia	10.1	15	Syria	3.9
2	Oman	7.3	16	Burundi	3.8
3	Israel	6.5	17	Uzbekistan	3.7
4	Iraq	6.0	18	Algeria	3.6
5	Yemen	5.8		Colombia	3.6
6	Jordan	5.4		Libya	3.6
7	United Arab Emirates	5.3		Singapore	3.6
8	Myanmar	4.9	22	Kuwait	3.5
9	United States	4.8		Morocco	3.5
10	Angola	4.5		Namibia	3.5
	Armenia	4.5	25	Bahrain	3.3
12	Botswana	4.3	26	Pakistan	3.2
13	Georgia	4.2	27	Guinea-Bissau	3.0
	Lebanon	4.2		Mauritania	3.0

Defence spending
$bn, 2010

			Per head, $, 2010		
1	United States	693.6	1	United Arab Emirates	3,227
2	China[a]	76.4	2	United States	2,250
3	United Kingdom	57.8	3	Israel	1,910
4	Japan	54.4	4	Kuwait	1,830
5	France	52.0	5	Qatar	1,813
6	Saudi Arabia	45.2	6	Saudi Arabia	1,755
7	Germany	44.1	7	Singapore	1,575
8	Russia	41.9	8	Oman	1,408
8	Brazil	33.4	9	Norway	1,268
10	India	30.9	10	Australia	1,098
11	South Korea	25.1	11	United Kingdom	927
12	Australia	23.6	12	Brunei	889
13	Italy	21.9	13	Denmark	817
14	Canada	20.2	14	France	803
15	Turkey	17.5	15	Greece	740

Armed forces
'000, 2010

		Regulars	Reserves			Regulars	Reserves
1	China	2,285	510	13	Brazil	318	1,340
2	United States	1,569	865	14	Thailand	306	200
3	India	1,325	1,155	15	Indonesia	302	400
4	North Korea	1,190	600	16	Syria	295	314
5	Russia	956	20,000	17	Taiwan	290	1,657
6	South Korea	655	4,500	18	Colombia	283	62
7	Pakistan	642	0	19	Mexico	280	87
8	Iran	523	350	20	Iraq	271	0
9	Turkey	511	379	21	Germany	251	40
10	Vietnam	482	5,000	22	Japan	248	56
11	Egypt	439	479	23	France	239	34
12	Myanmar	406	0	24	Saudi Arabia	234	0

a Official budget only at market exchange rates.

Arms exporters

$m, 2011

1	United States	9,984
2	Russia	7,874
3	France	2,437
4	China	1,356
5	Germany	1,206
6	United Kingdom	1,070
7	Italy	1,046
8	Spain	927
9	Sweden	686
10	Netherlands	538
11	Israel	531
12	Ukraine	484
13	Switzerland	297
14	Canada	292
15	South Korea	225
16	Australia	126
17	Bosnia	119
18	Belgium	111
19	Norway	108
20	Uzbekistan	90

Arms importers

$m, 2011

1	India	3,582
2	Australia	1,749
3	Pakistan	1,675
4	Morocco	1,558
5	United Arab Emirates	1,444
6	South Korea	1,422
7	China	1,112
8	Saudi Arabia	1,095
9	Turkey	1,010
10	Vietnam	1,009
11	United Sates	946
12	Singapore	921
13	Afghanistan	835
14	Algeria	783
15	Iraq	722
16	Norway	650
17	Venezuela	560
18	Egypt	545
19	United Kingom	412
20	Thailand	360

Global Peace Index[a]

Most peaceful, 2012

1	Iceland	1.113
2	Denmark	1.239
2	New Zealand	1.239
4	Canada	1.317
5	Japan	1.326
6	Austria	1.328
	Ireland	1.328
8	Slovenia	1.330
9	Finland	1.348
10	Switzerland	1.349
11	Belgium	1.376
12	Qatar	1.395
13	Czech Republic	1.396
14	Sweden	1.419
15	Germany	1.424
16	Portugal	1.470
17	Hungary	1.476
18	Norway	1.480
19	Bhutan	1.481
20	Malaysia	1.485
21	Mauritius	1.487
22	Australia	1.494
23	Singapore	1.521
24	Poland	1.524

Least peaceful, 2012

1	Somalia	3.392
2	Afghanistan	3.252
2	Sudan	3.193
4	Iraq	3.192
5	Congo-Kinshasa	3.073
6	Russia	2.938
7	North Korea	2.932
8	Central African Rep.	2.872
9	Israel	2.842
10	Pakistan	2.833
11	Libya	2.830
	Syria	2.830
13	Nigeria	2.801
14	Chad	2.671
15	Colombia	2.625
16	Yemen	2.601
17	India	2.549
18	Georgia	2.541
19	Zimbabwe	2.538
20	Myanmar	2.525
21	Burundi	2.524
22	Ethiopia	2.504
23	Lebanon	2.459
24	Mexico	2.445

a Ranks 158 countries using 23 indicators which gauge the level of safety and security in society, the extent of domestic or international conflict and the degree of militarisation.

Environment

Environmental Performance Index[a]
Best performers, scores, 2010

1	Switzerland	76.7		21	Denmark	63.6
2	Latvia	70.4		22	Poland	63.5
3	Norway	69.9		23	Japan	63.4
4	Luxembourg	69.2		24	Belgium	63.0
5	Costa Rica	69.0		25	Brunei	62.5
	France	69.0			Malaysia	62.5
7	Austria	68.9		27	Colombia	62.3
	Italy	68.9			Slovenia	62.3
9	Sweden	68.8		29	Taiwan	62.2
	United Kingdom	68.8		30	Brazil	60.9
11	Germany	66.9		31	Ecuador	60.6
12	Slovakia	66.6		32	Spain	60.3
13	Iceland	66.3		33	Greece	60.0
14	New Zealand	66.0		34	Thailand	59.9
15	Albania	65.9		35	Nicaragua	59.2
16	Netherlands	65.7		36	Ireland	58.7
17	Lithuania	65.5		37	Canada	58.4
18	Czech Republic	64.8		38	Nepal	58.0
19	Finland	64.4		39	Gabon	57.9
20	Croatia	64.2			Panama	57.9

Trend Environmental Performance Index[a]
Improvements over various indicators between 2000 and 2010, scores[b]

	Best			Worst	
1	Latvia	18.0	1	Russia	-12.8
2	Azerbaijan	17.8	2	Kuwait	-7.4
3	Romania	16.9	3	Saudi Arabia	-6.5
4	Albania	16.8	4	Bosnia	-4.7
5	Egypt	16.3	5	Estonia	-3.9
6	Angola	15.6	6	Kyrgyzstan	-3.3
7	Slovakia	14.5	7	Kazakhstan	-3.1
8	Ireland	13.8	8	Iraq	-2.7
9	Belgium	12.4		South Africa	-2.7
10	Thailand	12.1	10	Turkmenistan	-2.4
11	Sri Lanka	11.7	11	Bolivia	-1.8
12	Italy	11.3	12	Qatar	-1.7
	Nepal	11.3	13	Benin	-1.4
	Nicaragua	11.3	14	Brunei	-1.3
	South Korea	11.3		Iran	-1.3
16	Bulgaria	11.2	16	Chile	-1.2
17	Turkey	11.1	17	Cyprus	-1.0
18	France	11.0	18	Trinidad & Tobago	-0.7
	Hungary	11.0		Uruguay	-0.7
	United Kingdom	11.0	20	Costa Rica	-0.5

a An overall rank on scores over various indicators that include environmental, public health and ecosystem vitality.
b Score range is -50 to 50.

Biggest emitters of carbon dioxide
Million tonnes, 2008

1	China	7,031.9	26	Malaysia	208.3
2	United States	5,461.0	27	Argentina	192.4
3	India	1,742.7	28	Netherlands	173.7
4	Russia	1,708.7	29	Venezuela	169.5
5	Japan	1,208.2	30	Pakistan	163.2
6	Germany	786.7	31	United Arab Emirates	155.1
7	Canada	544.1	32	Vietnam	127.4
8	Iran	538.4	33	Uzbekistan	124.9
9	United Kingdom	522.9	34	Czech Republic	117.0
10	South Korea	509.2	35	Algeria	111.3
11	Mexico	475.8	36	Belgium	104.9
12	Italy	445.1	37	Iraq	102.9
13	South Africa	435.9	38	Greece	97.8
14	Saudi Arabia	433.6	39	Nigeria	95.8
15	Indonesia	406.0	40	Romania	94.7
16	Australia	399.2	41	Philippines	83.2
17	Brazil	393.2	42	North Korea	78.4
18	France	377.0	43	Kuwait	76.7
19	Spain	329.3	44	Chile	73.1
20	Ukraine	323.5	45	Syria	71.6
21	Poland	316.1	46	Qatar	68.5
22	Thailand	285.7	47	Austria	67.7
23	Turkey	284.0		Colombia	67.7
24	Kazakhstan	237.0	49	Belarus	62.8
25	Egypt	210.3	50	Libya	58.3

Largest amount of carbon dioxide emitted per person
Tonnes, 2008

1	Qatar	49.1	23	Japan	9.5
2	Trinidad & Tobago	37.4		Libya	9.5
3	Kuwait	30.1	25	South Africa	8.9
4	United Arab Emirates	25.0	26	Greece	8.7
5	Bahrain	21.4	27	Slovenia	8.5
6	Australia	18.6		United Kingdom	8.5
7	United States	18.0	29	Denmark	8.4
8	Oman	17.3	30	Bosnia	8.3
9	Saudi Arabia	16.6		Poland	8.3
10	Canada	16.3	32	Austria	8.1
11	Kazakhstan	15.1	33	Cyprus	7.9
12	Estonia	13.6	34	New Zealand	7.8
13	Russia	12.0	35	Malaysia	7.6
14	Czech Republic	11.2	36	Iran	7.4
15	Finland	10.6		Italy	7.4
	Netherlands	10.6	38	Spain	7.2
17	Norway	10.5	39	Ukraine	7.0
	South Korea	10.5	40	Slovakia	6.9
19	Ireland	9.9	41	Serbia	6.8
20	Belgium	9.8	42	Singapore	6.7
21	Turkmenistan	9.7	43	Bulgaria	6.6
22	Germany	9.6	44	Belarus	6.5

Sources of carbon dioxide emissions
As % of total emissions in each country, 2008
Electricity, heat, energy industry

1	Estonia	75.8	19	Poland	55.8
2	Singapore	71.4	20	Bahrain	54.2
3	Bosnia	69.5	21	Greece	53.4
4	Kuwait	68.2	22	Cuba	53.3
5	Hong Kong	68.1	23	Belarus	52.9
	Macedonia	68.1	24	South Korea	52.4
7	Israel	66.6	25	Qatar	52.1
8	South Africa	64.5	26	China	51.9
9	Bulgaria	64.3	27	Gabon	22.0
10	Serbia	63.3	28	Malaysia	20.5
11	Australia	62.9	29	Cameroon	19.9
12	Mongolia	62.6	30	Thailand	19.0
13	Libya	62.1	31	Spain	18.2
14	India	59.9	32	Paraguay	17.6
15	Russia	59.5	33	Chile	16.2
16	Czech Republic	56.9	34	France	16.0
17	Zimbabwe	56.8	35	Laos	15.8
18	Oman	56.7	36	Zimbabwe	15.6

Manufacturing and construction

1	North Korea	62.9	15	Brazil	29.7
2	Trinidad & Tobago	56.6	16	United Arab Emirates	29.4
3	Zambia	49.1	17	Thailand	29.2
4	Gabon	38.9	18	Kyrgyzstan	28.5
5	Congo-Kinshasa	35.3	19	Cyprus	28.3
6	Vietnam	35.1	20	Venezuela	28.0
7	Indonesia	34.0	21	Botswana	26.8
8	Nepal	33.9	22	Peru	26.6
9	China	33.3	23	Slovakia	25.7
10	Pakistan	32.4	24	Myanmar	25.4
11	Colombia	31.7	25	Belgium	24.7
12	Qatar	31.5	26	Bangladesh	24.5
13	Bahrain	31.1		Ethiopia	24.5
14	United Kingdom	29.8			

Transport

1	Paraguay	92.1	14	Cameroon	50.6
2	Congo-Brazzaville	87.2	15	Andorra	50.3
3	Togo	78.2	16	Ghana	49.8
4	Mozambique	69.9	17	Ecuador	49.2
5	Costa Rica	65.5	18	Namibia	48.6
6	Belgium	61.2		Nigeria	48.6
7	Albania	59.6	20	Sri Lanka	48.2
8	Haiti	57.3	21	Panama	47.6
9	Tanzania	56.8	22	Senegal	46.2
10	Ethiopia	56.7	23	Latvia	44.9
11	Sudan	55.6	24	Botswana	43.6
12	Guatemala	51.3	25	New Zealand	41.7
13	Sweden	50.7	26	Brazil	41.0

Renewable sources[a] of energy
As % of electricity production, 2009

1	Guatemala	34.0	16	Netherlands	9.5
2	El Salvador	30.3	17	Uruguay	9.3
3	Denmark	27.6	18	Hong Kong	7.4
4	Kenya	24.4	19	Chile	7.2
5	Nicaragua	22.3	20	Italy	7.0
6	Portugal	20.2	21	Indonesia	6.0
7	Costa Rica	17.4	22	Estonia	5.8
8	Philippines	16.8	23	Belgium	5.7
9	Spain	16.2	24	United Kingdom	5.4
10	New Zealand	15.9	25	Brazil	5.2
11	Germany	12.8	26	Greece	4.6
12	Finland	12.5	27	Poland	4.2
13	Ireland	11.2	28	Thailand	4.0
14	Sweden	10.2	29	Mexico	3.9
15	Austria	9.6	30	United States	3.7

Air quality[b]
Concentration of particulate matter[c], micrograms per cubic metre, 2009

Urban areas			Cities		
1	Uruguay	142	1	Delhi, India	118
2	Sudan	137	2	Xian, China	115
3	Bangladesh	121	3	Cairo, Egypt	112
4	Iraq	110	4	Tianjin, China	103
5	Mali	106	5	Chongqing, China	101
6	Saudi Arabia	103		Kolkata, India	101
7	Mongolia	101	7	Buenos Aires, Argentina	92
	Pakistan	101	8	Kanpur, India	86
9	Togo	98		Lucknow, India	86
10	Kuwait	95	10	Shenyang, China	83
11	Niger	92	11	Zhenzhou, China	80
12	Egypt	88	12	Jinan, China	77
13	Chad	82	13	Lanzhou, China	75
	Oman	82	14	Beijing, China	73
15	Libya	81	15	Chengdu, China	71
16	Senegal	80	16	Jakarta, Indonesia	70
17	Algeria	75	17	Anshan, China	68
18	Sri Lanka	71	18	Ahmedabad, India	66
	Syria	71	19	Nanchang, China	65
20	Guatemala	68		Wuhan, China	65
	Indonesia	68	21	Harbin, China	63
	Mauritania	68	22	Changchun, China	61
23	Botswana	66		Zibo, China	61
24	Paraguay	65	24	Bangkok, Thailand	60
25	Eritrea	64		Santiago, Chile	60
26	Burkina Faso	63		Shanghai, China	60
27	United Arab Emirates	62	27	Guiyang, China	58
28	Armenia	61		Kunming, China	58
	Gambia, The	61	29	Foshan, China	56

a Includes geothermal, solar, municipal waste, biofuels.   b Data are weighted for the size of a country's urban population.   c Less than 10 microns in diameter.

Number of species under threat, 2011

Mammals

1	Indonesia	184		Vietnam	54
2	Mexico	100	12	Colombia	52
3	India	94	13	Laos	45
4	Brazil	81		Myanmar	45
5	China	75	15	Ecuador	43
6	Malaysia	70	16	Papua New Guinea	39
7	Madagascar	65	17	Argentina	38
8	Thailand	57		Cameroon	38
9	Australia	55		Philippines	38
10	Peru	54			

Birds

1	Brazil	122	11	Mexico	56
2	Indonesia	119	12	Australia	52
3	Peru	98	13	Argentina	49
4	Colombia	94		Russia	49
5	China	86	15	Thailand	46
6	India	78	16	Malaysia	45
7	United States	76	17	Myanmar	43
8	Philippines	74		Vietnam	43
9	Ecuador	73	19	Tanzania	42
10	New Zealand	70	20	South Africa	40

Fish

1	India	212	11	South Africa	87
2	United States	183	12	Madagascar	85
3	Tanzania	174	13	Brazil	84
4	Mexico	152	14	Congo-Kinshasa	83
5	Indonesia	140	15	Greece	75
6	China	113	16	Philippines	71
7	Cameroon	112		Spain	71
8	Australia	103	18	Turkey	70
9	Malawi	101	19	Kenya	68
10	Thailand	97		Vietnam	68

Nationally protected areas[a]

As % of total land, 2011

1	Venezuela	53.8	13	Brazil	26.3
2	Germany	42.4	14	New Zealand	26.2
3	Hong Kong	41.8	15	Cambodia	25.8
4	Nicaragua	36.7	16	Ecuador	25.1
5	Zambia	36.0	17	Switzerland	24.9
6	Saudi Arabia	31.3	18	Senegal	24.1
7	Trinidad & Tobago	31.2	19	Benin	23.8
8	Botswana	30.9	20	Slovakia	23.2
9	Guatemala	30.6	21	Austria	22.9
10	Zimbabwe	28.0	22	Côte d'Ivoire	22.6
11	Tanzania	27.5	23	Poland	22.4
12	United Kingdom	26.4	24	Dominican Republic	22.2

a Includes wildlife reserves, scientific reserves and national parks.

Country
profiles

ALGERIA

Area	2,381,741 sq km	Capital	Algiers
Arable as % of total land	3.1	Currency	Algerian dinar (AD)

People

Population	35.4m	Life expectancy: men	71.9 yrs
Pop. per sq km	14.9	women	75.0 yrs
Av. ann. growth		Adult literacy	72.6%
in pop. 2010–15	1.35%	Fertility rate (per woman)	2.1
Pop. under 15	27.0%	Urban population	76.2%
Pop. over 60	6.9%		per 1,000 pop.
No. of men per 100 women	101.9	Crude birth rate	19.2
Human Development Index	69.8	Crude death rate	4.9

The economy

GDP	AD12,049bn	GDP per head	$4,570
GDP	$162bn	GDP per head in purchasing	
Av. ann. growth in real		power parity (USA=100)	17.9
GDP 2005–10	2.6%	Economic freedom index	51.0

Origins of GDP		Components of GDP	
	% of total		% of total
Agriculture	7	Private consumption	35
Industry, of which:	62	Public consumption	14
manufacturing	6	Investment	41
Services	31	Exports	31
		Imports	-21

Structure of employment

	% of total		% of labour force
Agriculture	21	Unemployed 2010	11.4
Industry	27	Av. ann. rate 1995–2010	21.1
Services	52		

Energy

	m TOE		
Total output	152.3	Net energy imports as %	
Total consumption	39.8	of energy use	-283
Consumption per head,			
kg oil equivalent	1,138		

Inflation and finance

Consumer price			av. ann. increase 2005–10
inflation 2011	4.5%	Narrow money (M1)	18.4%
Av. ann. inflation 2006–11	4.5%	Broad money	14.9%
Treasury bill rate, 2011	0.21%		

Exchange rates

	end 2011		2011
AD per $	76.06	Effective rates	2005 = 100
AD per SDR	116.77	– nominal	94.3
AD per €	98.41	– real	103.9

Trade

Principal exports		Principal imports	
	$bn fob		*$bn cif*
Hydrocarbons	56.1	Capital goods	14.8
Semi-finished goods	0.4	Semi-finished goods	9.4
Raw materials	0.2	Food	5.7
Total incl. others	**57.1**	Consumer goods	5.7
		Total incl. others	**40.2**

Main export destinations		Main origins of imports	
	% of total		*% of total*
United States	24.2	France	15.2
Italy	15.4	Italy	11.0
Spain	10.4	China	10.1
Netherlands	7.3	Spain	6.6

Balance of payments, reserves and debt, $bn

Visible exports fob	57.1	Change in reserves	15.3
Visible imports fob	-38.9	Level of reserves	
Trade balance	18.2	end Dec.	170.5
Invisibles inflows	8.2	No. months of import cover	36.7
Invisibles outflows	-16.9	Official gold holdings, m oz	5.6
Net transfers	2.7	Foreign debt	5.3
Current account balance	12.1	– as % of GDP	3.0
– as % of GDP	7.3	– as % of total exports	5.4
Capital balance	3.4	Debt service ratio[a]	1.0
Overall balance	15.6		

Health and education

Health spending, % of GDP	4.2	Education spending, % of GDP	4.3
Doctors per 1,000 pop.	1.2	Enrolment, %: primary	110
Hospital beds per 1,000 pop.	1.6	secondary	95
Improved-water source access,		tertiary	31
% of pop.	83		

Society

No. of households	6.2m	Colour TV households, % with:	
Av. no. per household	5.7	cable	0
Marriages per 1,000 pop.	9.2	satellite	93.0
Divorces per 1,000 pop.	...	Telephone lines per 100 pop.	8.2
Cost of living, Dec. 2011		Mobile telephone subscribers	
New York = 100	59	per 100 pop.	92.4
Cars per 1,000 pop.	...	Broadband subs per 100 pop.	2.5
		Internet hosts per 1,000 pop.	0.1

a 2008

ARGENTINA

Area	2,766,889 sq km	Capital	Buenos Aires
Arable as % of total land	11.3	Currency	Peso (P)

People

Population	40.7m	Life expectancy: men	72.4 yrs
Pop. per sq km	14.7	women	79.9 yrs
Av. ann. growth		Adult literacy	97.7%
in pop. 2010–15	0.85%	Fertility rate (per woman)	2.1
Pop. under 15	24.9%	Urban population	93.1%
Pop. over 60	14.7%		per 1,000 pop.
No. of men per 100 women	95.8	Crude birth rate	16.8
Human Development Index	79.7	Crude death rate	7.7

The economy

GDP	P1,443bn	GDP per head	$9,120
GDP	$369bn	GDP per head in purchasing	
Av. ann. growth in real		power parity (USA=100)	34.0
GDP 2005–10	6.7%	Economic freedom index	48.0

Origins of GDP		Components of GDP	
	% of total		% of total
Agriculture	10	Private consumption	60
Industry, of which:	31	Public consumption	15
manufacturing	21	Investment	22
Services	59	Exports	22
		Imports	-18

Structure of employment

	% of total		% of labour force
Agriculture	1	Unemployed 2010	8.6
Industry	23	Av. ann. rate 1995–2010	14.0
Services	76		

Energy

	m TOE		
Total output	80.8	Net energy imports as %	
Total consumption	74.2	of energy use	-9
Consumption per head			
kg oil equivalent	1,853		

Inflation and finance

Consumer price		av. ann. increase 2005–10	
inflation 2011	9.5%	Narrow money (M1)	19.4%
Av. ann. inflation 2006–11	8.8%	Broad money	20.3%
Money market rate, 2011	9.98%		

Exchange rates

	end 2011		2011
P per $	4.28	Effective rates	2005 = 100
P per SDR	6.48	– nominal	...
P per €	5.54	– real	...

Trade

Principal exports	$bn fob	Principal imports	$bn cif
Manufactures	23.9	Intermediate goods	17.7
Agricultural products	22.7	Capital goods	11.7
Primary products	15.2	Consumer goods	6.6
Fuels	6.5	Fuels	4.5
Total incl. others	**68.1**	Total incl. others	**48.0**

Main export destinations	% of total	Main origins of imports	% of total
Brazil	21.2	Brazil	37.3
China	8.5	China	15.9
Chile	6.6	United States	12.7
United States	5.4	Germany	6.7

Balance of payments, reserves and debt, $bn

Visible exports fob	68.1	Change in reserves	4.2
Visible imports fob	-53.9	Level of reserves	
Trade balance	14.3	end Dec.	52.2
Invisibles inflows	15.9	No. months of import cover	7.8
Invisibles outflows	-26.8	Official gold holdings, m oz	1.8
Net transfers	-0.3	Foreign debt	127.8
Current account balance	3.1	– as % of GDP	37.5
– as % of GDP	0.8	– as % of total exports	150.3
Capital balance	9.3	Debt service ratio	16.7
Overall balance	10.8		

Health and education

Health spending, % of GDP	4.7	Education spending, % of GDP	6.0
Doctors per 1,000 pop.	...	Enrolment, %: primary	118
Hospital beds per 1,000 pop.	4.5	secondary	89
Improved-water source access, % of pop.	97	tertiary	71

Society

No. of households	11.2m	Colour TV households, % with:	
Av. no. per household	3.6	cable	59.6
Marriages per 1,000 pop.	2.9	satellite	13.0
Divorces per 1,000 pop.	...	Telephone lines per 100 pop.	24.7
Cost of living, Dec. 2011		Mobile telephone subscribers	
New York = 100	71	per 100 pop.	141.2
Cars per 1,000 pop.	136	Broadband subs per 100 pop.	9.6
		Internet hosts per 1,000 pop.	273.3

AUSTRALIA

Area	7,682,300 sq km	Capital	Canberra
Arable as % of total land	6.1	Currency	Australian dollar (A$)

People

Population	21.5m	Life expectancy:	men	79.9 yrs
Pop. per sq km	2.9		women	84.3 yrs
Av. ann. growth		Adult literacy		...
in pop. 2010–15	1.32%	Fertility rate (per woman)		2.0
Pop. under 15	18.9%	Urban population		89.8%
Pop. over 60	19.5%			per 1,000 pop.
No. of men per 100 women	99.3	Crude birth rate		13.5
Human Development Index	92.9	Crude death rate		6.8

The economy

GDP	A$1,285bn	GDP per head	$50,750
GDP	$1,132bn	GDP per head in purchasing	
Av. ann. growth in real		power parity (USA=100)	80.9
GDP 2005–10	2.7%	Economic freedom index	83.1

Origins of GDP		Components of GDP	
	% of total		% of total
Agriculture	2	Private consumption	54
Industry, of which:	20	Public consumption	18
manufacturing	9	Investment	28
Services	78	Exports	20
		Imports	-20

Structure of employment

	% of total		% of labour force
Agriculture	3	Unemployed 2010	5.2
Industry	21	Av. ann. rate 1995–2010	6.3
Services	76		

Energy

	m TOE		
Total output	310.7	Net energy imports as %	
Total consumption	131.1	of energy use	-137
Consumption per head,			
kg oil equivalent	5,971		

Inflation and finance

Consumer price		av. ann. increase 2005–10	
inflation 2011	3.4%	Narrow money (M1)	9.1%
Av. ann. inflation 2006–11	2.9%	Broad money	13.4%
Money market rate, 2011	4.69%	Household saving rate, 2011	9.7%

Exchange rates

	end 2011		2011
A$ per $	0.98	Effective rates	2005 = 100
A$ per SDR	1.51	– nominal	99.8
A$ per €	1.27	– real	110.1

Trade

Principal exports		Principal imports	
	$bn fob		*$bn cif*
Coal	39.4	Intermediate & other goods	99.9
Meat & meat products	9.4	Capital goods	53.2
Wheat	3.8	Consumption goods	40.4
Total incl. others	**212.9**	**Total**	**193.5**

Main export destinations		Main origins of imports	
	% of total		*% of total*
China	25.0	China	20.6
Japan	18.8	United States	12.2
South Korea	8.9	Japan	9.5
India	7.1	Thailand	5.7
United States	4.0	Singapore	5.6

Balance of payments, reserves and aid, $bn

Visible exports fob	212.9	Overall balance	0.4
Visible imports fob	-194.7	Change in reserves	0.5
Trade balance	18.2	Level of reserves	
Invisibles inflows	87.1	end Dec.	42.3
Invisibles outflows	-135.9	No. months of import cover	1.5
Net transfers	-1.4	Official gold holdings, m oz	2.6
Current account balance	-32.0	Aid given	3.83
– as % of GDP	-2.8	– as % of GDP	0.32
Capital balance	32.7		

Health and education

Health spending, % of GDP	8.7	Education spending, % of GDP	4.5
Doctors per 1,000 pop.	3.0	Enrolment, %: primary	106
Hospital beds per 1,000 pop.	4.5	secondary	149
Improved-water source access,		tertiary	77
% of pop.	100		

Society

No. of households	8.0m	Colour TV households, % with:	
Av. no. per household	2.7	cable	24.6
Marriages per 1,000 pop.	5.1	satellite	13.7
Divorces per 1,000 pop.	2.2	Telephone lines per 100 pop.	38.7
Cost of living, Dec. 2011		Mobile telephone subscribers	
New York = 100	147	per 100 pop.	101
Cars per 1,000 pop.	554	Broadband subs per 100 pop.	24.1
		Internet hosts per 1,000 pop.	793.5

AUSTRIA

Area	83,855 sq km	Capital	Vienna
Arable as % of total land	16.6	Currency	Euro (€)

People

Population	8.4m	Life expectancy:	men	78.4 yrs
Pop. per sq km	100.1		women	83.6 yrs
Av. ann. growth		Adult literacy		...
in pop. 2010–15	0.16%	Fertility rate (per woman)		1.4
Pop. under 15	14.7%	Urban population		68.5%
Pop. over 60	23.1%			per 1,000 pop.
No. of men per 100 women	95.3	Crude birth rate		8.6
Human Development Index	88.5	Crude death rate		9.4

The economy

GDP	€286bn	GDP per head	$45,180
GDP	$379bn	GDP per head in purchasing	
Av. ann. growth in real		power parity (USA=100)	84.8
GDP 2005–10	1.4%	Economic freedom index	70.3

Origins of GDP		Components of GDP	
	% of total		% of total
Agriculture	2	Private consumption	55
Industry, of which:	29	Public consumption	19
manufacturing	19	Investment	22
Services	69	Exports	54
		Imports	-50

Structure of employment

	% of total		% of labour force
Agriculture	5	Unemployed 2010	4.4
Industry	25	Av. ann. rate 1995–2010	4.2
Services	70		

Energy

	m TOE		
Total output	11.4	Net energy imports as %	
Total consumption	31.7	of energy use	64
Consumption per head,			
kg oil equivalent	3,784		

Inflation and finance

Consumer price		av. ann. increase 2005–10	
inflation 2011	3.3%	Euro area:	
Av. ann. inflation 2006–11	2.2%	Narrow money (M1)	6.3%
Deposit rate, h'holds, 2011	1.39%	Broad money	5.9%
		Household saving rate, 2011	7.5%

Exchange rates

	end 2011		December 2011
€ per $	0.77	Effective rates	2005 = 100
€ per SDR	1.19	– nominal	100
		– real	98.6

Trade

Principal exports

	$bn fob
Machinery & transport equip.	56.9
Chemicals & related products	18.5
Food, drink & tobacco	10.4
Mineral fuels & lubricants	4.7
Raw materials	5.2
Total incl. others	**145.0**

Principal imports

	$bn cif
Machinery & transport equip.	52.0
Chemicals & related products	19.2
Mineral fuels & lubricants	15.8
Food, drink & tobacco	10.8
Raw materials	8.2
Total incl. others	**150.7**

Main export destinations

	% of total
Germany	33.0
Italy	8.1
Switzerland	4.9
France	4.3
EU27	71.3

Main origins of imports

	% of total
Germany	45.9
Italy	7.1
Switzerland	6.1
Netherlands	4.3
EU27	77.5

Balance of payments, reserves and aid, $bn

Visible exports fob	147.7	Overall balance	1.4
Visible imports fob	-152.0	Change in reserves	4.4
Trade balance	-4.3	Level of reserves	
Invisibles inflows	91.2	end Dec.	22.3
Invisibles outflows	-72.8	No. months of import cover	1.2
Net transfers	-2.7	Official gold holdings, m oz	9.0
Current account balance	11.5	Aid given	1.21
– as % of GDP	3.0	– as % of GDP	0.32
Capital balance	-2.0		

Health and education

Health spending, % of GDP	11.0	Education spending, % of GDP	5.5
Doctors per 1,000 pop.	4.9	Enrolment, %: primary	100
Hospital beds per 1,000 pop.	7.7	secondary	100
Improved-water source access,		tertiary	60
% of pop.	100		

Society

No. of households	3.6m	Colour TV households, % with:	
Av. no. per household	2.3	cable	46.7
Marriages per 1,000 pop.	4.5	satellite	53.9
Divorces per 1,000 pop.	2.1	Telephone lines per 100 pop.	38.7
Cost of living, Dec. 2011		Mobile telephone subscribers	
New York = 100	120	per 100 pop.	145.8
Cars per 1,000 pop.	524	Broadband subs per 100 pop.	23.9
		Internet hosts per 1,000 pop.	415.2

BANGLADESH

Area	143,998 sq km	Capital	Dhaka
Arable as % of total land	58.1	Currency	Taka (Tk)

People

Population	164.4m	Life expectancy: men		68.5 yrs
Pop. per sq km	1,141.7	women		70.2 yrs
Av. ann. growth		Adult literacy		55.9%
in pop. 2010–15	1.25%	Fertility rate (per woman)		2.2
Pop. under 15	30.9%	Urban population		30.4%
Pop. over 60	6.2%			per 1,000 pop.
No. of men per 100 women	102.6	Crude birth rate		19.5
Human Development Index	50.0	Crude death rate		6.0

The economy

GDP	Tk6,943bn	GDP per head	$680
GDP	$100.4bn	GDP per head in purchasing	
Av. ann. growth in real		power parity (USA=100)	3.5
GDP 2005–10	6.2%	Economic freedom index	53.2

Origins of GDP		**Components of GDP**	
	% of total		% of total
Agriculture	19	Private consumption	77
Industry, of which:	28	Public consumption	5
manufacturing	18	Investment	24
Services	53	Exports	18
		Imports	-25

Structure of employment

	% of total		% of labour force
Agriculture	...	Unemployed 2009	5.0
Industry	...	Av. ann. rate 1995–2009	2.9
Services	...		

Energy

			m TOE
Total output	24.8	Net energy imports as %	
Total consumption	29.6	of energy use	16
Consumption per head,			
kg oil equivalent	201		

Inflation and finance

Consumer price		av. ann. increase 2005–10	
inflation 2010	8.1%	Narrow money (M1)	21.3%
Av. ann. inflation 2006–10	7.9%	Broad money	22.9%
Deposit rate, 2011	10.02%		

Exchange rates

	end 2011		2011
Tk per $	81.85	Effective rates	2005 = 100
Tk per SDR	125.67	– nominal	...
Tk per €	105.90	– real	...

Trade

Principal exports[a]		**Principal imports**[a]	
	$bn fob		*$bn cif*
Clothing	13.6	Capital goods	4.5
Jute goods	0.5	Textiles & yarns	4.3
Fish & fish products	0.5	Fuels	2.6
Leather	0.4	Iron & steel	1.5
Total incl. others	**14.8**	Total incl. others	**23.7**

Main export destinations		**Main origins of imports**	
	% of total		*% of total*
United States	22.1	India	16.9
Germany	14.1	China	13.9
United Kingdom	8.5	Kuwait	5.4
France	6.8	Singapore	4.7
Netherlands	6.1	Hong Kong	4.2

Balance of payments, reserves and debt, $bn

Visible exports fob	19.2	Change in reserves	0.8
Visible imports fob	-24.7	Level of reserves	
Trade balance	-5.5	end Dec.	11.2
Invisibles inflows	2.3	No. months of import cover	4.4
Invisibles outflows	-5.9	Official gold holdings, m oz	0.4
Net transfers	11.4	Foreign debt	25.0
Current account balance	2.5	– as % of GDP	16.2
– as % of GDP	2.5	– as % of total exports	84.3
Capital balance	-1.2	Debt service ratio	4.7
Overall balance	1.0		

Health and education

Health spending, % of GDP	3.5	Education spending, % of GDP	2.2
Doctors per 1,000 pop.	0.3	Enrolment, %: primary	103
Hospital beds per 1,000 pop.	...	secondary	49
Improved-water source access,		tertiary	11
% of pop.	81		

Society

No. of households	35.5m	Colour TV households, % with:	
Av. no. per household	4.2	cable	...
Marriages per 1,000 pop.	...	satellite	...
Divorces per 1,000 pop.	...	Telephone lines per 100 pop.	0.6
Cost of living, Dec. 2011		Mobile telephone subscribers	
New York = 100	61	per 100 pop.	32.3
Cars per 1,000 pop.	2	Broadband subs per 100 pop.	0.04
		Internet hosts per 1,000 pop.	0.5

a Fiscal year ending June 30 2010.

BELGIUM

Area	30,520 sq km	Capital	Brussels
Arable as % of total land	27.7	Currency	Euro (€)

People

Population	10.7m	Life expectancy:	men	77.2 yrs
Pop. per sq km	350.9		women	82.8 yrs
Av. ann. growth		Adult literacy		...
in pop. 2010–15	0.29%	Fertility rate (per woman)		1.8
Pop. under 15	16.7%	Urban population		97.6%
Pop. over 60	23.4%			per 1,000 pop.
No. of men per 100 women	96	Crude birth rate		11.4
Human Development Index	88.6	Crude death rate		10.3

The economy

GDP	€354bn	GDP per head	$43,080
GDP	$469bn	GDP per head in purchasing	
Av. ann. growth in real		power parity (USA=100)	79.8
GDP 2005–10	1.2%	Economic freedom index	69.0

Origins of GDP		Components of GDP	
	% of total		% of total
Agriculture	1	Private consumption	53
Industry, of which:	22	Public consumption	24
manufacturing	14	Investment	20
Services	78	Exports	80
		Imports	-77

Structure of employment

	% of total		% of labour force
Agriculture	1	Unemployed 2010	8.3
Industry	23	Av. ann. rate 1995–2010	8.1
Services	76		

Energy

	m TOE		
Total output	15.3	Net energy imports as %	
Total consumption	57.2	of energy use	73
Consumption per head,			
kg oil equivalent	5,300		

Inflation and finance

Consumer price		av. ann. increase 2005–10	
inflation 2011	3.5%	Euro area:	
Av. ann. inflation 2006–11	2.4%	Narrow money (M1)	6.3%
Treasury bill rate, 2011	0.78%	Broad money	5.9%
		Household saving rate, 2011	11.2%

Exchange rates

	end 2011		2011
€ per $	0.77	Effective rates	2005 = 100
€ per SDR	1.19	– nominal	101.5
		– real	100.8

Trade

Principal exports	
	$bn fob
Chemicals & related products	126.9
Machinery & transport equip.	81.8
Minerals, fuels & lubricants	35.5
Food, drink & tobacco	33.9
Raw materials	11.9
Total incl. others	**409.5**

Principal imports	
	$bn cif
Chemicals & related products	97.4
Machinery & transport equip.	90.2
Minerals, fuels & lubricants	53.0
Food, drink & tobacco	28.7
Raw materials	17.9
Total incl. others	**393.7**

Main export destinations	
	% of total
Germany	18.5
France	16.6
Netherlands	11.9
United Kingdom	7.0
EU27	73.0

Main origins of imports	
	% of total
Netherlands	18.6
Germany	16.1
France	11.1
United Kingdom	5.6
EU27	69.3

Balance of payments, reserves and aid, $bn

Visible exports fob	279.7	Overall balance	0.8
Visible imports fob	-284.4	Change in reserves	2.9
Trade balance	-4.7	Level of reserves	
Invisibles inflows	156.3	end Dec.	26.8
Invisibles outflows	-136.8	No. months of import cover	0.8
Net transfers	-8.4	Official gold holdings, m oz	7.3
Current account balance	6.3	Aid given	3.00
– as % of GDP	1.4	– as % of GDP	0.64
Capital balance	-6.7		

Health and education

Health spending, % of GDP	10.7	Education spending, % of GDP	6.4
Doctors per 1,000 pop.	3.0	Enrolment, %: primary	105
Hospital beds per 1,000 pop.	6.5	secondary	111
Improved-water source access,		tertiary	67
% of pop.	100		

Society

No. of households	4.6m	Colour TV households, % with:	
Av. no. per household	2.3	cable	95.6
Marriages per 1,000 pop.	4.3	satellite	11.8
Divorces per 1,000 pop.	3.0	Telephone lines per 100 pop.	43.3
Cost of living, Dec. 2011		Mobile telephone subscribers	
New York = 100	117	per 100 pop.	113.5
Cars per 1,000 pop.	483	Broadband subs per 100 pop.	31.5
		Internet hosts per 1,000 pop.	487.5

BRAZIL

Area	8,511,965 sq km	Capital	Brasilia
Arable as % of total land	7.2	Currency	Real (R)

People

Population	195.4m	Life expectancy:	men	70.7 yrs
Pop. per sq km	23.0		women	77.4 yrs
Av. ann. growth		Adult literacy		90.0%
in pop. 2010–15	0.84%	Fertility rate (per woman)		1.8
Pop. under 15	25.5%	Urban population		85.7%
Pop. over 60	10.2%			per 1,000 pop.
No. of men per 100 women	96.9	Crude birth rate		15.0
Human Development Index	71.8	Crude death rate		6.4

The economy

GDP	R3,675bn	GDP per head	$10,710
GDP	$2,088bn	GDP per head in purchasing	
Av. ann. growth in real		power parity (USA=100)	23.8
GDP 2005–10	4.5%	Economic freedom index	57.9

Origins of GDP		Components of GDP	
	% of total		% of total
Agriculture	6	Private consumption	61
Industry, of which:	27	Public consumption	21
manufacturing	16	Investment	19
Services	67	Exports	11
		Imports	-12

Structure of employment

	% of total		% of labour force
Agriculture	17	Unemployed 2010	8.3
Industry	22	Av. ann. rate 1995–2010	8.4
Services	61		

Energy

			m TOE
Total output	230.3	Net energy imports as %	
Total consumption	240.2	of energy use	4
Consumption per head,			
kg oil equivalent	2,305		

Inflation and finance

			av. ann. increase 2005–10
Consumer price			
inflation 2011	6.6%	Narrow money (M1)	14.3%
Av. ann. inflation 2006–11	5.2%	Broad money	19.4%
Money market rate, 2011	11.66%		

Exchange rates

	end 2011		2011
R per $	1.86	Effective rates	2005 = 100
R per sdr	2.85	– nominal	129.0
R per €	2.41	– real	145.6

Trade

Principal exports		Principal imports	
	$bn fob		*$bn cif*
Primary products	90.0	Intermediate products and raw	
Manufactured products	79.6	materials	84.0
Semi-manufactured products	28.2	Capital goods	41.0
		Consumer goods	31.4
		Fuels and lubricants	25.3
Total incl. others	**201.9**	Total	**181.6**

Main export destinations		Main origins of imports	
	% of total		*% of total*
China	15.2	United States	16.5
United States	9.6	China	15.5
Argentina	9.2	Argentina	8.7
Netherlands	5.1	Germany	7.6

Balance of payments, reserves and debt, $bn

Visible exports fob	201.9	Change in reserves	50.0
Visible imports fob	-181.7	Level of reserves	
Trade balance	20.2	end Dec.	288.6
Invisibles inflows	39.2	No. months of import cover	11.9
Invisibles outflows	-109.5	Official gold holdings, m oz	1.1
Net transfers	2.8	Foreign debt	347.0
Current account balance	-47.4	– as % of GDP	18.8
– as % of GDP	-2.3	– as % of total exports	146.0
Capital balance	99.7	Debt service ratio	19.0
Overall balance	49.1		

Health and education

Health spending, % of GDP	9.0	Education spending, % of GDP	5.4
Doctors per 1,000 pop.	1.8	Enrolment, %: primary	127
Hospital beds per 1,000 pop.	2.4	secondary	101
Improved-water source access,		tertiary	36
% of pop.	98		

Society

No. of households	55.5m	Colour TV households, % with:	
Av. no. per household	3.4	cable	8.5
Marriages per 1,000 pop.	3.9	satellite	4.3
Divorces per 1,000 pop.	0.8	Telephone lines per 100 pop.	21.6
Cost of living, Dec. 2011		Mobile telephone subscribers	
New York = 100	104	per 100 pop.	104.1
Cars per 1,000 pop.	136	Broadband subs per 100 pop.	6.8
		Internet hosts per 1,000 pop.	124.4

BULGARIA

Area	110,994 sq km	Capital	Sofia
Arable as % of total land	28.9	Currency	Lev (BGL)

People

Population	7.5m	Life expectancy: men	70.3 yrs
Pop. per sq km	67.6	women	77.1 yrs
Av. ann. growth		Adult literacy	98.3%
in pop. 2010–15	-0.66%	Fertility rate (per woman)	1.6
Pop. under 15	13.5%	Urban population	75.3%
Pop. over 60	24.5%		per 1,000 pop.
No. of men per 100 women	93.6	Crude birth rate	10.0
Human Development Index	77.1	Crude death rate	15.2

The economy

GDP	BGL70.5bn	GDP per head	$6,330
GDP	$47.7bn	GDP per head in purchasing	
Av. ann. growth in real		power parity (USA=100)	29.5
GDP 2005–10	2.7%	Economic freedom index	64.7

Origins of GDP		Components of GDP	
	% of total		% of total
Agriculture	5	Private consumption	61
Industry, of which:	31	Public consumption	16
manufacturing	16	Investment	25
Services	63	Exports	58
		Imports	-60

Structure of employment

	% of total		% of labour force
Agriculture	7	Unemployed 2010	10.2
Industry	33	Av. ann. rate 1995–2010	12.5
Services	60		

Energy

		m TOE	
Total output	9.8	Net energy imports as %	
Total consumption	17.5	of energy use	44
Consumption per head,			
kg oil equivalent	2,305		

Inflation and finance

		av. ann. change 2005–10	
Consumer price			
inflation 2011	4.2%	Narrow money (M1)	8.0%
Av. ann. inflation 2006–11	6.0%	Broad money	22.2%
Money market rate, 2011	0.20%		

Exchange rates

	end 2011		2011
BGL per $	1.51	Effective rates	2005 = 100
BGL per SDR	2.32	– nominal	105.7
BGL per €	1.95	– real	122.9

Trade

Principal exports		Principal imports	
	$bn fob		$bn cif
Other metals	2.4	Crude oil & natural gas	4.1
Clothing and footwear	1.8	Chemicals, plastics & rubber	1.8
Iron & steel	0.9	Machinery & equipment	1.8
Chemicals, plastics & rubber	0.8	Textiles	1.2
Total incl. others	**20.6**	Total incl. others	**24.3**

Main export destinations		Main origins of imports	
	% of total		% of total
Germany	10.7	Russia	17.0
Italy	9.7	Germany	12.2
Romania	9.1	Italy	7.7
Greece	7.9	Romania	7.3
EU27	60.9	EU27	58.5

Balance of payments, reserves and debt, $bn

Visible exports fob	20.6	Change in reserves	-1.3
Visible imports fob	-24.3	Level of reserves	
Trade balance	-3.7	end Dec.	17.2
Invisibles inflows	7.6	No. months of import cover	6.7
Invisibles outflows	-6.7	Official gold holdings, m oz	1.3
Net transfers	2.0	Foreign debt	48.1
Current account balance	-0.7	– as % of GDP	95.0
– as % of GDP	-1.5	– as % of total exports	159
Capital balance	0.1	Debt service ratio	14
Overall balance	-0.6		

Health and education

Health spending, % of GDP	6.9	Education spending, % of GDP	4.4
Doctors per 1,000 pop.	3.7	Enrolment, %: primary	103
Hospital beds per 1,000 pop.	6.6	secondary	89
Improved-water source access,		tertiary	53
% of pop.	100		

Society

No. of households	2.9m	Colour TV households, % with:	
Av. no. per household	2.6	cable	46.1
Marriages per 1,000 pop.	3.2	satellite	12.1
Divorces per 1,000 pop.	1.5	Telephone lines per 100 pop.	29.7
Cost of living, Dec. 2011		Mobile telephone subscribers	
New York = 100	71	per 100 pop.	136.1
Cars per 1,000 pop.	339	Broadband subs per 100 pop.	14.5
		Internet hosts per 1,000 pop.	139.6

CAMEROON

Area	475,442 sq km	Capital	Yaoundé
Arable as % of total land	12.6	Currency	CFA franc (CFAfr)

People

Population	20.0m	Life expectancy: men	51.4 yrs
Pop. per sq km	42.0	women	53.6 yrs
Av. ann. growth		Adult literacy	70.7%
in pop. 2010–15	2.14%	Fertility rate (per woman)	4.3
Pop. under 15	40.8%	Urban population	54.4%
Pop. over 60	5.4%		per 1,000 pop.
No. of men per 100 women	99.7	Crude birth rate	34.9
Human Development Index	48.2	Crude death rate	13.4

The economy

GDP	CFAfr11,134bn	GDP per head	$1,150
GDP	$22.5bn	GDP per head in purchasing	
Av. ann. growth in real		power parity (USA=100)	4.9
GDP 2005–10	2.8%	Economic freedom index	51.8

Origins of GDP		Components of GDP	
	% of total		% of total
Agriculture	22	Private consumption	75
Industry, of which:	28	Public consumption	12
manufacturing	15	Investment	19
Services	51	Exports	17
		Imports	-23

Structure of employment

	% of total		% of labour force
Agriculture	...	Unemployed 2007	2.9
Industry	...	Av. ann. rate 1995–2007	5.2
Services	...		

Energy

	m TOE		
Total output	8.8	Net energy imports as %	
Total consumption	6.9	of energy use	-28
Consumption per head,			
kg oil equivalent	361		

Inflation and finance

		av. ann. change 2005–10	
Consumer price			
inflation 2011	2.9%	Narrow money (M1)	13.7%
Av. ann. inflation 2006–11	2.7%	Broad money	11.3%
Deposit rate, 2011	3.25%		

Exchange rates

	end 2011		2011
CFAfr per $	506.96	Effective rates	2005 = 100
CFAfr per SDR	778.32	– nominal	100.6
CFAfr per €	655.92	– real	98.1

Trade

Principal exports[a]		Principal imports[a]	
	$bn fob		$bn cif
Oil & petroleum products	1.9	Machinery & electrical goods	0.7
Timber	0.5	Fuels	0.7
Agricultural products	0.3	Grain & cereal products	0.5
Metal products	0.1	Chemicals	0.4
Total incl. others	**3.3**	Total incl. others	**4.2**

Main export destinations		Main origins of imports	
	% of total		% of total
Spain	14.8	France	19.0
Netherlands	12.6	China	13.3
China	9.3	Belgium	5.6
Italy	9.1	Germany	4.0

Balance of payments, reserves and debt, $bn

Visible exports fob	4.5	Change in reserves	-3.7
Visible imports fob	-4.7	Level of reserves	
Trade balance	-0.2	end Dec.	0.0
Invisible inflows	1.3	No. months of import cover	0
Invisible outflows	-2.2	Official gold holdings, m oz	0
Net transfers	0.1	Foreign debt	3.0
Current account balance	-0.9	– as % of GDP	5
– as % of GDP	-3.8	– as % of total exports	19
Capital balance	0.7	Debt service ratio	4
Overall balance	0.0		

Health and education

Health spending, % of GDP	5.1	Education spending, % of GDP	3.5
Doctors per 1,000 pop.	...	Enrolment, %: primary	120
Hospital beds per 1,000 pop.	1.3	secondary	42
Improved-water source access,		tertiary	11
% of pop.	77		

Society

No. of households	4.0m	Colour TV households, % with:	
Av. no. per household	5.0	cable	0.0
Marriages per 1,000 pop.	...	satellite	2.3
Divorces per 1,000 pop.	...	Telephone lines per 100 pop.	2.8
Cost of living, Dec. 2011		Mobile telephone subscribers	
New York = 100	...	per 100 pop.	44.1
Cars per 1,000 pop.	10	Broadband subs per 100 pop.	0.01
		Internet hosts per 1,000 pop.	0.5

a 2009

CANADA

Area[a]	9,970,610 sq km	Capital	Ottawa
Arable as % of total land	5.0	Currency	Canadian dollar (C$)

People

Population	33.9m	Life expectancy: men		78.9 yrs
Pop. per sq km	3.4		women	85.3 yrs
Av. ann. growth		Adult literacy		...
in pop. 2010–15	0.92%	Fertility rate (per woman)		1.7
Pop. under 15	16.3%	Urban population		81.1%
Pop. over 60	20.0%			*per 1,000 pop.*
No. of men per 100 women	98.4	Crude birth rate		11.3
Human Development Index	90.8	Crude death rate		7.7

The economy

GDP	C$1,625bn	GDP per head	$46,210
GDP	$1,577bn	GDP per head in purchasing	
Av. ann. growth in real		power parity (USA=100)	82.8
GDP 2005–10	1.2%	Economic freedom index	79.9

Origins of GDP		**Components of GDP**	
	% of total		*% of total*
Agriculture	2	Private consumption	58
Industry, of which:	28	Public consumption	22
manufacturing & mining	...	Investment	22
Services	70	Exports	29
		Imports	-31

Structure of employment

	% of total		*% of labour force*
Agriculture	2	Unemployed 2010	8.0
Industry	22	Av. ann. rate 1995–2010	10.7
Services	76		

Energy

	m TOE		
Total output	389.8	Net energy imports as %	
Total consumption	254.1	of energy use	-53
Consumption per head,			
kg oil equivalent	7,534		

Inflation and finance

Consumer price		*av. ann. increase 2005–10*	
inflation 2011	2.9%	Narrow money (M1)	10.5%
Av. ann. inflation 2006–11	1.9%	Broad money	7.8%
Money market rate, 2011	1.00%	Household saving rate, 2011	3.8%

Exchange rates

	end 2011		*December 2011*
			2005 = 100
C$ per $	1.02	Effective rates	
C$ per SDR	1.57	– nominal	114.5
C$ per €	1.32	– real	111.4

Trade

Principal exports	$bn fob	Principal imports	$bn fob
Industrial goods & materials	93.7	Machinery & equipment	110.5
Energy products	88.2	Industrial goods & materials	84.4
Machinery & equipment	73.9	Motor vehicles & parts	66.7
Motor vehicles & parts	55.1	Consumer goods	56.1
Agricultural & fishing products	35.9	Energy products	39.4
Total incl. others	**393.0**	Total incl. others	**401.7**

Main export destinations	% of total	Main origins of imports	% of total
United States	74.9	United States	50.4
United Kingdom	4.1	China	11.0
China	3.3	Mexico	5.5
Japan	2.3	Japan	3.3
EU27	8.6	EU 27	11.9

Balance of payments, reserves and aid, $bn

Visible exports fob	393.2	Overall balance	3.8
Visible imports fob	-401.9	Change in reserves	2.8
Trade balance	-8.7	Level of reserves	
Invisibles inflows	129.2	end Dec.	57.2
Invisibles outflows	-167.2	No. months of import cover	1.2
Net transfers	-2.6	Official gold holdings, m oz	0.1
Current account balance	-49.3	Aid given	5.20
– as % of GDP	-3.1	– as % of GDP	0.34
Capital balance	42.0		

Health and education

Health spending, % of GDP	11.3	Education spending, % of GDP	4.8
Doctors per 1,000 pop.	2.0	Enrolment, %: primary	99
Hospital beds per 1,000 pop.	3.2	secondary	101
Improved-water source access,		tertiary	62
% of pop.	100		

Society

No. of households	13.1m	Colour TV households, % with:	
Av. no. per household	2.6	cable	67.4
Marriages per 1,000 pop.	4.4	satellite	24.5
Divorces per 1,000 pop.	2.1	Telephone lines per 100 pop.	50.0
Cost of living, Dec. 2011		Mobile telephone subscribers	
New York = 100	108	per 100 pop.	70.7
Cars per 1,000 pop.	410	Broadband subs per 100 pop.	29.8
		Internet hosts per 1,000 pop.	264.0

a Including freshwater.

CHILE

Area	756,945 sq km	Capital	Santiago
Arable as % of total land	1.7	Currency	Chilean peso (Ps)

People

Population	17.1m	Life expectancy: men		76.2 yrs
Pop. per sq km	22.6		women	82.4 yrs
Av. ann. growth		Adult literacy		98.6%
in pop. 2010–15	0.86%	Fertility rate (per woman)		1.8
Pop. under 15	22.3%	Urban population		90.0%
Pop. over 60	13.2%			per 1,000 pop.
No. of men per 100 women	97.8	Crude birth rate		14.0
Human Development Index	80.5	Crude death rate		5.7

The economy

GDP	108.6trn pesos	GDP per head	$12,430
GDP	$213bn	GDP per head in purchasing	
Av. ann. growth in real		power parity (USA=100)	33.5
GDP 2005–10	3.8%	Economic freedom index	78.3

Origins of GDP		Components of GDP	
	% of total		% of total
Agriculture	3	Private consumption	59
Industry, of which:	43	Public consumption	12
manufacturing	12	Investment	21
Services	54	Exports	39
		Imports	-32

Structure of employment

	% of total		% of labour force
Agriculture	11	Unemployed 2010	8.1
Industry	23	Av. ann. rate 1995–2010	7.3
Services	66		

Energy

	m TOE		
Total output	9.3	Net energy imports as %	
Total consumption	28.8	of energy use	68
Consumption per head,			
kg oil equivalent	1,698		

Inflation and finance

Consumer price			av. ann. increase 2005–10
inflation 2011	3.3%	Narrow money (M1)	14.9%
Av. ann. inflation 2006–11	3.8%	Broad money	12.2%
Money market rate, 2011	4.67%		

Exchange rates

	end 2011		2011
Ps per $	521.46	Effective rates	2005 = 100
Ps per SDR	800.58	– nominal	101.1
Ps per €	674.68	– real	105.1

Trade

Principal exports	
	$bn fob
Copper	39.3
Fresh fruit	3.7
Paper products	3.1
Total incl. others	**70.9**

Principal imports	
	$bn cif
Intermediate goods	30.6
Consumer goods	13.4
Capital goods	9.7
Total incl. others	**59.4**

Main export destinations	
	% of total
China	24.5
Japan	10.7
United States	9.9
Brazil	6.1
South Korea	5.7

Main origins of imports	
	% of total
China	16.7
United States	16.6
Argentina	7.9
Brazil	7.8
South Korea	5.9

Balance of payments, reserves and debt, $bn

Visible exports fob	71.0	Change in reserves	0.0
Visible imports fob	-55.2	Level of reserves	
Trade balance	15.9	end Dec.	25.3
Invisibles inflows	16.8	No. months of import cover	3.4
Invisibles outflows	-33.2	Official gold holdings, m oz	0.0
Net transfers	4.4	Foreign debt	86.3
Current account balance	3.8	– as % of GDP	48
– as % of GDP	1.8	– as % of total exports	99
Capital balance	-0.2	Debt service ratio	15
Overall balance	3.0		

Health and education

Health spending, % of GDP	8.0	Education spending, % of GDP	4.5
Doctors per 1,000 pop.	1.0	Enrolment, %: primary	106
Hospital beds per 1,000 pop.	2.1	secondary	88
Improved-water source access,		tertiary	59
% of pop.	96		

Society

No. of households	4.7m	Colour TV households, % with:	
Av. no. per household	3.6	cable	32.8
Marriages per 1,000 pop.	3.1	satellite	5.0
Divorces per 1,000 pop.	0.5	Telephone lines per 100 pop.	20.2
Cost of living, Dec. 2011		Mobile telephone subscribers	
New York = 100	84	per 100 pop.	116.0
Cars per 1,000 pop.	97	Broadband subs per 100 pop.	10.5
		Internet hosts per 1,000 pop.	109.5

CHINA

Area	9,560,900 sq km	Capital	Beijing
Arable as % of total land	11.8	Currency	Yuan

People

Population	1,354.1m	Life expectancy: men		72.1 yrs
Pop. per sq km	141.6	women		75.6 yrs
Av. ann. growth		Adult literacy		94.0%
in pop. 2010–15	0.42%	Fertility rate (per woman)		1.6
Pop. under 15	19.9%	Urban population		55.6%
Pop. over 60	12.3%		per 1,000 pop.	
No. of men per 100 women	108.0	Crude birth rate		11.9
Human Development Index	68.7	Crude death rate		7.5

The economy

GDP	Yuan40.1trn	GDP per head	$4,430
GDP	$5,927bn	GDP per head in purchasing	
Av. ann. growth in real		power parity (USA=100)	16.1
GDP 2005–10	11.2%	Economic freedom index	51.2

Origins of GDP

	% of total
Agriculture	10
Industry, of which:	47
manufacturing	30
Services	43

Components of GDP

	% of total
Private consumption	35
Public consumption	13
Investment	48
Exports	30
Imports	-26

Structure of employment

	% of total		% of labour force
Agriculture	40	Unemployed 2010	4.3
Industry	27	Av. ann. rate 1995–2010	3.6
Services	33		

Energy

	m TOE		
Total output	2,084.9	Net energy imports as %	
Total consumption	2,257.1	of energy use	8
Consumption per head,			
kg oil equivalent	1,695		

Inflation and finance

		av. ann. increase 2005–10	
Consumer price			
inflation 2011	5.4%	Narrow money (M1)	20.1%
Av. ann. inflation 2006–11	3.7%	Broad money	20.7%
Deposit rate, 2011	3.50%		

Exchange rates

	end 2011		2011
			2005 = 100
Yuan per $	6.30	Effective rates	
Yuan per SDR	9.67	– nominal	118.7
Yuan per €	8.15	– real	127.2

Trade

Principal exports		Principal imports	
	$bn fob		*$bn cif*
Office machinery	196.3	Electrical machinery	262.2
Telecoms equipment	190.2	Petroleum & products	163.6
Electrical goods	189.3	Metal ores & scrap	130.4
Clothing & apparel	129.8	Professional instruments	75.0
Total incl. others	**1,577.8**	Total incl. others	**1,396.0**

Main export destinations		Main origins of imports	
	% of total		*% of total*
United States	18.0	Japan	12.6
Hong Kong	13.8	South Korea	8.8
Japan	7.6	Taiwan	8.3
South Korea	4.4	United States	7.3
EU27[a]	19.7	EU27[a]	12.7

Balance of payments, reserves and debt, $bn

Visible exports fob	1,581	Change in reserves	461
Visible imports fob	-1,327	Level of reserves	
Trade balance	254	end Dec.	2,914
Invisibles inflows	316	No. months of import cover	21.4
Invisibles outflows	-308	Official gold holdings, m oz	33.9
Net transfers	43	Foreign debt	548.6
Current account balance	305	– as % of GDP	10
– as % of GDP	5.2	– as % of total exports	31
Capital balance	226	Debt service ratio	3
Overall balance	472		

Health and education

Health spending, % of GDP	5.1	Education spending, % of GDP	...
Doctors per 1,000 pop.	1.4	Enrolment, %: primary	111
Hospital beds per 1,000 pop.	4.2	secondary	81
Improved-water source access,		tertiary	26
% of pop.	91		

Society

No. of households	393.1m	Colour TV households, % with:	
Av. no. per household	3.4	cable	53.0
Marriages per 1,000 pop.	5.7	satellite	0.0
Divorces per 1,000 pop.	1.6	Telephone lines per 100 pop.	22.0
Cost of living, Dec. 2011		Mobile telephone subscribers	
New York = 100	91	per 100 pop.	64.0
Cars per 1,000 pop.	18	Broadband subs per 100 pop.	9.4
		Internet hosts per 1,000 pop.	14.9

Note: Data excludes Special Administrative Regions ie, Hong Kong and Macau.
a 2009

COLOMBIA

Area	1,141,748 sq km	Capital	Bogota
Arable as % of total land	1.6	Currency	Colombian peso (peso)

People

Population	46.3m	Life expectancy: men	70.4 yrs
Pop. per sq km	40.6	women	77.7 yrs
Av. ann. growth		Adult literacy	93.2%
in pop. 2010–15	1.28%	Fertility rate (per woman)	2.3
Pop. under 15	28.6%	Urban population	76.4%
Pop. over 60	8.6%		per 1,000 pop.
No. of men per 100 women	96.8	Crude birth rate	18.9
Human Development Index	71.0	Crude death rate	5.5

The economy

GDP	548trn pesos	GDP per head	$6,240
GDP	$289bn	GDP per head in purchasing	
Av. ann. growth in real		power parity (USA=100)	20.0
GDP 2005–10	3.8%	Economic freedom index	68.0

Origins of GDP		Components of GDP	
	% of total		% of total
Agriculture	7	Private consumption	62
Industry, of which:	36	Public consumption	16
manufacturing	15	Investment	24
Services	57	Exports	16
		Imports	-18

Structure of employment

	% of total		% of labour force
Agriculture	18	Unemployed 2010	11.6
Industry	20	Av. ann. rate 1995–2010	13.7
Services	62		

Energy

	m TOE		
Total output	99.1	Net energy imports as %	
Total consumption	31.8	of energy use	-211
Consumption per head,			
kg oil equivalent	697		

Inflation and finance

		av. ann. increase 2005–10	
Consumer price			
inflation 2011	3.4%	Narrow money (M1)	12.5%
Av. ann. inflation 2006–11	4.5%	Broad money	14.6%
Money market rate, 2011	4.03%		

Exchange rates

	end 2011		2011
Peso per $	1,943	Effective rates	2005 = 100
Peso per SDR	2,983	– nominal	121.8
Peso per €	2,514	– real	120.3

Trade

Principal exports	$bn fob	Principal imports	$bn cif
Petroleum & products	16.5	Intermediate goods & raw	
Coal	6.0	materials	15.8
Nickel	6.0	Capital goods	13.5
Coffee	1.9	Consumer goods	8.2
Total incl. others	**39.8**	**Total**	**40.7**

Main export destinations	% of total	Main origins of imports	% of total
United States	42.6	United States	25.9
China	4.9	China	13.5
Ecuador	4.6	Mexico	9.5
Netherlands	4.1	Brazil	5.8

Balance of payments, reserves and debt, $bn

Visible exports fob	40.8	Change in reserves	3.1
Visible imports fob	-38.6	Level of reserves	
Trade balance	2.2	end Dec.	28.1
Invisibles inflows	6.0	No. months of import cover	5.6
Invisibles outflows	-21.5	Official gold holdings, m oz	0.2
Net transfers	4.5	Foreign debt	63.1
Current account balance	-8.9	– as % of GDP	38
– as % of GDP	-3.1	– as % of total exports	212
Capital balance	11.8	Debt service ratio	21
Overall balance	3.1		

Health and education

Health spending, % of GDP	7.6	Education spending, % of GDP	4.8
Doctors per 1,000 pop.	1.3	Enrolment, %: primary	115
Hospital beds per 1,000 pop.	1.0	secondary	96
Improved-water source access,		tertiary	39
% of pop.	92		

Society

No. of households	12.3m	Colour TV households, % with:	
Av. no. per household	3.8	cable	59.3
Marriages per 1,000 pop.	1.7	satellite	7.0
Divorces per 1,000 pop.	...	Telephone lines per 100 pop.	15.5
Cost of living, Dec. 2011		Mobile telephone subscribers	
New York = 100	95	per 100 pop.	96.1
Cars per 1,000 pop.	35	Broadband subs per 100 pop.	5.6
		Internet hosts per 1,000 pop.	98.2

CÔTE D'IVOIRE

Area	322,463 sq km	Capital	Abidjan/Yamoussoukro
Arable as % of total land	8.8	Currency	CFA franc (CFAfr)

People

Population	21.6m	Life expectancy: men		55.3 yrs
Pop. per sq km	67.0		women	57.7 yrs
Av. ann. growth		Adult literacy		55.3%
in pop. 2010–15	2.18%	Fertility rate (per woman)		4.2
Pop. under 15	40.4%	Urban population		54.2%
Pop. over 60	6.1%			per 1,000 pop.
No. of men per 100 women	103.9	Crude birth rate		33.0
Human Development Index	40.0	Crude death rate		11.2

The economy

GDP	CFAfr11,283bn	GDP per head	$1,150
GDP	$22.8bn	GDP per head in purchasing	
Av. ann. growth in real		power parity (USA=100)	4.0
GDP 2005–10	2.2%	Economic freedom index	54.3

Origins of GDP		**Components of GDP**	
	% of total		% of total
Agriculture	23	Private consumption	73
Industry, of which:	27	Public consumption	9
manufacturing	19	Investment	14
Services	50	Exports	41
		Imports	-36

Structure of employment

	% of total		% of labour force
Agriculture	...	Unemployed 2010	...
Industry	...	Av. ann. rate 1995–2010	...
Services	...		

Energy

	m TOE		
Total output	11.9	Net energy imports as %	
Total consumption	10.4	of energy use	-15
Consumption per head,			
kg oil equivalent	535		

Inflation and finance

			av. ann. change 2005–10
Consumer price			
inflation 2011	4.9%	Narrow money (M1)	14.4%
Av. ann. inflation 2006–11	3.1%	Broad money	14.8%
Money market rate, 2011	3.29%		

Exchange rates

	end 2011		2011
CFAfr per $	506.96	Effective rates	2005 = 100
CFAfr per SDR	778.32	– nominal	98.8
CFAfr per €	655.92	– real	98.5

Trade

Principal exports[a]

	$bn fob
Petroleum products	3.0
Cocoa beans & products	2.7
Timber	0.3
Coffee & products	0.2
Total incl. others	**10.5**

Principal imports[a]

	$bn cif
Fuel & lubricants	1.8
Capital equipment & raw materials	3.0
Foodstuffs	1.2
Total incl. others	**7.4**

Main export destinations

	% of total
Netherlands	14.1
United States	10.4
France	6.9
Nigeria	6.5
Germany	5.1

Main origins of imports

	% of total
Nigeria	25.6
France	11.5
China	6.7
Thailand	4.0
Colombia	3.3

Balance of payments[a], reserves and debt, $bn

Visible exports fob	10.5	Change in reserves	-3.3
Visible imports fob	-6.3	Level of reserves	
Trade balance	4.2	end Dec.	0.0
Invisibles inflows	1.2	No. months of import cover	0.0
Invisibles outflows	-3.6	Official gold holdings, m oz	0.0
Net transfers	-0.1	Foreign debt	11.4
Current account balance	1.7	– as % of GDP	48
– as % of GDP	7.2	– as % of total exports	88
Capital balance	-0.7	Debt service ratio	10
Overall balance	1.0		

Health and education

Health spending, % of GDP	5.3	Education spending, % of GDP	4.6
Doctors per 1,000 pop.	0.1	Enrolment, %: primary	88
Hospital beds per 1,000 pop.	...	secondary	...
Improved-water source access, % of pop.	80	tertiary	9

Society

No. of households	3.6m	Colour TV households, % with:	
Av. no. per household	5.5	cable	...
Marriages per 1,000 pop.	...	satellite	...
Divorces per 1,000 pop.	...	Telephone lines per 100 pop.	1.4
Cost of living, Dec. 2011		Mobile telephone subscribers	
New York = 100	80	per 100 pop.	76.1
Cars per 1,000 pop.	16	Broadband subs per 100 pop.	0.04
		Internet hosts per 1,000 pop.	0.4

a 2009

CZECH REPUBLIC

Area	78,864 sq km	Capital	Prague
Arable as % of total land	41.2	Currency	Koruna (Kc)

People

Population	10.4m	Life expectancy: men		74.7 yrs
Pop. per sq km	133.0		women	81.0 yrs
Av. ann. growth		Adult literacy		...
in pop. 2010–15	0.27%	Fertility rate (per woman)		1.5
Pop. under 15	14.1%	Urban population		73.4%
Pop. over 60	22.2%			per 1,000 pop.
No. of men per 100 women	96.3	Crude birth rate		10.9
Human Development Index	86.5	Crude death rate		10.3

The economy

GDP	Kc3,667bn	GDP per head	$18,250
GDP	$192bn	GDP per head in purchasing	
Av. ann. growth in real		power parity (USA=100)	52.0
GDP 2005–10	2.7%	Economic freedom index	69.9

Origins of GDP		**Components of GDP**	
	% of total		% of total
Agriculture	2	Private consumption	51
Industry, of which:	38	Public consumption	22
manufacturing	24	Investment	23
Services	60	Exports	79
		Imports	-75

Structure of employment

	% of total		% of labour force
Agriculture	3	Unemployed 2010	7.3
Industry	38	Av. ann. rate 1995–2010	6.7
Services	59		

Energy

	m TOE		
Total output	31.2	Net energy imports as %	
Total consumption	42.0	of energy use	26
Consumption per head,			
kg oil equivalent	4,004		

Inflation and finance

Consumer price		av. ann. increase 2005–10	
inflation 2011	1.9%	Narrow money (M1)	11.7%
Av. ann. inflation 2006–11	2.7%	Broad money	8.7%
Money market rate, 2011	1.17%	Household saving rate, 2011	4.2%

Exchange rates

	end 2011		2011
Kc per $	19.94	Effective rates	2005 = 100
Kc per SDR	30.61	– nominal	117.4
Kc per €	25.80	– real	120.5

Trade

Principal exports	$bn fob	Principal imports	$bn cif
Machinery & transport equipment	72.1	Machinery & transport equipment	54.8
Semi-manufactures	23.2	Semi-manufactures	22.7
Raw materials & fuels	8.9	Raw materials & fuels	15.6
Chemicals	8.6	Chemicals	13.4
Total incl. others	**133.0**	Total incl. others	**126.6**

Main export destinations	% of total	Main origins of imports	% of total
Germany	32.4	Germany	29.6
Slovakia	8.6	China	17.4
Poland	6.1	Poland	6.8
France	5.3	Slovakia	6.5
EU27	84.0	EU27	74.9

Balance of payments, reserves and debt, $bn

Visible exports fob	116.7	Change in reserves	0.7
Visible imports fob	-113.9	Level of reserves	
Trade balance	2.8	end Dec.	42.3
Invisibles inflows	25.8	No. months of import cover	3.4
Invisibles outflows	-35.1	Official gold holdings, m oz	0.4
Net transfers	0.5	Foreign debt	86.0
Current account balance	-6.0	– as % of GDP	43
– as % of GDP	-3.1	– as % of total exports	60
Capital balance	11.2	Debt service ratio	11
Overall balance	2.1	Aid given	0.23
		– as % of GDP	0.13

Health and education

Health spending, % of GDP	7.9	Education spending, % of GDP	4.1
Doctors per 1,000 pop.	3.7	Enrolment, %: primary	106
Hospital beds per 1,000 pop.	7.1	secondary	90
Improved-water source access, % of pop.	100	tertiary	61

Society

No. of households	4.5m	Colour TV households, % with:	
Av. no. per household	2.3	cable	25.7
Marriages per 1,000 pop.	4.4	satellite	25.9
Divorces per 1,000 pop.	2.9	Telephone lines per 100 pop.	22.9
Cost of living, Dec. 2011		Mobile telephone subscribers	
New York = 100	99	per 100 pop.	137.2
Cars per 1,000 pop.	433	Broadband subs per 100 pop.	14.5
		Internet hosts per 1,000 pop.	401.9

DENMARK

Area	43,075 sq km	Capital	Copenhagen
Arable as % of total land	57.3	Currency	Danish krone (DKr)

People

Population	5.5m	Life expectancy: men		76.7 yrs
Pop. per sq km	128.8	women		87.4 yrs
Av. ann. growth		Adult literacy		...
in pop. 2010–15	0.35%	Fertility rate (per woman)		1.9
Pop. under 15	18.0%	Urban population		87.5%
Pop. over 60	23.4%			per 1,000 pop.
No. of men per 100 women	98.3	Crude birth rate		11.3
Human Development Index	89.5	Crude death rate		10.1

The economy

GDP	DKr1,755bn	GDP per head	$56,240
GDP	$312bn	GDP per head in purchasing	
Av. ann. growth in real		power parity (USA=100)	85.2
GDP 2005–10	-0.1%	Economic freedom index	76.2

Origins of GDP		**Components of GDP**	
	% of total		% of total
Agriculture	1	Private consumption	48
Industry, of which:	22	Public consumption	29
manufacturing	12	Investment	17
Services	77	Exports	50
		Imports	-45

Structure of employment

	% of total		% of labour force
Agriculture	2	Unemployed 2010	7.4
Industry	20	Av. ann. rate 1995–2010	5.4
Services	78		

Energy

	m TOE		
Total output	23.9	Net energy imports as %	
Total consumption	18.6	of energy use	-29
Consumption per head,			
kg oil equivalent	3,369		

Inflation and finance

Consumer price		av. ann. increase 2005–10	
inflation 2011	2.8%	Narrow money (M1)	5.1%
Av. ann. inflation 2006–11	2.3%	Broad money	9.9%
Money market rate, 2011	1.06%	Household saving rate, 2011	-1.3%

Exchange rates

	end 2011		2011
DKr per $	5.75	Effective rates	2005 = 100
DKr per SDR	8.80	– nominal	100.7
DKr per €	7.44	– real	100.6

Trade

Principal exports		Principal imports	
	$bn fob		*$bn cif*
Machinery & transport equip.	23.7	Machinery & transport equip.	26.3
Food, drink & tobacco	17.8	Food, drink & tobacco	11.3
Chemicals & related products	15.6	Chemicals & related products	10.1
Minerals, fuels & lubricants	9.1	Minerals, fuels & lubricants	5.8
Total incl. others	**96.5**	Total incl. others	**84.5**

Main export destinations		Main origins of imports	
	% of total		*% of total*
Germany	17.1	Germany	20.8
Sweden	13.6	Sweden	13.4
United Kingdom	8.1	Netherlands	7.2
United States	5.9	China	6.7
Norway	5.6	United Kingdom	6.0
EU27	65.9	EU27	70.5

Balance of payments, reserves and aid, $bn

Visible exports fob	95.8	Overall balance	4.3
Visible imports fob	-87.1	Change in reserves	-0.1
Trade balance	8.6	Level of reserves	
Invisibles inflows	87.6	end Dec.	76.5
Invisibles outflows	-73.3	No. months of import cover	5.7
Net transfers	-5.8	Official gold holdings, m oz	2.1
Current account balance	17.1	Aid given	2.87
– as % of GDP	5.5	– as % of GDP	0.91
Capital balance	1.3		

Health and education

Health spending, % of GDP	11.4	Education spending, % of GDP	7.7
Doctors per 1,000 pop.	3.4	Enrolment, %: primary	99
Hospital beds per 1,000 pop.	3.5	secondary	117
Improved-water source access,		tertiary	74
% of pop.	100		

Society

No. of households	2.6m	Colour TV households, % with:	
Av. no. per household	2.2	cable	65.7
Marriages per 1,000 pop.	5.6	satellite	17.4
Divorces per 1,000 pop.	2.6	Telephone lines per 100 pop.	47.4
Cost of living, Dec. 2011		Mobile telephone subscribers	
New York = 100	133	per 100 pop.	125.0
Cars per 1,000 pop.	392	Broadband subs per 100 pop.	37.7
		Internet hosts per 1,000 pop.	784.5

EGYPT

Area	1,000,250 sq km	Capital	Cairo
Arable as % of total land	2.9	Currency	Egyptian pound (£E)

People

Population	84.5m	Life expectancy: men	71.6 yrs
Pop. per sq km	84.5	women	75.5 yrs
Av. ann. growth		Adult literacy	66.4%
in pop. 2010–15	1.67%	Fertility rate (per woman)	2.6
Pop. under 15	32.1%	Urban population	44.2%
Pop. over 60	7.5%		per 1,000 pop.
No. of men per 100 women	100.9	Crude birth rate	22.3
Human Development Index	64.4	Crude death rate	5.1

The economy

GDP	£E1,207bn	GDP per head	$2,700
GDP	$219bn	GDP per head in purchasing	
Av. ann. growth in real		power parity (USA=100)	13.1
GDP 2005–10	6.2%	Economic freedom index	57.9

Origins of GDP

Components of GDP

	% of total		% of total
Agriculture	14	Private consumption	75
Industry, of which:	38	Public consumption	11
manufacturing	16	Investment	19
Services	48	Exports	21
		Imports	-26

Structure of employment

	% of total		% of labour force
Agriculture	32	Unemployed 2010	9.4
Industry	23	Av. ann. rate 1995–2010	9.8
Services	45		

Energy

	m TOE		
Total output	88.2	Net energy imports as %	
Total consumption	72.0	of energy use	-22
Consumption per head,			
kg oil equivalent	903		

Inflation and finance

Consumer price		av. ann. increase 2005–10	
inflation 2011	10.1%	Narrow money (M1)	17.3%
Av. ann. inflation 2006–11	12.1%	Broad money	13.2%
Treasury bill rate, 2011	13.95%		

Exchange rates

	end 2011		2011
£E per $	6.02	Effective rates	2005 = 100
£E per SDR	9.24	– nominal	...
£E per €	7.79	– real	...

Trade

Principal exports[a]	$bn fob	Principal imports[a]	$bn fob
Petroleum & products	10.8	Intermediate goods	12.9
Finished goods incl. textiles	10.1	Consumer goods	12.9
Semi-finished products	1.8	Capital goods	10.5
Iron & steel	0.6	Fuels	2.9
Total incl. others	**25.0**	Total incl. others	**52.7**

Main export destinations	% of total	Main origins of imports	% of total
Italy	8.3	United States	9.4
Spain	6.1	China	9.2
Saudi Arabia	6.0	Germany	7.6
United States	5.9	Italy	5.6

Balance of payments, reserves and debt, $bn

Visible exports fob	25.0	Change in reserves	2.1
Visible imports fob	-45.1	Level of reserves	
Trade balance	-20.1	end Dec.	37.0
Invisibles inflows	24.3	No. months of import cover	6.7
Invisibles outflows	-21.2	Official gold holdings, m oz	2.4
Net transfers	12.4	Foreign debt	34.8
Current account balance	-4.5	– as % of GDP	15
– as % of GDP	-2.1	– as % of total exports	46
Capital balance	6.4	Debt service ratio	6
Overall balance	-0.2		

Health and education

Health spending, % of GDP	4.7	Education spending, % of GDP	3.8
Doctors per 1,000 pop.	2.8	Enrolment, %: primary	106
Hospital beds per 1,000 pop.	1.7	secondary	...
Improved-water source access,		tertiary	30
% of pop.	99		

Society

No. of households	19.5m	Colour TV households, % with:	
Av. no. per household	4.0	cable	0.0
Marriages per 1,000 pop.	6.1	satellite	68.1
Divorces per 1,000 pop.	0.6	Telephone lines per 100 pop.	11.9
Cost of living, Dec. 2011		Mobile telephone subscribers	
New York = 100	69	per 100 pop.	87.1
Cars per 1,000 pop.	27	Broadband subs per 100 pop.	1.8
		Internet hosts per 1,000 pop.	2.6

a   Year ending June 30, 2010.

ESTONIA

Area	45,200 sq km	Capital	Tallinn
Arable as % of total land	14.1	Currency	Kroon (EEK)/Euro (€)[a]

People

Population	1.3m	Life expectancy: men	69.8 yrs
Pop. per sq km	29.7	women	80.0 yrs
Av. ann. growth		Adult literacy	99.8%
in pop. 2010–15	-0.07%	Fertility rate (per woman)	1.7
Pop. under 15	15.4%	Urban population	69.7%
Pop. over 60	22.6%		per 1,000 pop.
No. of men per 100 women	85.5	Crude birth rate	12.1
Human Development Index	83.5	Crude death rate	12.7

The economy

GDP	EEK227bn	GDP per head	$14,340
GDP	$19.2bn	GDP per head in purchasing	
Av. ann. growth in real		power parity (USA=100)	43.8
GDP 2005–10	0.0%	Economic freedom index	73.2

Origins of GDP		Components of GDP	
	% of total		% of total
Agriculture	3	Private consumption	53
Industry, of which:	29	Public consumption	21
manufacturing	17	Investment	20
Services	68	Exports	78
		Imports	-72

Structure of employment

	% of total		% of labour force
Agriculture	4	Unemployed 2010	16.9
Industry	30	Av. ann. rate 1995–2010	10.1
Services	66		

Energy

	m TOE		
Total output	4.2	Net energy imports as %	
Total consumption	4.7	of energy use	12
Consumption per head,			
kg oil equivalent	3,534		

Inflation and finance

Consumer price		av. ann. increase 2005–10	
inflation 2011	5.0%	Narrow money (M1)	6.1%
Av. ann. inflation 2006–11	4.9%	Broad money (M2)	9.9%
Deposit rate, h'holds, 2011	1.70%	Household saving rate, 2011	1.4%

Exchange rates

	end 2011		2011
€ per $	0.77	Effective rates	2005 = 100
€ per SDR	1.19	– nominal	...
		– real	...

Trade

Principal exports		Principal imports	
	$bn fob		*$bn cif*
Machinery & equipment	2.6	Machinery & equipment	2.9
Mineral products	1.8	Mineral products	2.1
Wood & paper	1.4	Chemicals	1.7
Non-precious metals & products	1.1	Transport equipment	0.9
Total incl. others	**11.6**	Total incl. others	**12.3**

Main export destinations		Main origins of imports	
	% of total		*% of total*
Finland	17.0	Finland	14.9
Sweden	15.6	Germany	11.2
Russia	9.7	Sweden	10.9
Latvia	9.0	Latvia	10.8
Germany	5.2	Russia	8.2
EU27	68.6	EU27	79.7

Balance of payments, reserves and debt, $bn

Visible exports fob	11.6	Change in reserves	-1.4
Visible imports fob	-12.0	Level of reserves	
Trade balance	-0.3	end Dec.	2.6
Invisibles inflows	5.4	No. months of import cover	1.8
Invisibles outflows	-4.8	Official gold holdings, m oz	0.0
Net transfers	0.3	Foreign debt	22.0
Current account balance	0.7	– as % of GDP	116.0
– as % of GDP	3.5	– as % of total exports	129
Capital balance	-1.5	Debt service ratio	14
Overall balance	-1.1		

Health and education

Health spending, % of GDP	...	Education spending, % of GDP	5.7
Doctors per 1,000 pop.	3.3	Enrolment, %: primary	99
Hospital beds per 1,000 pop.	5.4	secondary	104
Improved-water source access,		tertiary	63
% of pop.	98		

Society

No. of households	0.6m	Colour TV households, % with:	
Av. no. per household	2.3	cable	59.3
Marriages per 1,000 pop.	3.8	satellite	24.6
Divorces per 1,000 pop.	2.2	Telephone lines per 100 pop.	36.0
Cost of living, Dec. 2011		Mobile telephone subscribers	
New York = 100	...	per 100 pop.	123.2
Cars per 1,000 pop.	428	Broadband subs per 100 pop.	25.1
		Internet hosts per 1,000 pop.	656.1

a Estonia joined the Euro area on January 1, 2011.

FINLAND

Area	338,145 sq km	Capital	Helsinki
Arable as % of total land	7.4	Currency	Euro (€)

People

Population	5.3m	Life expectancy:	men	77.2 yrs
Pop. per sq km	15.9		women	83.3 yrs
Av. ann. growth		Adult literacy		...
in pop. 2010–15	0.32%	Fertility rate (per woman)		1.9
Pop. under 15	16.6%	Urban population		84.2%
Pop. over 60	24.7%			*per 1,000 pop.*
No. of men per 100 women	96.3	Crude birth rate		11.4
Human Development Index	88.2	Crude death rate		9.8

The economy

GDP	€179bn	GDP per head	$44,380
GDP	$238bn	GDP per head in purchasing	
Av. ann. growth in real		power parity (USA=100)	77.3
GDP 2005–10	1.0%	Economic freedom index	72.3

Origins of GDP		Components of GDP	
	% of total		*% of total*
Agriculture	3	Private consumption	55
Industry, of which:	29	Public consumption	25
manuf., mining & utilities	19	Investment	19
Services	68	Exports	40
		Imports	-39

Structure of employment

	% of total		*% of labour force*
Agriculture	4	Unemployed 2010	8.4
Industry	23	Av. ann. rate 1995–2010	9.7
Services	73		

Energy

	m TOE		
Total output	16.6	Net energy imports as %	
Total consumption	33.2	of energy use	50
Consumption per head,			
kg oil equivalent	6,213		

Inflation and finance

Consumer price		*av. ann. increase 2005–10*	
inflation 2011	3.5%	Euro area:	
Av. ann. inflation 2006–11	2.2%	Narrow money (M1)	6.3%
Money market rate, 2011	1.39%	Broad money	5.9%
		Household saving rate, 2011	2.2%

Exchange rates

	end 2011		*2011*
€ per $	0.77	Effective rates	*2005 = 100*
€ per SDR	1.19	– nominal	100.3
		– real	96.9

Trade

Principal exports	$bn fob	Principal imports	$bn cif
Machinery & transport equipment	22.7	Machinery & transport equipment	20.9
Chemicals & related products	5.9	Minerals & fuels	12.4
Mineral fuels & lubricants	5.7	Chemicals & related products	7.4
Raw materials	4.7	Raw materials	6.1
Total incl. others	**69.6**	Total incl. others	**66.2**

Main export destinations	% of total	Main origins of imports	% of total
Sweden	11.4	Russia	17.8
Germany	10.1	Germany	15.1
Russia	8.4	Sweden	15.0
United States	6.9	Netherlands	8.5
Netherlands	6.7	China	4.6
China	5.0	France	3.7
EU27	54.3	EU27	64.2

Balance of payments, reserves and aid, $bn

Visible exports fob	70.1	Overall balance	-2.2
Visible imports fob	-66.2	Change in reserves	-1.9
Trade balance	3.9	Level of reserves	
Invisibles inflows	46.2	end Dec.	9.5
Invisibles outflows	-43.5	No. months of import cover	1.0
Net transfers	-2.2	Official gold holdings, m oz	1.6
Current account balance	4.5	Aid given	1.33
– as % of GDP	1.9	– as % of GDP	0.55
Capital balance	3.8		

Health and education

Health spending, % of GDP	9.0	Education spending, % of GDP	6.1
Doctors per 1,000 pop.	2.9	Enrolment, %: primary	99
Hospital beds per 1,000 pop.	6.2	secondary	108
Improved-water source access, % of pop.	100	tertiary	92

Society

No. of households	2.6m	Colour TV households, % with:	
Av. no. per household	2.1	cable	57.1
Marriages per 1,000 pop.	5.6	satellite	26.2
Divorces per 1,000 pop.	2.6	Telephone lines per 100 pop.	23.3
Cost of living, Dec. 2011		Mobile telephone subscribers	
New York = 100	128	per 100 pop.	156.4
Cars per 1,000 pop.	530	Broadband subs per 100 pop.	28.6
		Internet hosts per 1,000 pop.	892.8

FRANCE

Area	543,965 sq km	Capital	Paris
Arable as % of total land	33.5	Currency	Euro (€)

People

Population	62.6m	Life expectancy: men		78.5 yrs
Pop. per sq km	115.0	women		84.9 yrs
Av. ann. growth		Adult literacy		...
in pop. 2010–15	0.51%	Fertility rate (per woman)		2.0
Pop. under 15	18.4%	Urban population		87.8%
Pop. over 60	23.2%			per 1,000 pop.
No. of men per 100 women	94.8	Crude birth rate		12.4
Human Development Index	88.4	Crude death rate		8.9

The economy

GDP	€1,933bn	GDP per head	$39,450
GDP	$2,560bn	GDP per head in purchasing	
Av. ann. growth in real		power parity (USA=100)	72.4
GDP 2005–10	0.7%	Economic freedom index	63.2

Origins of GDP		Components of GDP	
	% of total		% of total
Agriculture	2	Private consumption	58
Industry, of which:	19	Public consumption	25
manufacturing	11	Investment	19
Services	79	Exports	25
		Imports	-28

Structure of employment

	% of total		% of labour force
Agriculture	3	Unemployed 2010	9.3
Industry	22	Av. ann. rate 1995–2010	9.9
Services	75		

Energy

	m TOE		
Total output	129.5	Net energy imports as %	
Total consumption	256.2	of energy use	49
Consumption per head,			
kg oil equivalent	3,970		

Inflation and finance

Consumer price		av. ann. increase 2005–10	
inflation 2011	2.1%	Euro area:	
Av. ann. inflation 2006–11	1.6%	Narrow money (M1)	6.3%
Treasury bill rate, 2011	0.69%	Broad money	5.9%
		Household saving rate[a], 2011	16.8%

Exchange rates

	end 2011		2011
€ per $	0.77	Effective rates	2005 = 100
€ per SDR	1.19	– nominal	100.5
		– real	96.8

Trade

Principal exports	
	$bn fob
Machinery & transport equip.	196.2
Chemicals & related products	96.3
Food, drink & tobacco	59.2
Mineral fuels & lubricants	20.2
Raw materials	14.0
Total incl. others	**515.3**

Principal imports	
	$bn cif
Machinery & transport equip.	202.4
Chemicals & related products	84.0
Mineral fuels & lubricants	81.6
Food, drink & tobacco	47.7
Raw materials	17.1
Total incl. others	**605.3**

Main export destinations	
	% of total
Germany	16.3
Italy	8.1
Belgium	7.6
Spain	7.6
United Kingdom	6.8
United States	5.1
EU27	60.9

Main origins of imports	
	% of total
Germany	19.0
Belgium	11.3
Italy	7.9
Netherlands	7.5
Spain	6.7
China	5.0
EU27	68.3

Balance of payments, reserves and aid, $bn

Visible exports fob	517.2	Overall balance	7.8
Visible imports fob	-588.4	Change in reserves	34.1
Trade balance	-71.2	Level of reserves	
Invisibles inflows	353.5	end Dec.	165.9
Invisibles outflows	-291.8	No. months of import cover	2.3
Net transfers	-35.0	Official gold holdings, m oz	78.3
Current account balance	-44.5	Aid given	12.92
– as % of GDP	-1.7	– as % of GDP	0.50
Capital balance	31.8		

Health and education

Health spending, % of GDP	11.9	Education spending, % of GDP	5.6
Doctors per 1,000 pop.	3.4	Enrolment, %: primary	111
Hospital beds per 1,000 pop.	6.9	secondary	113
Improved-water source access,		tertiary	55
% of pop.	100		

Society

No. of households	27.2m	Colour TV households, % with:	
Av. no. per household	2.3	cable	14.8
Marriages per 1,000 pop.	3.8	satellite	30.2
Divorces per 1,000 pop.	2.3	Telephone lines per 100 pop.	56.2
Cost of living, Dec. 2011		Mobile telephone subscribers	
New York = 100	150	per 100 pop.	100.7
Cars per 1,000 pop.	502	Broadband subs per 100 pop.	34.0
		Internet hosts per 1,000 pop.	270.7

a Gross.

GERMANY

Area	357,868 sq km	Capital	Berlin
Arable as % of total land	34.3	Currency	Euro (€)

People

Population	82.1m	Life expectancy: men	78.2 yrs
Pop. per sq km	229.4	women	83.0 yrs
Av. ann. growth		Adult literacy	...
in pop. 2010–15	-0.20%	Fertility rate (per woman)	1.5
Pop. under 15	13.4%	Urban population	74.5%
Pop. over 60	26.0%		per 1,000 pop.
No. of men per 100 women	96.1	Crude birth rate	8.7
Human Development Index	90.5	Crude death rate	10.9

The economy

GDP	€2,477bn	GDP per head	$40,120
GDP	$3,281bn	GDP per head in purchasing	
Av. ann. growth in real		power parity (USA=100)	79.3
GDP 2005–10	1.3%	Economic freedom index	71.0

Origins of GDP

	% of total
Agriculture	1
Industry, of which:	28
manufacturing	21
Services	71

Components of GDP

	% of total
Private consumption	57
Public consumption	20
Investment	17
Exports	47
Imports	-41

Structure of employment

	% of total		% of labour force
Agriculture	2	Unemployed 2010	7.1
Industry	28	Av. ann. rate 1995–2010	8.9
Services	70		

Energy

	m TOE		
Total output	127.1	Net energy imports as %	
Total consumption	318.5	of energy use	60
Consumption per head,			
kg oil equivalent	3,889		

Inflation and finance

Consumer price			av. ann. increase 2005–10
inflation 2011	2.3%	Euro area:	
Av. ann. inflation 2006–11	1.7%	Narrow money (M1)	6.3%
Money market rate, 2011	0.81%	Broad money	5.9%
		Household saving rate, 2011	11.0%

Exchange rates

	end 2011		2011
€ per $	0.77	Effective rates	2005 = 100
€ per SDR	1.19	– nominal	100.1
		– real	95.1

Trade

Principal exports	
	$bn fob
Machinery & transport equip.	594.3
Chemicals & related products	196.3
Food, drink & tobacco	64.5
Raw materials	27.3
Mineral fuels & lubricants	26.5
Total incl. others	**1,255.5**

Principal imports	
	$bn cif
Machinery & transport equip.	374.1
Chemicals & related products	139.9
Mineral fuels & lubricants	123.3
Food, drink & tobacco	73.2
Raw materials	47.4
Total incl. others	**1,054.0**

Main export destinations	
	% of total
France	9.5
Netherlands	6.6
United Kingdom	6.2
Italy	6.2
Austria	5.5
United States	5.2
Belgium	4.8
EU27	60.1

Main origins of imports	
	% of total
Netherlands	13.4
France	7.9
China	7.8
Belgium	6.6
Italy	5.3
United Kingdom	4.6
Austria	4.4
EU27	63.2

Balance of payments, reserves and aid, $bn

Visible exports fob	1,303	Overall balance	2.1
Visible imports fob	-1,099	Change in reserves	36.4
Trade balance	205	Level of reserves	
Invisibles inflows	468	end Dec.	216.0
Invisibles outflows	-434	No. months of import cover	1.7
Net transfers	-51	Official gold holdings, m oz	109.3
Current account balance	188	Aid given	12.99
– as % of GDP	5.7	– as % of GDP	0.39
Capital balance	-184		

Health and education

Health spending, % of GDP	11.6	Education spending, % of GDP	4.6
Doctors per 1,000 pop.	3.6	Enrolment, %: primary	102
Hospital beds per 1,000 pop.	8.2	secondary	103
Improved-water source access,		tertiary	46
% of pop.	100		

Society

No. of households	40.0m	Colour TV households, % with:	
Av. no. per household	2.0	cable	50.5
Marriages per 1,000 pop.	5.0	satellite	44.3
Divorces per 1,000 pop.	2.3	Telephone lines per 100 pop.	55.5
Cost of living, Dec. 2011		Mobile telephone subscribers	
New York = 100	109	per 100 pop.	127.0
Cars per 1,000 pop.	502	Broadband subs per 100 pop.	31.7
		Internet hosts per 1,000 pop.	251.4

GREECE

Area	131,957 sq km	Capital	Athens
Arable as % of total land	19.8	Currency	Euro (€)

People

Population	11.2m	Life expectancy: men	77.6 yrs
Pop. per sq km	86.1	women	82.6 yrs
Av. ann. growth		Adult literacy	97.2%
in pop. 2010–15	0.23%	Fertility rate (per woman)	1.5
Pop. under 15	14.2%	Urban population	62.4%
Pop. over 60	24.3%		per 1,000 pop.
No. of men per 100 women	97.9	Crude birth rate	10.1
Human Development Index	86.1	Crude death rate	10.5

The economy

GDP	€227bn	GDP per head	$26,610
GDP	$301bn	GDP per head in purchasing	
Av. ann. growth in real		power parity (USA=100)	60.2
GDP 2005–10	0.1%	Economic freedom index	55.4

Origins of GDP

	% of total
Agriculture	3
Industry, of which:	18
mining & manufacturing	...
Services	79

Components of GDP

	% of total
Private consumption	75
Public consumption	18
Investment	16
Exports	22
Imports	-30

Structure of employment

	% of total		% of labour force
Agriculture	13	Unemployed 2010	12.5
Industry	20	Av. ann. rate 1995–2010	10.0
Services	67		

Energy

	m TOE		
Total output	10.1	Net energy imports as %	
Total consumption	29.4	of energy use	66
Consumption per head,			
kg oil equivalent	2,669		

Inflation and finance

Consumer price		av. ann. increase 2005–10	
inflation 2011	3.3%	Euro area:	
Av. ann. inflation 2006–11	3.3%	Narrow money (M1)	6.3%
Treasury bill rate, 2011	2.01%	Broad money	5.9%

Exchange rates

	end 2011		2011
€ per $	0.77	Effective rates	2005 = 100
€ per SDR	1.19	– nominal	101.5
		– real	106.2

Trade

Principal exports		Principal imports	
	$bn fob		*$bn cif*
Food, drink & tobacco	4.7	Mineral fuels & lubricants	15.0
Chemicals & related products	3.1	Machinery & transport equip.	15.0
Machinery & transport equip.	2.5	Chemicals & related products	9.5
Mineral fuels & lubricants	2.4	Food, drink & tobacco	7.2
Raw materials	1.6	Raw materials	1.8
Total incl. others	**21.7**	Total incl. others	**63.4**

Main export destinations		Main origins of imports	
	% of total		*% of total*
Germany	11.1	Germany	10.6
Italy	11.0	Italy	9.9
Cyprus	7.3	Russia	9.8
Bulgaria	6.5	China	6.0
United Kingdom	5.3	Netherlands	5.3
EU27	62.6	EU27	51.1

Balance of payments, reserves and debt, $bn

Visible exports fob	22.6	Overall balance	-13.9
Visible imports fob	-60.2	Change in reserves	0.9
Trade balance	-37.5	Level of reserves	
Invisibles inflows	42.2	end Dec.	6.4
Invisibles outflows	-35.7	No. months of import cover	0.8
Net transfers	1.0	Official gold holdings, m oz	3.6
Current account balance	-30.9	Aid given	0.51
– as % of GDP	-10.3	– as % of GDP	0.17
Capital balance	17.5		

Health and education

Health spending, % of GDP	10.2	Education spending, % of GDP	...
Doctors per 1,000 pop.	6.2	Enrolment, %: primary	100
Hospital beds per 1,000 pop.	4.8	secondary	101
Improved-water source access,		tertiary	89
% of pop.	100		

Society

No. of households	4.0m	Colour TV households, % with:	
Av. no. per household	2.8	cable	0.8
Marriages per 1,000 pop.	5.2	satellite	16.6
Divorces per 1,000 pop.	1.3	Telephone lines per 100 pop.	45.8
Cost of living, Dec. 2011		Mobile telephone subscribers	
New York = 100	94	per 100 pop.	108.2
Cars per 1,000 pop.	497	Broadband subs per 100 pop.	19.9
		Internet hosts per 1,000 pop.	279.4

HONG KONG

Area	1,075 sq km	Capital	Victoria
Arable as % of total land	...	Currency	Hong Kong dollar (HK$)

People

Population	7.1m	Life expectancy: men	80.2 yrs
Pop. per sq km	6,604.7	women	86.4 yrs
Av. ann. growth		Adult literacy	...
in pop. 2010–15	1.04%	Fertility rate (per woman)	1.1
Pop. under 15	11.5%	Urban population	100.0%
Pop. over 60	18.4%		per 1,000 pop.
No. of men per 100 women	90	Crude birth rate	8.8
Human Development Index	89.8	Crude death rate	6.3

The economy

GDP	HK$1,744bn	GDP per head	$31,760
GDP	$224bn	GDP per head in purchasing	
Av. ann. growth in real		power parity (USA=100)	98.6
GDP 2005–10	4.0%	Economic freedom index	89.9

Origins of GDP		Components of GDP	
	% of total		% of total
Agriculture	0	Private consumption	62
Industry, of which:	7	Public consumption	8
manufacturing	2	Investment	24
Services	93	Exports	223
		Imports	-217

Structure of employment

	% of total		% of labour force
Agriculture	0	Unemployed 2009	5.2
Industry	12	Av. ann. rate 1995–2009	5.0
Services	88		

Energy

	m TOE		
Total output	0.1	Net energy imports as %	
Total consumption	14.9	of energy use	100
Consumption per head,			
kg oil equivalent	2,133		

Inflation and finance

			av. ann. increase 2005–10
Consumer price			
inflation 2011	5.3%	Narrow money (M1)	15.1%
Av. ann. inflation 2006–11	2.9%	Broad money	10.2%
Money market rate, 2011	0.13%		

Exchange rates

	end 2011		2011
HK$ per $	7.77	Effective rates	2005 = 100
HK$ per SDR	11.92	– nominal	...
HK$ per €	10.05	– real	...

Trade

Principal exports[a]	$bn fob	Principal imports[a]	$bn cif
Capital goods	137.7	Raw materials & semi-manufactures	159.3
Raw materials & semi manufactures	133.1	Capital goods	137.7
Consumer goods	105.3	Consumer goods	104.4
Foodstufs	4.3	Foodstuffs	15.8
Total incl. others	**390.4**	Total	**433.5**

Main export destinations	% of total	Main origins of imports	% of total
China	52.7	China	45.4
United States	10.9	Japan	9.1
Japan	4.2	Singapore	7.0
Germany	2.7	Taiwan	6.7

Balance of payments, reserves and debt, $bn

Visible exports fob	394.0	Change in reserves	12.9
Visible imports fob	-437.0	Level of reserves	
Trade balance	-43.0	end Dec.	268.7
Invisibles inflows	230.0	No. months of import cover	5.4
Invisibles outflows	-162.7	Official gold holdings, m oz	0.1
Net transfers	-3.4	Foreign debt	55.0
Current account balance	13.9	– as % of GDP	25.0
– as % of GDP	6.2	– as % of total exports	9
Capital balance	-8.5	Debt service ratio	1
Overall balance	9.2		

Health and education

Health spending, % of GDP	...	Education spending, % of GDP	3.6
Doctors per 1,000 pop.	1.3	Enrolment, %: primary	102
Hospital beds per 1,000 pop.	5.0	secondary	83
Improved-water source access, % of pop.	...	tertiary	60

Society

No. of households	2.4m	Colour TV households, % with:	
Av. no. per household	3.0	cable	92.4
Marriages per 1,000 pop.	6.4	satellite	0.1
Divorces per 1,000 pop.	2.9	Telephone lines per 100 pop.	61.8
Cost of living, Dec. 2011		Mobile telephone subscribers	
New York = 100	115	per 100 pop.	195.6
Cars per 1,000 pop.	52	Broadband subs per 100 pop.	29.9
		Internet hosts per 1,000 pop.	121.9

a Including re-exports.
Note: Hong Kong became a Special Administrative Region of China on July 1 1997.

HUNGARY

Area	93,030 sq km	Capital	Budapest
Arable as % of total land	50.6	Currency	Forint (Ft)

People

Population	10.0m	Life expectancy: men		70.8 yrs
Pop. per sq km	107.3	women		78.5 yrs
Av. ann. growth		Adult literacy		99.4
in pop. 2010–15	-0.16%	Fertility rate (per woman)		1.4
Pop. under 15	14.7%	Urban population		71.3%
Pop. over 60	22.4%			per 1,000 pop.
No. of men per 100 women	90.4	Crude birth rate		10.1
Human Development Index	81.6	Crude death rate		13.2

The economy

GDP	Ft26,748bn	GDP per head	$12,860
GDP	$129bn	GDP per head in purchasing	
Av. ann. growth in real		power parity (USA=100)	43.6
GDP 2005–10	-0.2%	Economic freedom index	67.1

Origins of GDP		Components of GDP	
	% of total		% of total
Agriculture	4	Private consumption	53
Industry, of which:	31	Public consumption	22
manufacturing	23	Investment	18
Services	65	Exports	87
		Imports	-80

Structure of employment

	% of total		% of labour force
Agriculture	5	Unemployed 2010	11.2
Industry	31	Av. ann. rate 1995–2010	7.6
Services	64		

Energy

	m TOE		
Total output	11.0	Net energy imports as %	
Total consumption	24.9	of energy use	56
Consumption per head,			
kg oil equivalent	2,480		

Inflation and finance

Consumer price		av. ann. increase 2005–10	
inflation 2011	4.1%	Narrow money (M1)	5.0%
Av. ann. inflation 2006–11	5.4%	Broad money	7.9%
Treasury bill rate, 2011	6.02%	Household saving rate, 2011	3.0%

Exchange rates

	end 2011		2011
			2005 = 100
Ft per $	240.68	Effective rates	
Ft per SDR	369.51	– nominal	82.3
Ft per €	311.40	– real	97.7

Trade

Principal exports		Principal imports	
	$bn fob		*$bn cif*
Machinery & equipment	57.1	Machinery & equipment	43.7
Other manufactures	26.0	Other manufactures	27.8
Food, drink & tobacco	6.5	Fuels	9.7
Raw materials	2.3	Food, drink & tobacco	4.3
Total incl. others	**94.7**	Total incl. others	**87.4**

Main export destinations		Main origins of imports	
	% of total		*% of total*
Germany	25.2	Germany	24.1
Italy	5.6	China	10.0
United Kingdom	5.5	Russia	7.9
Romania	5.4	Austria	6.3
EU27	77.2	EU27	67.7

Balance of payments, reserves and debt, $bn

Visible exports fob	91.4	Change in reserves	0.8
Visible imports fob	-87.2	Level of reserves	
Trade balance	4.3	end Dec.	45.0
Invisibles inflows	35.4	No. months of import cover	4.3
Invisibles outflows	-38.7	Official gold holdings, m oz	0.1
Net transfers	0.5	Foreign debt	179.0
Current account balance	1.4	– as % of GDP	139
– as % of GDP	1.1	– as % of total exports	150
Capital balance	4.4	Debt service ratio	32
Overall balance	4.2	Aid given	0.11
		% of GDP	0.09

Health and education

Health spending, % of GDP	7.3	Education spending, % of GDP	5.1
Doctors per 1,000 pop.	3.0	Enrolment, %: primary	102
Hospital beds per 1,000 pop.	6.7	secondary	98
Improved-water source access,		tertiary	62
% of pop.	100		

Society

No. of households	4.2m	Colour TV households, % with:	
Av. no. per household	2.4	cable	52.0
Marriages per 1,000 pop.	4.2	satellite	21.5
Divorces per 1,000 pop.	2.4	Telephone lines per 100 pop.	29.8
Cost of living, Dec. 2011		Mobile telephone subscribers	
New York = 100	82	per 100 pop.	120.3
Cars per 1,000 pop.	313	Broadband subs per 100 pop.	19.6
		Internet hosts per 1,000 pop.	307.9

INDIA

Area	3,287,263 sq km	Capital	New Delhi
Arable as % of total land	53.1	Currency	Indian rupee (Rs)

People

Population	1,214.5m	Life expectancy:	men	64.4 yrs
Pop. per sq km	369.5		women	67.6 yrs
Av. ann. growth		Adult literacy		...
in pop. 2010–15	1.32%	Fertility rate (per woman)		2.5
Pop. under 15	30.8%	Urban population		32.8%
Pop. over 60	7.5%			per 1,000 pop.
No. of men per 100 women	106.8	Crude birth rate		21.3
Human Development Index	54.7	Crude death rate		7.9

The economy

GDP	Rs78.8trn	GDP per head	$1,410
GDP	$1,727bn	GDP per head in purchasing	
Av. ann. growth in real		power parity (USA=100)	7.3
GDP 2005–10	8.6%	Economic freedom index	54.6

Origins of GDP		Components of GDP	
	% of total		% of total
Agriculture	19	Private consumption	57
Industry, of which:	26	Public consumption	12
manufacturing	14	Investment	35
Services	55	Exports	22
		Imports	-25

Structure of employment

	% of total		% of labour force
Agriculture	51	Unemployed 2005	4.4
Industry	22	Av. ann. rate 1995–2005	3.5
Services	27		

Energy

	m TOE		
Total output	502.5	Net energy imports as %	
Total consumption	675.8	of energy use	26
Consumption per head,			
kg oil equivalent	560		

Inflation and finance

Consumer price		av. ann. increase 2005–10	
inflation 2011	8.9%	Narrow money (M1)	16.1%
Av. ann. inflation 2006–11	9.3%	Broad money	20.0%
Lending rate, 2011	10.17%		

Exchange rates

	end 2011		2011
Rs per $	53.26	Effective rates	2005 = 100
Rs per SDR	81.77	– nominal	...
Rs per €	68.91	– real	...

Trade

Principal exports[a]	$bn fob	Principal imports[a]	$bn cif
Engineering goods	68.8	Petroleum & products	106.1
Petroleum & products	41.9	Gold & silver	35.6
Gems & jewellery	40.8	Gems	31.3
Agricultural goods	24.7	Machinery	23.3
Textiles	23.3	Electronic goods	21.5
Total incl. others	**254.4**	Total incl. others	**352.6**

Main export destinations	% of total	Main origins of imports	% of total
United Arab Emirates	11.6	China	11.7
United States	9.3	United Arab Emirates	8.8
China	6.9	Switzerland	6.3
Hong Kong	3.7	Saudi Arabia	5.8

Balance of payments, reserves and debt, $bn

Visible exports fob	225.5	Change in reserves	15.8
Visible imports fob	-323.4	Level of reserves	
Trade balance	-97.9	end Dec.	300.5
Invisibles inflows	133.4	No. months of import cover	7.8
Invisibles outflows	-139.4	Official gold holdings, m oz	17.9
Net transfers	52.2	Foreign debt	290.3
Current account balance	-51.8	– as % of GDP	18
– as % of GDP	-3.0	– as % of total exports	79
Capital balance	68.5	Debt service ratio	6
Overall balance	1.0		

Health and education

Health spending, % of GDP	4.1	Education spending, % of GDP	...
Doctors per 1,000 pop.	0.6	Enrolment, %: primary	118
Hospital beds per 1,000 pop.	...	secondary	60
Improved-water source access,		tertiary	16
% of pop.	92		

Society

No. of households	225.8m	Colour TV households, % with:	
Av. no. per household	5.3	cable	58.5
Marriages per 1,000 pop.	...	satellite	7.4
Divorces per 1,000 pop.	...	Telephone lines per 100 pop.	2.9
Cost of living, Dec. 2011		Mobile telephone subscribers	
New York = 100	56	per 100 pop.	61.4
Cars per 1,000 pop.	15	Broadband subs per 100 pop.	0.9
		Internet hosts per 1,000 pop.	5.6

a Year ending March 31, 2011.

INDONESIA

Area	1,904,443 sq km	Capital	Jakarta
Arable as % of total land	13.0	Currency	Rupiah (Rp)

People

Population	232.5m	Life expectancy: men	68.3 yrs
Pop. per sq km	122.0	women	71.8 yrs
Av. ann. growth		Adult literacy	92.2%
in pop. 2010–15	0.98%	Fertility rate (per woman)	2.1
Pop. under 15	26.7%	Urban population	53.7%
Pop. over 60	8.9%		per 1,000 pop.
No. of men per 100 women	99.5	Crude birth rate	17.4
Human Development Index	61.7	Crude death rate	6.8

The economy

GDP	Rp6,423trn	GDP per head	$2,950
GDP	$707bn	GDP per head in purchasing	
Av. ann. growth in real		power parity (USA=100)	9.2
GDP 2005–10	5.7%	Economic freedom index	56.4

Origins of GDP		Components of GDP	
	% of total		% of total
Agriculture	15	Private consumption	57
Industry, of which:	47	Public consumption	9
manufacturing	25	Investment	32
Services	38	Exports	25
		Imports	-23

Structure of employment

	% of total		% of labour force
Agriculture	38	Unemployed 2010	7.1
Industry	19	Av. ann. rate 1995–2010	7.5
Services	43		

Energy

	m TOE		
Total output	351.8	Net energy imports as %	
Total consumption	202.0	of energy use	-74
Consumption per head,			
kg oil equivalent	851		

Inflation and finance

Consumer price		av. ann. increase 2005–10	
inflation 2011	5.4%	Narrow money (M1)	12.3%
Av. ann. inflation 2006–11	6.3%	Broad money	15.5%
Money market rate, 2011	5.62%		

Exchange rates

	end 2011		2011
Rp per $	9,068	Effective rates	2005 = 100
Rp per SDR	13,922	– nominal	...
Rp per €	11,732	– real	...

Trade

Principal exports

	$bn fob
Mineral fuels	46.8
Manufactured goods	21.9
Raw materials	20.3
Machinery & transport equip.	19.6
Total incl. others	**157.8**

Principal imports

	$bn cif
Machinery & transport equip.	48.5
Mineral fuels	27.5
Manufactured goods	20.5
Chemicals	16.7
Total incl. others	**135.7**

Main export destinations

	% of total
Japan	16.3
China	9.9
United States	9.1
Singapore	8.7

Main origins of imports

	% of total
China	15.1
Singapore	14.9
Japan	12.5
United States	6.9

Balance of payments, reserves and debt, $bn

Visible exports fob	158.1	Change in reserves	30.1
Visible imports fob	-127.4	Level of reserves	
Trade balance	30.6	end Dec.	96.2
Invisibles inflows	18.7	No. months of import cover	6.6
Invisibles outflows	-48.3	Official gold holdings, m oz	2.4
Net transfers	4.6	Foreign debt	179.1
Current account balance	5.6	– as % of GDP	28
– as % of GDP	0.8	– as % of total exports	102
Capital balance	26.2	Debt service ratio	17
Overall balance	30.3		

Health and education

Health spending, % of GDP	2.6	Education spending, % of GDP	4.6
Doctors per 1,000 pop.	0.3	Enrolment, %: primary	118
Hospital beds per 1,000 pop.	...	secondary	77
Improved-water source access,		tertiary	23
% of pop.	82		

Society

No. of households	67.4m	Colour TV households, % with:	
Av. no. per household	3.4	cable	1.4
Marriages per 1,000 pop.	7.0	satellite	10.8
Divorces per 1,000 pop.	0.9	Telephone lines per 100 pop.	15.8
Cost of living, Dec. 2011		Mobile telephone subscribers	
New York = 100	85	per 100 pop.	91.7
Cars per 1,000 pop.	...	Broadband subs per 100 pop.	0.8
		Internet hosts per 1,000 pop.	6.0

IRAN

Area	1,648,000 sq km	Capital	Tehran
Arable as % of total land	10.6	Currency	Rial (IR)

People

Population	75.1m	Life expectancy: men	71.5 yrs
Pop. per sq km	45.6	women	75.3 yrs
Av. ann. growth		Adult literacy	85.0%
in pop. 2010–15	1.04%	Fertility rate (per woman)	1.6
Pop. under 15	23.8%	Urban population	69.7%
Pop. over 60	7.1%		per 1,000 pop.
No. of men per 100 women	103.0	Crude birth rate	16.2
Human Development Index	70.7	Crude death rate	5.4

The economy

GDP	IR3,965trn	GDP per head	$5,230
GDP	$387bn	GDP per head in purchasing	
Av. ann. growth in real		power parity (USA=100)	24.5
GDP 2005–10	4.6%	Economic freedom index	42.3

Origins of GDP[a]		Components of GDP[a]	
	% of total		% of total
Agriculture	10	Private consumption	50
Industry, of which:	39	Public consumption	12
manufacturing	12	Investment	29
Services	51	Exports	26
		Imports	-17

Structure of employment

	% of total		% of labour force
Agriculture	21	Unemployed 2008	10.5
Industry	32	Av. ann. rate 2000-2008	12.1
Services	47		

Energy

	m TOE		
Total output	349.8	Net energy imports as %	
Total consumption	215.9	of energy use	-62
Consumption per head,			
kg oil equivalent	2,951		

Inflation and finance

Consumer price		av. ann. increase 2005–09	
inflation 2011	22.7%	Narrow money (M1)	16.5%
Av. ann. inflation 2006–11	17.7%	Broad money	23.5%
Deposit rate, March 2011	12.07%		

Exchange rates

	end 2011		2011
IR per $	11,165	Effective rates	2005 = 100
IR per SDR	17,141	– nominal	79.3
IR per €	14,446	– real	179.1

Trade

Principal exports[b]		Principal imports[b]	
	$bn fob		$bn cif
Oil & gas	69.8	Machinery & transport equipment	18.0
Industrial goods excl. oil & gas products	12.7	Iron & steel	8.1
Agricultural & traditional goods	4.0	Foodstuffs & live animals	6.4
Metallic mineral ores	0.7	Chemicals	6.0
		Mineral products & fuels	5.8
Total incl. others	**87.5**	Total incl. others	**55.2**

Main export destinations		Main origins of imports	
	% of total		% of total
China	16.7	United Arab Emirates	33.8
India	10.2	China	8.6
Japan	10.2	Germany	6.8
Turkey	7.0	Turkey	5.7
South Korea	6.4	South Korea	5.6

Balance of payments[c], reserves and debt, $bn

Visible exports fob	108.6	Change in reserves	4.7
Visible imports fob	-68.4	Level of reserves	
Trade balance	40.2	end Dec.	84.3
Net invisibles	-15.2	No. months of import cover	15.2
Net transfers	0.5	Official gold holdings, m oz	...
Current account balance	25.5	Foreign debt	13.0
– as % of GDP	6.6	– as % of GDP	3
Capital balance	-16.5	– as % of total exports	...
Overall balance	-0.9	Debt service ratio[a]	2

Health and education

Health spending, % of GDP	5.6	Education spending, % of GDP	4.7
Doctors per 1,000 pop.	...	Enrolment, %: primary	108
Hospital beds per 1,000 pop.	...	secondary	84
Improved-water source access, % of pop.	96	tertiary	43

Society

No. of households	20.5m	Colour TV households, % with:	
Av. no. per household	3.7	cable	0.0
Marriages per 1,000 pop.	11.4	satellite	39.3
Divorces per 1,000 pop.	1.7	Telephone lines per 100 pop.	36.3
Cost of living, Dec. 2011		Mobile telephone subscribers	
New York = 100	54	per 100 pop.	91.3
Cars per 1,000 pop.	24	Broadband subs per 100 pop.	0.7
		Internet hosts per 1,000 pop.	2.2

a   2009
b   Iranian year ending March 20, 2010.
c   Iranian year ending March 20, 2011.

IRELAND

Area	70,282 sq km	Capital	Dublin
Arable as % of total land	15.8	Currency	Euro (€)

People

Population	4.6m	Life expectancy: men	78.4 yrs
Pop. per sq km	65.5	women	83.2 yrs
Av. ann. growth		Adult literacy	...
in pop. 2010–15	1.14%	Fertility rate (per woman)	2.1
Pop. under 15	20.8%	Urban population	63.4%
Pop. over 60	16.1%		per 1,000 pop.
No. of men per 100 women	100.1	Crude birth rate	15.6
Human Development Index	90.8	Crude death rate	6.4

The economy

GDP	€156bn	GDP per head	$46,170
GDP	$207bn	GDP per head in purchasing	
Av. ann. growth in real		power parity (USA=100)	85.8
GDP 2005–10	-0.1%	Economic freedom index	76.9

Origins of GDP		**Components of GDP**	
	% of total		% of total
Agriculture	1	Private consumption	51
Industry, of which:	32	Public consumption	19
manufacturing	24	Investment	11
Services	67	Exports	101
		Imports	-82

Structure of employment

	% of total		% of labour force
Agriculture	5	Unemployed 2010	13.5
Industry	20	Av. ann. rate 1995–2010	7.1
Services	75		

Energy

	m TOE		
Total output	1.5	Net energy imports as %	
Total consumption	14.3	of energy use	89
Consumption per head,			
kg oil equivalent	3,216		

Inflation and finance

Consumer price		av. ann. increase 2005–10	
inflation 2011	2.6%	Euro area:	
Av. ann. inflation 2006–11	1.2%	Narrow money (M1)	6.3%
Money market rate, 2011	1.14%	Broad money	5.9%
		Household saving rate, 2011	9.4%

Exchange rates

	end 2011		2011
€ per $	0.77	Effective rates	2005 = 100
€ per SDR	1.19	– nominal	101.2
		– real	97.5

Trade

Principal exports		Principal imports	
	$bn fob		*$bn cif*
Chemicals & related products	68.0	Machinery & transport equip.	15.8
Machinery & transport equip.	13.2	Chemicals	11.4
Food, drink & tobacco	10.4	Food, drink & tobacco	7.3
Raw materials	1.9	Minerals, fuels & lubricants	7.0
Total incl. others	**118.3**	Total incl. others	**60.7**

Main export destinations		Main origins of imports	
	% of total		*% of total*
United States	21.0	United Kingdom	37.4
United Kingdom	15.3	United States	13.6
Belgium	15.2	Germany	7.5
Germany	6.8	Netherlands	5.6
France	5.0	China	4.1
Switzerland	3.9	France	3.8
EU27	58.1	EU27	67.3

Balance of payments, reserves and aid, $bn

Visible exports fob	109.9	Overall balance	-0.0
Visible imports fob	-61.6	Change in reserves	0.0
Trade balance	48.3	Level of reserves	
Invisibles inflows	174.3	end Dec.	2.1
Invisibles outflows	-220.0	No. months of import cover	0.1
Net transfers	-1.6	Official gold holdings, m oz	0.2
Current account balance	1.0	Aid given	0.90
– as % of GDP	0.5	– as % of GDP	0.52
Capital balance	14.5		

Health and education

Health spending, % of GDP	9.2	Education spending, % of GDP	5.7
Doctors per 1,000 pop.	3.2	Enrolment, %: primary	108
Hospital beds per 1,000 pop.	4.9	secondary	117
Improved-water source access,		tertiary	61
% of pop.	100		

Society

No. of households	1.7m	Colour TV households, % with:	
Av. no. per household	2.7	cable	36.0
Marriages per 1,000 pop.	4.7	satellite	41.2
Divorces per 1,000 pop.	0.7	Telephone lines per 100 pop.	46.5
Cost of living, Dec. 2011		Mobile telephone subscribers	
New York = 100	111	per 100 pop.	105.2
Cars per 1,000 pop.	446	Broadband subs per 100 pop.	21.1
		Internet hosts per 1,000 pop.	302.3

ISRAEL

Area	20,770 sq km	Capital	Jerusalem[a]
Arable as % of total land	14.0	Currency	New Shekel (NIS)

People

Population	7.3m	Life expectancy: men	79.6 yrs
Pop. per sq km	351.5	women	84.2 yrs
Av. ann. growth		Adult literacy	...
in pop. 2010–15	1.66%	Fertility rate (per woman)	2.9
Pop. under 15	27.6%	Urban population	92.1%
Pop. over 60	14.6%		per 1,000 pop.
No. of men per 100 women	97.4	Crude birth rate	20.5
Human Development Index	88.8	Crude death rate	5.4

The economy

GDP	NIS813bn	GDP per head	$28,510
GDP	$217bn	GDP per head in purchasing	
Av. ann. growth in real		power parity (USA=100)	60.6
GDP 2005–10	4.1%	Economic freedom index	67.8

Origins of GDP[b]		Components of GDP	
	% of total		% of total
Agriculture	3	Private consumption	58
Industry, of which:	32	Public consumption	24
manufacturing	22	Investment	16
Services	64	Exports	37
		Imports	-35

Structure of employment

	% of total		% of labour force
Agriculture	2	Unemployed 2010	6.6
Industry	20	Av. ann. rate 1995–2010	8.2
Services	78		

Energy

	m TOE		
Total output	3.3	Net energy imports as %	
Total consumption	21.5	of energy use	85
Consumption per head,			
kg oil equivalent	2,878		

Inflation and finance

		av. ann. increase 2005–09	
Consumer price			
inflation 2011	3.5%	Narrow money (M1)	20.2%
Av. ann. inflation 2006–11	2.9%	Broad money	7.9%
Treasury bill rate, 2011	3.05%		

Exchange rates

	end 2011		2011
NIS per $	3.82	Effective rates	2005 = 100
NIS per SDR	5.87	– nominal	113.8
NIS per €	4.94	– real	113.1

Trade

Principal exports		Principal imports	
	$bn fob		*$bn fob*
Chemicals & chemical products	13.9	Fuel	10.4
Polished diamonds	8.9	Diamonds	8.0
Communications, medical &		Machinery & equipment	5.7
scientific equipment	7.8	Chemicals	4.9
Electronics	4.2		
Total incl. others	**50.8**	Total incl. others	**58.7**

Main export destinations		Main origins of imports	
	% of total		*% of total*
United States	36.4	United States	11.4
Hong Kong	7.7	China	8.1
Belgium	6.1	Germany	6.3
India	5.7	Belgium	6.1
United Kingdom	4.5	Switzerland	5.5

Balance of payments, reserves and debt, $bn

Visible exports fob	56.1	Change in reserves	10.3
Visible imports fob	-58.0	Level of reserves	
Trade balance	-1.9	end Dec.	70.9
Invisibles inflows	30.1	No. months of import cover	9.6
Invisibles outflows	-30.2	Official gold holdings, m oz	0.0
Net transfers	8.4	Foreign debt	106.0
Current account balance	6.3	– as % of GDP	49
– as % of GDP	2.9	– as % of total exports	118
Capital balance	2.2	Debt service ratio	12
Overall balance	11.6	Aid given	0.14
		% of GDP	0.07

Health and education

Health spending, % of GDP	7.6	Education spending, % of GDP	5.9
Doctors per 1,000 pop.	3.7	Enrolment, %: primary	113
Hospital beds per 1,000 pop.	3.5	secondary	91
Improved-water source access,		tertiary	62
% of pop.	100		

Society

No. of households	2.2m	Colour TV households, % with:	
Av. no. per household	3.4	cable	94.3
Marriages per 1,000 pop.	4.8	satellite	45.3
Divorces per 1,000 pop.	1.6	Telephone lines per 100 pop.	44.2
Cost of living, Dec. 2011		Mobile telephone subscribers	
New York = 100	112	per 100 pop.	133.1
Cars per 1,000 pop.	267	Broadband subs per 100 pop.	25.1
		Internet hosts per 1,000 pop.	305.0

a Sovereignty over the city is disputed.
b 2006

ITALY

Area	301,245 sq km	Capital	Rome
Arable as % of total land	23.4	Currency	Euro (€)

People

Population	60.1m	Life expectancy: men	79.2 yrs
Pop. per sq km	199.5	women	84.6 yrs
Av. ann. growth		Adult literacy	98.9%
in pop. 2010–15	0.23%	Fertility rate (per woman)	1.5
Pop. under 15	14.2%	Urban population	69.1%
Pop. over 60	26.7%		*per 1,000 pop.*
No. of men per 100 women	95.7	Crude birth rate	9.1
Human Development Index	87.4	Crude death rate	10.2

The economy

GDP	€1,556bn	GDP per head	$34,080
GDP	$2,061bn	GDP per head in purchasing	
Av. ann. growth in real		power parity (USA=100)	67.8
GDP 2005–10	-0.2%	Economic freedom index	58.8

Origins of GDP

Components of GDP

	% of total		% of total
Agriculture	2	Private consumption	60
Industry, of which:	25	Public consumption	21
manufacturing	17	Investment	20
Services	73	Exports	27
		Imports	-29

Structure of employment

	% of total		% of labour force
Agriculture	4	Unemployed 2010	8.4
Industry	29	Av. ann. rate 1995–2010	9.2
Services	67		

Energy

	m TOE		
Total output	27.0	Net energy imports as %	
Total consumption	164.6	of energy use	84
Consumption per head,			
kg oil equivalent	2,735		

Inflation and finance

Consumer price		*av. ann. increase 2005–10*	
inflation 2011	2.7%	Euro area:	
Av. ann. inflation 2006–11	2.0%	Narrow money (M1)	6.3%
Money market rate, 2011	2.73%	Broad money	5.9%
		Household saving rate, 2011	4.5%

Exchange rates

	end 2011		2011
€ per $	0.77	Effective rates	2005 = 100
€ per SDR	1.19	– nominal	100.5
		– real	98.6

Trade

Principal exports		Principal imports	
	$bn fob		*$bn cif*
Machinery & transport equip.	157.1	Machinery & transport equip.	130.7
Chemicals & related products	50.7	Mineral fuels & lubricants	90.6
Food, drink & tobacco	32.5	Chemicals & related products	65.2
Mineral fuels & lubricants	22.4	Food, drink & tobacco	39.3
Total incl. others	**446.9**	Total incl. others	**487.0**

Main export destinations		Main origins of imports	
	% of total		*% of total*
Germany	13.0	Germany	15.9
France	11.6	France	8.3
United States	6.0	Netherlands	5.3
United Kingdom	5.3	United Kingdom	3.3
EU27	57.3	EU27	54.8

Balance of payments, reserves and aid, $bn

Visible exports fob	448.4	Overall balance	1.3
Visible imports fob	-475.7	Change in reserves	27.0
Trade balance	-27.3	Level of reserves	
Invisibles inflows	172.7	end Dec.	158.5
Invisibles outflows	-196.3	No. months of import cover	2.8
Net transfers	-21.1	Official gold holdings, m oz	78.8
Current account balance	-72.0	Aid given	3.00
– as % of GDP	-3.5	– as % of GDP	0.15
Capital balance	114.7		

Health and education

Health spending, % of GDP	9.5	Education spending, % of GDP	4.6
Doctors per 1,000 pop.	3.5	Enrolment, %: primary	103
Hospital beds per 1,000 pop.	3.6	secondary	99
Improved-water source access,		tertiary	66
% of pop.	100		

Society

No. of households	24.5m	Colour TV households, % with:	
Av. no. per household	2.5	cable	1.0
Marriages per 1,000 pop.	4.3	satellite	31.5
Divorces per 1,000 pop.	0.9	Telephone lines per 100 pop.	35.5
Cost of living, Dec. 2011		Mobile telephone subscribers	
New York = 100	110	per 100 pop.	149.6
Cars per 1,000 pop.	614	Broadband subs per 100 pop.	21.9
		Internet hosts per 1,000 pop.	424.7

JAPAN

Area	377,727 sq km	Capital	Tokyo
Arable as % of total land	11.8	Currency	Yen (¥)

People

Population	127.0m	Life expectancy:	men	80.1 yrs
Pop. per sq km	336.2		women	87.1 yrs
Av. ann. growth		Adult literacy		...
in pop. 2010–15	-0.07%	Fertility rate (per woman)		1.4
Pop. under 15	13.2%	Urban population		93.5%
Pop. over 60	30.5%			per 1,000 pop.
No. of men per 100 women	95.0	Crude birth rate		8.5
Human Development Index	90.1	Crude death rate		9.6

The economy

GDP	¥479trn	GDP per head	$42,830
GDP	$5,459bn	GDP per head in purchasing	
Av. ann. growth in real		power parity (USA=100)	71.5
GDP 2005–10	0.3%	Economic freedom index	71.6

Origins of GDP		**Components of GDP**	
	% of total		% of total
Agriculture	1	Private consumption	59
Industry, of which:	27	Public consumption	20
manufacturing	18	Investment	20
Services	72	Exports	15
		Imports	-14

Structure of employment

	% of total		% of labour force
Agriculture	4	Unemployed 2010	5.0
Industry	25	Av. ann. rate 1995–2010	4.4
Services	71		

Energy

	m TOE		
Total output	93.8	Net energy imports as %	
Total consumption	472.0	of energy use	80
Consumption per head,			
kg oil equivalent	3,788		

Inflation and finance

		av. ann. increase 2005–10	
Consumer price			
inflation 2011	-0.3%	Narrow money (M1)	0.8%
Av. ann. inflation 2006–11	-0.2%	Broad money	0.9%
Money market rate, 2011	0.08%	Household saving rate, 2011	2.9%

Exchange rates

	end 2011		2011
¥ per $	77.72	Effective rates	2005 = 100
¥ per SDR	119.32	– nominal	129.0
¥ per €	100.56	– real	107.1

Trade

Principal exports		Principal imports	
	$bn fob		*$bn cif*
Capital equipment	404.5	Industrial supplies	362.5
Industrial supplies	192.1	Capital equipment	163.1
Consumer durable goods	114.5	Food & direct consumer goods	58.9
Consumer nondurable goods	5.1	Consumer durable goods	45.5
Total incl. others	**770.1**	Total incl. others	**694.3**

Main export destinations		Main origins of imports	
	% of total		*% of total*
China	19.4	China	22.1
United States	15.6	United States	9.9
South Korea	8.1	Australia	6.5
Hong Kong	5.5	Saudi Arabia	5.2
Thailand	4.4	United Arab Emirates	4.2

Balance of payments, reserves and aid, $bn

Visible exports fob	730.1	Overall balance	43.9
Visible imports fob	-639.1	Change in reserves	47.1
Trade balance	91.0	Level of reserves	
Invisibles inflows	315.1	end Dec.	1,096.1
Invisibles outflows	-198.0	No. months of import cover	15.7
Net transfers	-12.4	Official gold holdings, m oz	24.6
Current account balance	195.8	Aid given	11.05
– as % of GDP	3.6	– as % of GDP	0.20
Capital balance	-135.5		

Health and education

Health spending, % of GDP	9.5	Education spending, % of GDP	3.8
Doctors per 1,000 pop.	2.1	Enrolment, %: primary	103
Hospital beds per 1,000 pop.	13.7	secondary	102
Improved-water source access,		tertiary	59
% of pop.	100		

Society

No. of households	50.8m	Colour TV households, % with:	
Av. no. per household	2.5	cable	65.0
Marriages per 1,000 pop.	5.5	satellite	40.5
Divorces per 1,000 pop.	1.9	Telephone lines per 100 pop.	31.9
Cost of living, Dec. 2011		Mobile telephone subscribers	
New York = 100	166	per 100 pop.	95.4
Cars per 1,000 pop.	317	Broadband subs per 100 pop.	26.9
		Internet hosts per 1,000 pop.	501.3

KENYA

Area	582,646 sq km	Capital	Nairobi
Arable as % of total land	9.5	Currency	Kenyan shilling (KSh)

People

Population	40.9m	Life expectancy: men	56.7 yrs
Pop. per sq km	70.2	women	59.2 yrs
Av. ann. growth		Adult literacy	87.0%
in pop. 2010–15	2.68%	Fertility rate (per woman)	4.6
Pop. under 15	42.8%	Urban population	25.6%
Pop. over 60	4.1%		per 1,000 pop.
No. of men per 100 women	99.8	Crude birth rate	36.9
Human Development Index	50.9	Crude death rate	9.9

The economy

GDP	KSh2,551bn	GDP per head	$790
GDP	$32.2bn	GDP per head in purchasing	
Av. ann. growth in real		power parity (USA=100)	3.5
GDP 2005–10	4.6%	Economic freedom index	57.5

Origins of GDP		Components of GDP	
	% of total		% of total
Agriculture	19	Private consumption	78
Industry, of which:	14	Public consumption	13
manufacturing	8	Investment	21
Other	67	Exports	26
		Imports	-39

Structure of employment

	% of total		% of labour force
Agriculture	...	Unemployed 2010	...
Industry	...	Av. ann. rate 1995–2010	...
Services	...		

Energy

	m TOE		
Total output	15.6	Net energy imports as %	
Total consumption	18.7	of energy use	17
Consumption per head,			
kg oil equivalent	474		

Inflation and finance

		av. ann. increase 2005–10	
Consumer price			
inflation 2011	14.0%	Narrow money (M1)	20.1%
Av. ann. inflation 2006–11	12.4%	Broad money	18.0%
Treasury bill rate, 2011	8.72%		

Exchange rates

	end 2011		2011
KSh per $	85.07	Effective rates	2005 = 100
KSh per SDR	130.60	– nominal	...
KSh per €	110.10	– real	...

Trade

Principal exports		Principal imports	
	$bn fob		*$bn cif*
Tea	1.2	Machinery & other capital equip.	3.8
Horticultural products	0.9	Food & drink	2.3
Coffee	0.2	Industrial supplies	0.8
Fish products	0.1	Transport equipment	0.8
Total incl. others	**5.2**	Total incl. others	**11.5**

Main export destinations		Main origins of imports	
	% of total		*% of total*
Uganda	10.0	India	14.7
Tanzania	9.7	China	13.1
United Kingdom	8.8	United Arab Emirates	9.4
Netherlands	8.2	South Africa	8.2

Balance of payments, reserves and debt, $bn

Visible exports fob	5.2	Change in reserves	-3.8
Visible imports fob	-11.5	Level of reserves	
Trade balance	-6.3	end Dec.	0.0
Invisibles inflows	3.8	No. months of import cover	0.0
Invisibles outflows	-2.3	Official gold holdings, m oz	0.0
Net transfers	2.3	Foreign debt	8.4
Current account balance	-2.5	– as % of GDP	20
– as % of GDP	-7.8	– as % of total exports	72
Capital balance	2.4	Debt service ratio	4
Overall balance	0.1		

Health and education

Health spending, % of GDP	4.8	Education spending, % of GDP	6.7
Doctors per 1,000 pop.	...	Enrolment, %: primary	113
Hospital beds per 1,000 pop.	...	secondary	60
Improved-water source access,		tertiary	4
% of pop.	59		

Society

No. of households	9.3m	Colour TV households, % with:	
Av. no. per household	4.4	cable	2.3
Marriages per 1,000 pop.	...	satellite	3.1
Divorces per 1,000 pop.	...	Telephone lines per 100 pop.	0.9
Cost of living, Dec. 2011		Mobile telephone subscribers	
New York = 100	69	per 100 pop.	61.6
Cars per 1,000 pop.	9	Broadband subs per 100 pop.	0.01
		Internet hosts per 1,000 pop.	2.3

LATVIA

Area	63,700 sq km	Capital	Riga
Arable as % of total land	18.8	Currency	Lats (LVL)

People

Population	2.2m	Life expectancy: men	68.8 yrs
Pop. per sq km	34.9	women	78.5 yrs
Av. ann. growth		Adult literacy	99.8%
in pop. 2010–15	-0.38%	Fertility rate (per woman)	1.5
Pop. under 15	13.8%	Urban population	67.7%
Pop. over 60	22.5%		per 1,000 pop.
No. of men per 100 women	85.2	Crude birth rate	11.0
Human Development Index	80.5	Crude death rate	13.8

The economy

GDP	LVL12.7bn	GDP per head	$10,720
GDP	$24.0bn	GDP per head in purchasing	
Av. ann. growth in real		power parity (USA=100)	34.7
GDP 2005–10	-0.8%	Economic freedom index	65.2

Origins of GDP		Components of GDP	
	% of total		% of total
Agriculture	4	Private consumption	63
Industry, of which:	22	Public consumption	17
manufacturing	12	Investment	21
Services	74	Exports	53
		Imports	-54

Structure of employment

	% of total		% of labour force
Agriculture	9	Unemployed 2010	18.7
Industry	24	Av. ann. rate 1995–2010	12.6
Services	67		

Energy

			m TOE
Total output	2.1	Net energy imports as %	
Total consumption	4.2	of energy use	50
Consumption per head, kg oil equivalent	2,512		

Inflation and finance

Consumer price		av. ann. increase 2005–10	
inflation 2011	4.4%	Narrow money (M1)	5.6%
Av. ann. inflation 2006–11	6.3%	Broad money	10.8%
Money market rate, 2011	0.31%		

Exchange rates

	end 2011		2011
		Effective rates	2005 = 100
LVL per $	0.54	– nominal	...
LVL per SDR	0.84	– real	...
LVL per €	0.70		

Trade

Principal exports	$bn fob	Principal imports	$bn cif
Wood & wood products	1.7	Mineral products	1.7
Metals	1.2	Machinery & equipment	1.8
Machinery & equipment	1.2	Chemicals	1.3
Foodstuffs	0.7	Metals	1.1
Total incl. others	**8.8**	Total incl. others	**11.2**

Main export destinations	% of total	Main origins of imports	% of total
Lithuania	16.2	Lithuania	17.1
Estonia	13.5	Germany	11.5
Russia	10.6	Russia	10.0
Germany	8.7	Poland	7.9
Sweden	6.3	Estonia	7.2
EU27	67.2	EU27	76.1

Balance of payments, reserves and debt, $bn

Visible exports fob	9.1	Change in reserves	0.7
Visible imports fob	-10.8	Level of reserves	
Trade balance	-1.7	end Dec.	7.6
Invisibles inflows	4.8	No. months of import cover	6.5
Invisibles outflows	-3.3	Official gold holdings, m oz	0.2
Net transfers	0.9	Foreign debt	39.6
Current account balance	0.7	– as % of GDP	129
– as % of GDP	3.0	– as % of total exports	260
Capital balance	-0.3	Debt service ratio	76
Overall balance	0.6		

Health and education

Health spending, % of GDP	6.7	Education spending, % of GDP	5.6
Doctors per 1,000 pop.	3.0	Enrolment, %: primary	101
Hospital beds per 1,000 pop.	6.4	secondary	95
Improved-water source access,		tertiary	60
% of pop.	99		

Society

No. of households	0.8m	Colour TV households, % with:	
Av. no. per household	2.8	cable	44.3
Marriages per 1,000 pop.	4.1	satellite	15.4
Divorces per 1,000 pop.	2.2	Telephone lines per 100 pop.	23.6
Cost of living, Dec. 2011		Mobile telephone subscribers	
New York = 100	...	per 100 pop.	102.4
Cars per 1,000 pop.	407	Broadband subs per 100 pop.	19.3
		Internet hosts per 1,000 pop.	145.2

LITHUANIA

Area	65,200 sq km	Capital	Vilnius
Arable as % of total land	32.8	Currency	Litas (LTL)

People

Population	3.3m	Life expectancy: men	67.2 yrs
Pop. per sq km	50.9	women	78.3 yrs
Av. ann. growth		Adult literacy	99.7%
in pop. 2010–15	-0.44%	Fertility rate (per woman)	1.5
Pop. under 15	14.6%	Urban population	67.6%
Pop. over 60	21.5%		per 1,000 pop.
No. of men per 100 women	86.8	Crude birth rate	10.8
Human Development Index	81.0	Crude death rate	13.5

The economy

GDP	LTL94.6bn	GDP per head	$11,050
GDP	$36.3bn	GDP per head in purchasing	
Av. ann. growth in real		power parity (USA=100)	39.0
GDP 2005–10	1.0%	Economic freedom index	71.5

Origins of GDP		Components of GDP	
	% of total		% of total
Agriculture	4	Private consumption	65
Industry, of which:	28	Public consumption	20
manufacturing	16	Investment	17
Services	68	Exports	68
		Imports	-70

Structure of employment

	% of total		% of labour force
Agriculture	9	Unemployed 2010	17.8
Industry	24	Av. ann. rate 1995–2010	12.7
Services	67		

Energy

		m TOE	
Total output	4.2	Net energy imports as %	
Total consumption	8.4	of energy use	50
Consumption per head,			
kg oil equivalent	2,512		

Inflation and finance

Consumer price		av. ann. increase 2005–10	
inflation 2011	4.1%	Narrow money (M1)	5.6%
Av. ann. inflation 2006–11	5.3%	Broad money	10.0%
Money market rate, 2011	0.31%		

Exchange rates

	end 2011		2011
LTL per $	2.67	Effective rates	2005 = 100
LTL per SDR	4.10	– nominal	...
LTL per €	3.45	– real	...

Trade

Principal exports	$bn fob	Principal imports	$bn cif
Mineral products	4.9	Mineral products	7.8
Machinery & equipment	2.2	Machinery & equipment	2.9
Chemicals	1.7	Chemicals	2.6
Transport equipment	1.6	Transport equipment	1.8
Total incl. others	**20.8**	Total incl. others	**23.4**

Main export destinations	% of total	Main origins of imports	% of total
Russia	15.7	Russia	32.6
Germany	9.9	Germany	10.9
Latvia	9.6	Poland	8.8
Poland	7.7	Latvia	6.3
Estonia	5.1	Netherlands	4.4
EU27	61.0	EU25	56.6

Balance of payments, reserves and debt, $bn

Visible exports fob	20.7	Change in reserves	0.2
Visible imports fob	-22.4	Level of reserves	
Trade balance	-1.7	end Dec.	6.8
Invisibles inflows	4.8	No. months of import cover	3.1
Invisibles outflows	-4.4	Official gold holdings, m oz	0.2
Net transfers	1.7	Foreign debt	29.6
Current account balance	0.5	– as % of GDP	69
– as % of GDP	1.5	– as % of total exports	107
Capital balance	0.2	Debt service ratio	34
Overall balance	0.7		

Health and education

Health spending, % of GDP	7.0	Education spending, % of GDP	4.9
Doctors per 1,000 pop.	3.6	Enrolment, %: primary	97
Hospital beds per 1,000 pop.	6.8	secondary	98
Improved-water source access, % of pop.	...	tertiary	77

Society

No. of households	1.4m	Colour TV households, % with:	
Av. no. per household	2.4	cable	49.7
Marriages per 1,000 pop.	5.7	satellite	11.5
Divorces per 1,000 pop.	3.0	Telephone lines per 100 pop.	22.1
Cost of living, Dec. 2011		Mobile telephone subscribers	
New York = 100	...	per 100 pop.	147.2
Cars per 1,000 pop.	547	Broadband subs per 100 pop.	20.6
		Internet hosts per 1,000 pop.	359.4

MALAYSIA

Area	332,665 sq km	Capital	Kuala Lumpur
Arable as % of total land	5.5	Currency	Malaysian dollar/ringgit (M$)

People

Population	27.9m	Life expectancy: men	72.5 yrs
Pop. per sq km	83.9	women	76.9 yrs
Av. ann. growth		Adult literacy	92.5%
in pop. 2010–15	1.57%	Fertility rate (per woman)	2.6
Pop. under 15	29.1%	Urban population	75.4%
Pop. over 60	7.8%		per 1,000 pop.
No. of men per 100 women	103.0	Crude birth rate	19.8
Human Development Index	76.1	Crude death rate	4.7

The economy

GDP	M$766bn	GDP per head	$8,370
GDP	$238bn	GDP per head in purchasing	
Av. ann. growth in real		power parity (USA=100)	31.2
GDP 2005–10	4.5%	Economic freedom index	66.4

Origins of GDP		Components of GDP	
	% of total		% of total
Agriculture	11	Private consumption	48
Industry, of which:	44	Public consumption	13
manufacturing	26	Investment	21
Services	45	Exports	97
		Imports	-79

Structure of employment

	% of total		% of labour force
Agriculture	14	Unemployed 2010	3.7
Industry	27	Av. ann. rate 1995–2010	3.3
Services	59		

Energy

	m TOE		
Total output	89.7	Net energy imports as %	
Total consumption	66.8	of energy use	-34
Consumption per head, kg oil equivalent	2,391		

Inflation and finance

		av. ann. increase 2005–10	
Consumer price inflation 2011	3.2%	Narrow money (M1)	12.6%
Av. ann. inflation 2006–11	2.6%	Broad money	9.4%
Money market rate, 2011	2.88%		

Exchange rates

	end 2011		2011
M$ per $	3.18	Effective rates	2005 = 100
M$ per SDR	4.88	– nominal	106.1
M$ per €	4.11	– real	106.6

Trade

Principal exports		Principal imports	
	$bn fob		*$bn cif*
Machinery & transport equip.	87.2	Machinery & transport equip.	81.2
Mineral fuels	31.2	Manufactured goods	20.4
Manufactured goods	17.5	Mineral fuels	16.4
Chemicals	12.6	Chemicals	14.9
Total incl. others	**198.6**	Total incl. others	**164.6**

Main export destinations		Main origins of imports	
	% of total		*% of total*
Singapore	13.4	China	12.6
China	12.6	Japan	12.6
Japan	10.4	Singapore	11.4
United States	9.6	United States	10.7
Thailand	5.3	Thailand	6.2

Balance of payments, reserves and debt, $bn

Visible exports fob	199.0	Change in reserves	9.8
Visible imports fob	-157.3	Level of reserves	
Trade balance	41.7	end Dec.	106.5
Invisibles inflows	44.8	No. months of import cover	6.1
Invisibles outflows	-52.3	Official gold holdings, m oz	1.2
Net transfers	-6.8	Foreign debt	81.5
Current account balance	27.3	– as % of GDP	36
– as % of GDP	11.5	– as % of total exports	33
Capital balance	-6.0	Debt service ratio	5
Overall balance	-0.0		

Health and education

Health spending, % of GDP	4.4	Education spending, % of GDP	5.8
Doctors per 1,000 pop.	0.9	Enrolment, %: primary	...
Hospital beds per 1,000 pop.	...	secondary	68
Improved-water source access,		tertiary	40
% of pop.	100		

Society

No. of households	6.5m	Colour TV households, % with:	
Av. no. per household	4.3	cable	12.2
Marriages per 1,000 pop.	5.7	satellite	54.1
Divorces per 1,000 pop.	...	Telephone lines per 100 pop.	16.1
Cost of living, Dec. 2011		Mobile telephone subscribers	
New York = 100	83	per 100 pop.	119.2
Cars per 1,000 pop.	308	Broadband subs per 100 pop.	7.3
		Internet hosts per 1,000 pop.	23.9

MEXICO

Area	1,972,545 sq km	Capital	Mexico city
Arable as % of total land	12.9	Currency	Mexican peso (PS)

People

Population	110.6m	Life expectancy: men	74.8 yrs
Pop. per sq km	56.0	women	79.6 yrs
Av. ann. growth		Adult literacy	93.4%
in pop. 2010–15	1.14%	Fertility rate (per woman)	2.2
Pop. under 15	27.9%	Urban population	79.2%
Pop. over 60	9.4%		per 1,000 pop.
No. of men per 100 women	97.3	Crude birth rate	18.5
Human Development Index	77.0	Crude death rate	4.8

The economy

GDP	PS13,089bn	GDP per head	$9,130
GDP	$1,036bn	GDP per head in purchasing	
Av. ann. growth in real		power parity (USA=100)	30.9
GDP 2005–10	1.7%	Economic freedom index	65.3

Origins of GDP		Components of GDP	
	% of total		% of total
Agriculture	4	Private consumption	65
Industry, of which:	34	Public consumption	12
manufacturing & mining	18	Investment	25
Services	62	Exports	30
		Imports	-32

Structure of employment

	% of total		% of labour force
Agriculture	13	Unemployed 2010	5.3
Industry	26	Av. ann. rate 1995–2010	3.2
Services	61		

Energy

	m TOE		
Total output	220.0	Net energy imports as %	
Total consumption	174.6	of energy use	-26
Consumption per head,			
kg oil equivalent	1,559		

Inflation and finance

Consumer price		av. ann. increase 2005–10	
inflation 2011	3.4%	Narrow money (M1)	11.4%
Av. ann. inflation 2006–11	4.4%	Broad money	12.0%
Money market rate, 2011	4.82%		

Exchange rates

	end 2011		2011
PS per $	14.00	Effective rates	2005 = 100
PS per SDR	21.48	– nominal	75.5
PS per €	18.11	– real	85.4

Trade

Principal exports	$bn fob	Principal imports	$bn fob
Manufactured products	245.7	Intermediate goods	229.8
Crude oil & products	41.7	Consumer goods	41.4
Agricultural products	8.6	Capital goods	30.2
Mining products	2.4		
Total	**298.5**	Total	**301.5**

Main export destinations	% of total	Main origins of imports	% of total
United States	80.0	United States	52.9
Canada	3.6	China	16.6
China	1.8	Japan	5.5
Spain	1.3	South Korea	4.7

Balance of payments, reserves and debt, $bn

Visible exports fob	298.9	Change in reserves	20.7
Visible imports fob	-301.9	Level of reserves	
Trade balance	-3.1	end Dec.	120.6
Invisibles inflows	20.2	No. months of import cover	4.2
Invisibles outflows	-44.4	Official gold holdings, m oz	0.2
Net transfers	21.5	Foreign debt	200.1
Current account balance	-5.7	– as % of GDP	18
– as % of GDP	-0.6	– as % of total exports	61
Capital balance	40.6	Debt service ratio	10
Overall balance	22.9		

Health and education

Health spending, % of GDP	6.3	Education spending, % of GDP	4.9
Doctors per 1,000 pop.	2.0	Enrolment, %: primary	115
Hospital beds per 1,000 pop.	...	secondary	87
Improved-water source access, % of pop.	94	tertiary	27

Society

No. of households	28.3m	Colour TV households, % with:	
Av. no. per household	3.9	cable	22.3
Marriages per 1,000 pop.	4.9	satellite	6.9
Divorces per 1,000 pop.	0.8	Telephone lines per 100 pop.	17.5
Cost of living, Dec. 2011		Mobile telephone subscribers	
New York = 100	91	per 100 pop.	80.6
Cars per 1,000 pop.	147	Broadband subs per 100 pop.	10.0
		Internet hosts per 1,000 pop.	140.2

MOROCCO

Area	446,550 sq km	Capital	Rabat
Arable as % of total land	18.0	Currency	Dirham (Dh)

People

Population	32.4m	Life expectancy: men	70.3 yrs
Pop. per sq km	72.6	women	74.9 yrs
Av. ann. growth		Adult literacy	56.1%
in pop. 2010–15	0.99%	Fertility rate (per woman)	2.2
Pop. under 15	28.0%	Urban population	58.5%
Pop. over 60	8.1%		per 1,000 pop.
No. of men per 100 women	96.2	Crude birth rate	18.7
Human Development Index	58.2	Crude death rate	5.8

The economy

GDP	Dh764bn	GDP per head	$2,800
GDP	$90.8bn	GDP per head in purchasing	
Av. ann. growth in real		power parity (USA=100)	10.0
GDP 2005–10	4.9%	Economic freedom index	60.2

Origins of GDP		Components of GDP	
	% of total		% of total
Agriculture	15	Private consumption	57
Industry, of which:	30	Public consumption	18
manufacturing	15	Investment	35
Services	55	Exports	33
		Imports	-43

Structure of employment

	% of total		% of labour force
Agriculture	41	Unemployed 2009	10.0
Industry	22	Av. ann. rate 1995–2009	13.4
Services	37		

Energy

	m TOE		
Total output	0.8	Net energy imports as %	
Total consumption	15.1	of energy use	95
Consumption per head,			
kg oil equivalent	477		

Inflation and finance

		av. ann. increase 2005–10	
Consumer price			
inflation 2011	0.9%	Narrow money (M1)	10.8%
Av. ann. inflation 2006–11	1.7%	Broad money	12.1%
Money market rate, 2011	3.29%		

Exchange rates

	end 2011		2011
			2005 = 100
Dh per $	8.58	Effective rates	
Dh per SDR	13.17	– nominal	102.1
Dh per €	11.10	– real	96.4

Trade

Principal exports		Principal imports	
	$bn fob		$bn cif
Clothing & textiles	2.1	Fuel & lubricants	8.1
Electrical cables & wires	1.6	Capital goods	7.9
Phosphoric acid	1.6	Semi-finished goods	7.4
Fertilisers	1.6	Consumer goods	6.6
Phosphate rock	1.1	Food, drink & tobacco	3.5
Total incl. others	**17.8**	Total incl. others	**35.4**

Main export destinations		Main origins of imports	
	% of total		% of total
France	21.6	France	15.4
Spain	17.1	Spain	11.8
India	5.9	China	8.0
Italy	4.5	Italy	7.1

Balance of payments, reserves and debt, $bn

Visible exports fob	17.6	Change in reserves	0.0
Visible imports fob	-32.6	Level of reserves	
Trade balance	-15.1	end Dec.	23.6
Invisibles inflows	13.4	No. months of import cover	6.7
Invisibles outflows	-9.5	Official gold holdings, m oz	0.7
Net transfers	7.0	Foreign debt	25.4
Current account balance	-4.2	– as % of GDP	23
– as % of GDP	-4.6	– as % of total exports	67
Capital balance	1.4	Debt service ratio	11
Overall balance	-3.0		

Health and education

Health spending, % of GDP	5.2	Education spending, % of GDP	5.4
Doctors per 1,000 pop.	0.6	Enrolment, %: primary	114
Hospital beds per 1,000 pop.	1.1	secondary	56
Improved-water source access,		tertiary	13
% of pop.	83		

Society

No. of households	6.5m	Colour TV households, % with:	
Av. no. per household	5.0	cable	0.0
Marriages per 1,000 pop.	...	satellite	67.9
Divorces per 1,000 pop.	...	Telephone lines per 100 pop.	11.7
Cost of living, Dec. 2011		Mobile telephone subscribers	
New York = 100	76	per 100 pop.	100.1
Cars per 1,000 pop.	46	Broadband subs per 100 pop.	1.6
		Internet hosts per 1,000 pop.	8.7

NETHERLANDS

Area[a]	41,526 sq km	Capital	Amsterdam
Arable as % of total land	31.2	Currency	Euro (€)

People

Population	16.7m	Life expectancy: men	78.9 yrs
Pop. per sq km	402.1	women	82.8 yrs
Av. ann. growth		Adult literacy	...
in pop. 2010–15	0.28%	Fertility rate (per woman)	1.8
Pop. under 15	17.6%	Urban population	84.7%
Pop. over 60	21.9%		per 1,000 pop.
No. of men per 100 women	98.5	Crude birth rate	10.8
Human Development Index	91.0	Crude death rate	8.6

The economy

GDP	€588bn	GDP per head	$46,900
GDP	$779bn	GDP per head in purchasing	
Av. ann. growth in real		power parity (USA=100)	89.4
GDP 2005–10	1.4%	Economic freedom index	73.3

Origins of GDP		Components of GDP	
	% of total		% of total
Agriculture	2	Private consumption	45
Industry, of which:	24	Public consumption	28
manufacturing	13	Investment	19
Services	74	Exports	78
		Imports	-71

Structure of employment

	% of total		% of labour force
Agriculture	3	Unemployed 2010	4.5
Industry	16	Av. ann. rate 1995–2010	4.3
Services	81		

Energy

	m TOE		
Total output	63.0	Net energy imports as %	
Total consumption	78.2	of energy use	19
Consumption per head,			
kg oil equivalent	4,729		

Inflation and finance

Consumer price			av. ann. increase 2005–10
inflation 2011	2.3%	Euro area:	
Av. ann. inflation 2006–11	1.8%	Narrow money (M1)	6.3%
Deposit rate, households, 2011	2.89%	Broad money	5.9%
		Household saving rate, 2011	5.5%

Exchange rates

	end 2011		2011
€ per $	0.77	Effective rates	2005 = 100
€ per SDR	1.19	– nominal	101.1
		– real	97.0

Trade

Principal exports		Principal imports	
	$bn fob		$bn cif
Machinery & transport equip.	172.7	Machinery & transport equip.	160.6
Mineral fuels & lubricants	83.5	Mineral fuels & lubricants	95.6
Chemicals & related products	82.4	Chemicals & related products	57.2
Food, drink & tobacco	69.6	Food, drink & tobacco	44.2
Total incl. others	**493.0**	Total incl. others	**440.3**

Main export destinations		Main origins of imports	
	% of total		% of total
Germany	30.1	Germany	18.0
Belgium	15.0	China	14.8
France	10.6	Belgium	9.7
United Kingdom	8.9	United States	7.9
EU27	77.2	EU27	46.6

Balance of payments, reserves and aid, $bn

Visible exports fob	480.3	Overall balance	0.2
Visible imports fob	-428.4	Change in reserves	6.6
Trade balance	51.9	Level of reserves	
Invisibles inflows	193.9	end Dec.	46.1
Invisibles outflows	-179.6	No. months of import cover	0.9
Net transfers	-14.5	Official gold holdings, m oz	19.7
Current account balance	51.6	Aid given	6.30
– as % of GDP	6.6	– as % of GDP	0.81
Capital balance	-30.1		

Health and education

Health spending, % of GDP	11.9	Education spending, % of GDP	5.5
Doctors per 1,000 pop.	2.9	Enrolment, %: primary	108
Hospital beds per 1,000 pop.	4.7	secondary	120
Improved-water source access,		tertiary	63
% of pop.	100		

Society

No. of households	7.3m	Colour TV households, % with:	
Av. no. per household	2.3	cable	74.9
Marriages per 1,000 pop.	4.1	satellite	13.8
Divorces per 1,000 pop.	1.7	Telephone lines per 100 pop.	43.5
Cost of living, Dec. 2011		Mobile telephone subscribers	
New York = 100	104	per 100 pop.	115.5
Cars per 1,000 pop.	488	Broadband subs per 100 pop.	38.1
		Internet hosts per 1,000 pop.	832.6

a Includes water.

NEW ZEALAND

Area	270,534 sq km	Capital	Wellington
Arable as % of total land	1.8	Currency	New Zealand dollar (NZ$)

People

Population	4.3m	Life expectancy:	men	78.9 yrs
Pop. per sq km	16.1		women	82.8 yrs
Av. ann. growth		Adult literacy		...
in pop. 2010–15	1.04%	Fertility rate (per woman)		2.1
Pop. under 15	20.2%	Urban population		86.4%
Pop. over 60	18.2%		per 1,000 pop.	
No. of men per 100 women	96.5	Crude birth rate		14.3
Human Development Index	90.8	Crude death rate		7.1

The economy

GDP	NZ$194bn	GDP per head	$32,370
GDP	$141bn	GDP per head in purchasing	
Av. ann. growth in real		power parity (USA=100)	62.6
GDP 2005–10	0.6%	Economic freedom index	82.1

Origins of GDP		**Components of GDP**	
	% of total		% of total
Agriculture & mining	5	Private consumption	58
Industry	24	Public consumption	21
Services	71	Investment	20
		Exports	29
		Imports	-27

Structure of employment

	% of total		% of labour force
Agriculture	7	Unemployed 2010	6.5
Industry	21	Av. ann. rate 1995–2010	5.4
Services	72		

Energy

	m TOE		
Total output	15.2	Net energy imports as %	
Total consumption	17.4	of energy use	13
Consumption per head,			
kg oil equivalent	4,632		

Inflation and finance

Consumer price		av. ann. increase 2005–10	
inflation 2011	2.9%	Narrow money (M1)	0.2%
Av. ann. inflation 2006–11	2.8%	Broad money	8.0%
Money market rate, 2011	2.50%	Household saving rate, 2011	0.8%

Exchange rates

	end 2011		2011
NZ$ per $	1.30	Effective rates	2005 = 100
NZ$ per SDR	1.99	– nominal	95.2
NZ$ per €	1.68	– real	98.5

Trade

Principal exports		**Principal imports**	
	$bn fob		*$bn cif*
Dairy produce	7.4	Machinery & equipment	6.1
Meat	3.7	Mineral fuels	4.5
Forestry products	3.0	Transport equipment	3.7
Wool	0.5		
Total incl. others	**31.3**	Total incl. others	**30.6**

Main export destinations		**Main origins of imports**	
	% of total		*% of total*
Australia	23.3	Australia	18.2
China	11.2	China	16.0
United States	8.7	United States	10.4
Japan	7.8	Japan	7.3

Balance of payments, reserves and aid, $bn

Visible exports fob	31.9	Overall balance	0.8
Visible imports fob	-29.5	Change in reserves	1.1
Trade balance	2.3	Level of reserves	
Invisibles inflows	12.8	end Dec.	16.7
Invisibles outflows	-20.1	No. months of import cover	4.0
Net transfers	0.0	Official gold holdings, m oz	0.0
Current account balance	-5.0	Aid given	0.34
– as % of GDP	-3.5	– as % of GDP	0.26
Capital balance	5.0		

Health and education

Health spending, % of GDP	10.1	Education spending, % of GDP	7.2
Doctors per 1,000 pop.	2.7	Enrolment, %: primary	101
Hospital beds per 1,000 pop.	...	secondary	119
Improved-water source access,		tertiary	83
% of pop.	100		

Society

No. of households	1.5m	Colour TV households, % with:	
Av. no. per household	2.9	cable	5.4
Marriages per 1,000 pop.	4.8	satellite	40.0
Divorces per 1,000 pop.	2.7	Telephone lines per 100 pop.	42.8
Cost of living, Dec. 2011		Mobile telephone subscribers	
New York = 100	117	per 100 pop.	114.9
Cars per 1,000 pop.	641	Broadband subs per 100 pop.	24.9
		Internet hosts per 1,000 pop.	715.8

NIGERIA

Area	923,768 sq km	Capital	Abuja
Arable as % of total land	37.3	Currency	Naira (N)

People

Population	158.3m	Life expectancy:	men	51.7 yrs
Pop. per sq km	171.4		women	53.4 yrs
Av. ann. growth		Adult literacy		60.8%
in pop. 2010–15	2.53%	Fertility rate (per woman)		5.4
Pop. under 15	42.4%	Urban population		52.1%
Pop. over 60	4.9%			per 1,000 pop.
No. of men per 100 women	102.5	Crude birth rate		39.3
Human Development Index	45.9	Crude death rate		13.7

The economy

GDP	N30,439bn	GDP per head	$1,280
GDP	$203bn	GDP per head in purchasing	
Av. ann. growth in real		power parity (USA=100)	5.1
GDP 2005–10	6.8%	Economic freedom index	56.3

Origins of GDP[a]		Components of GDP	
	% of total		% of total
Agriculture	33	Private consumption	60
Industry, of which:	41	Public consumption	15
manufacturing	3	Investment	14
Services	27	Exports	46
		Imports	-33

Structure of employment

	% of total		% of labour force
Agriculture	...	Unemployed 2001	3.9
Industry	...	Av. ann. rate 1995–2001	3.7
Services	...		

Energy

	m TOE		
Total output	228.7	Net energy imports as %	
Total consumption	108.3	of energy use	-111
Consumption per head,			
kg oil equivalent	701		

Inflation and finance

Consumer price		av. ann. increase 2005–10	
inflation 2011	10.8%	Narrow money (M1)	27.7%
Av. ann. inflation 2006–11	10.6%	Broad money (M2)	35.6%
Treasury bill rate, Nov. 2011	14.53%		

Exchange rates

	end 2011		2011
N per $	158.27	Effective rates	2005 = 100
N per SDR	242.98	– nominal	82.3
N per €	204.77	– real	129.9

Trade

Principal exports		Principal imports	
	$bn fob		$bn cif
Mineral products, incl. oil & gas	76.0	Industrial goods	13.8
Raw hides & skins	3.1	Capital goods	13.4
Prepared foodstuffs, beverages		Transport equipment & parts	10.7
& tobacco	1.6	Food & beverages	4.2
Vegetable products	1.2		
Total incl. others	**86.6**	Total incl. others	**44.2**

Main export destinations		Main origins of imports	
	% of total		% of total
United States	36.1	China	15.4
India	11.8	Netherlands	9.5
Brazil	7.5	United States	9.3
Spain	6.5	France	4.8

Balance of payments, reserves and debt, $bn

Visible exports fob	73.7	Change in reserves	-10.6
Visible imports fob	-53.5	Level of reserves	
Trade balance	20.2	end Dec.	34.9
Invisibles inflows	4.1	No. months of import cover	4.4
Invisibles outflows	-41.9	Official gold holdings, m oz	0.7
Net transfers	20.1	Foreign debt	7.9
Current account balance	2.5	– as % of GDP	3
– as % of GDP	1.2	– as % of total exports	7
Capital balance	-7.0	Debt service ratio	1
Overall balance	-9.7		

Health and education

Health spending, % of GDP	5.1	Education spending, % of GDP	...
Doctors per 1,000 pop.	0.4	Enrolment, %: primary	83
Hospital beds per 1,000 pop.	...	secondary	44
Improved-water source access,		tertiary	10
% of pop.	58		

Society

No. of households	32.2m	Colour TV households, % with:	
Av. no. per household	4.9	cable	1.8
Marriages per 1,000 pop.	...	satellite	2.4
Divorces per 1,000 pop.	...	Telephone lines per 100 pop.	0.7
Cost of living, Dec. 2011		Mobile telephone subscribers	
New York = 100	68	per 100 pop.	55.1
Cars per 1,000 pop.	13	Broadband subs per 100 pop.	0.1
		Internet hosts per 1,000 pop.	...

a 2009

NORWAY

Area	323,878 sq km	Capital	Oslo
Arable as % of total land	2.7	Currency	Norwegian krone (Nkr)

People

Population	4.9m	Life expectancy: men	79.1 yrs
Pop. per sq km	15.1	women	83.5 yrs
Av. ann. growth		Adult literacy	...
in pop. 2010–15	0.69%	Fertility rate (per woman)	2.0
Pop. under 15	18.8%	Urban population	80.5%
Pop. over 60	21.1%		per 1,000 pop.
No. of men per 100 women	100.1	Crude birth rate	12.3
Human Development Index	94.3	Crude death rate	8.4

The economy

GDP	Nkr2,523bn	GDP per head	$85,390
GDP	$417bn	GDP per head in purchasing	
Av. ann. growth in real		power parity (USA=100)	121.4
GDP 2005–10	0.8%	Economic freedom index	68.8

Origins of GDP		**Components of GDP**	
	% of total		% of total
Agriculture	2	Private consumption	43
Industry, of which:	40	Public consumption	22
manufacturing	9	Investment	22
Services	58	Exports	41
		Imports	-29

Structure of employment

	% of total		% of labour force
Agriculture	3	Unemployed 2010	3.6
Industry	20	Av. ann. rate 1995–2010	3.7
Services	77		

Energy

	m TOE		
Total output	213.6	Net energy imports as %	
Total consumption	28.2	of energy use	-656
Consumption per head,			
kg oil equivalent	5,849		

Inflation and finance

Consumer price		av. ann. increase 2005–10	
inflation 2011	1.3%	Narrow money (M1)	...
Av. ann. inflation 2006–11	2.1%	Broad money	8.2%
Interbank rate, 2011	2.87%	Household saving rate, 2011	8.0%

Exchange rates

	end 2011		2011
Nkr per $	5.99	Effective rates	2005 = 100
Nkr per SDR	9.22	– nominal	102.8
Nkr per €	7.75	– real	101.6

Trade

Principal exports		Principal imports	
	$bn fob		*$bn cif*
Mineral fuels & lubricants	83.9	Machinery & transport equip.	29.7
Machinery & transport equip.	12.4	Manufactured goods	11.3
Manufactured goods	12.4	Chemicals & mineral products	7.9
Food & beverages	9.2	Food & beverages	4.6
Total incl. others	**131.5**	Total incl. others	**77.3**

Main export destinations		Main origins of imports	
	% of total		*% of total*
United Kingdom	27.0	Sweden	14.0
Netherlands	11.9	Germany	12.3
Germany	11.3	China	8.5
Sweden	7.0	Denmark	6.2
France	6.6	United Kingdom	5.9
United States	5.0	United States	5.5
EU27	81.2	EU27	63.9

Balance of payments, reserves and aid, $bn

Visible exports fob	132.7	Overall balance	4.2
Visible imports fob	-74.3	Change in reserves	4.0
Trade balance	58.4	Level of reserves	
Invisibles inflows	67.8	end Dec.	52.9
Invisibles outflows	-70.0	No. months of import cover	4.4
Net transfers	-4.7	Official gold holdings, m oz	0.0
Current account balance	51.4	Aid given	4.58
– as % of GDP	12.3	– as % of GDP	1.10
Capital balance	-42.4		

Health and education

Health spending, % of GDP	9.5	Education spending, % of GDP	6.5
Doctors per 1,000 pop.	4.2	Enrolment, %: primary	99
Hospital beds per 1,000 pop.	3.3	secondary	110
Improved-water source access,		tertiary	74
% of pop.	100		

Society

No. of households	2.1m	Colour TV households, % with:	
Av. no. per household	2.3	cable	45.9
Marriages per 1,000 pop.	4.8	satellite	37.6
Divorces per 1,000 pop.	2.4	Telephone lines per 100 pop.	33.8
Cost of living, Dec. 2011		Mobile telephone subscribers	
New York = 100	156	per 100 pop.	115.7
Cars per 1,000 pop.	465	Broadband subs per 100 pop.	35.3
		Internet hosts per 1,000 pop.	740.7

PAKISTAN

Area	803,940 sq km	Capital	Islamabad
Arable as % of total land	26.5	Currency	Pakistan rupee (PRs)

People

Population	184.8m	Life expectancy: men		64.9 yrs
Pop. per sq km	229.9		women	66.9 yrs
Av. ann. growth		Adult literacy		55.5%
in pop. 2010–15	1.77%	Fertility rate (per woman)		3.2
Pop. under 15	36.6%	Urban population		37.6%
Pop. over 60	6.2%			per 1,000 pop.
No. of men per 100 women	103.4	Crude birth rate		26.3
Human Development Index	50.4	Crude death rate		7.3

The economy

GDP	PRs14,837bn	GDP per head	$1,020
GDP	$177bn	GDP per head in purchasing	
Av. ann. growth in real		power parity (USA=100)	5.7
GDP 2005–10	4.3%	Economic freedom index	54.7

Origins of GDP		Components of GDP	
	% of total		% of total
Agriculture	21	Private consumption	82
Industry, of which:	25	Public consumption	8
manufacturing	17	Investment	15
Services	53	Exports	14
		Imports	-19

Structure of employment

	% of total		% of labour force
Agriculture	45	Unemployed 2008	5.0
Industry	20	Av. ann. rate 1995–2008	6.3
Services	35		

Energy

	m TOE		
Total output	64.9	Net energy imports as %	
Total consumption	85.5	of energy use	24
Consumption per head,			
kg oil equivalent	502		

Inflation and finance

Consumer price		av. ann. increase 2005–10	
inflation 2011	11.9%	Narrow money (M1)	13.0%
Av. ann. inflation 2006–11	13.4%	Broad money (M2)	13.8%
Money market rate, 2011	12.47%		

Exchange rates

	end 2011		2011
PRs per $	89.97	Effective rates	2005 = 100
PRs per SDR	138.13	– nominal	61.5
PRs per €	116.41	– real	108.3

Trade[a]

Principal exports	$bn fob	Principal imports	$bn fob
Knitwear	2.1	Mineral fuels	10.5
Rice	2.1	Machinery & transport equip.	5.5
Cotton fabrics	1.9	Chemicals	5.2
Bedwear	1.6	Foodstuffs	3.1
Cotton yarn & thread	1.2	Metals & metal products	2.0
Total incl. others	**19.7**	Total incl. others	**31.2**

Main export destinations	% of total	Main origins of imports	% of total
United States	15.8	China	20.2
Afghanistan	8.1	Saudi Arabia	12.1
United Arab Emirates	7.9	United Arab Emirates	12.0
China	7.3	Malaysia	6.8
United Kingdom	4.3	India	6.6

Balance of payments, reserves and debt, $bn

Visible exports fob	21.5	Change in reserves	3.3
Visible imports fob	-32.9	Level of reserves	
Trade balance	-11.4	end Dec.	17.3
Invisibles inflows	7.1	No. months of import cover	4.7
Invisibles outflows	-11.0	Official gold holdings, m oz	2.1
Net transfers	13.8	Foreign debt	56.8
Current account balance	-1.5	– as % of GDP	24
– as % of GDP	-0.8	– as % of total exports	159
Capital balance	2.7	Debt service ratio	15
Overall balance	0.7		

Health and education

Health spending, % of GDP	2.2	Education spending, % of GDP	2.4
Doctors per 1,000 pop.	0.8	Enrolment, %: primary	95
Hospital beds per 1,000 pop.	...	secondary	34
Improved-water source access,		tertiary	5
% of pop.	92		

Society

No. of households	25.1	Colour TV households, % with:	
Av. no. per household	7.2	cable	1.1
Marriages per 1,000 pop.	...	satellite	15.2
Divorces per 1,000 pop.	...	Telephone lines per 100 pop.	2.0
Cost of living, Dec. 2011		Mobile telephone subscribers	
New York = 100	46	per 100 pop.	57.1
Cars per 1,000 pop.	9	Broadband subs per 100 pop.	0.3
		Internet hosts per 1,000 pop.	2.6

a Fiscal year ending June 30, 2010.

PERU

Area	1,285,216 sq km	Capital	Lima
Arable as % of total land	2.9	Currency	Nuevo Sol (New Sol)

People

Population	29.5m	Life expectancy:	men	71.7 yrs
Pop. per sq km	23.0		women	76.9 yrs
Av. ann. growth		Adult literacy		89.6%
in pop. 2010–15	1.13%	Fertility rate (per woman)		2.4
Pop. under 15	29.9%	Urban population		78.6%
Pop. over 60	8.7%			per 1,000 pop.
No. of men per 100 women	100.4	Crude birth rate		19.6
Human Development Index	72.5	Crude death rate		5.5

The economy

GDP	New Soles 444bn	GDP per head	$5,400
GDP	$157bn	GDP per head in purchasing	
Av. ann. growth in real		power parity (USA=100)	20.2
GDP 2005–10	7.2%	Economic freedom index	68.7

Origins of GDP		**Components of GDP**	
	% of total		% of total
Agriculture	8	Private consumption	63
Industry, of which:	34	Public consumption	10
manufacturing	17	Investment	24
Services	57	Exports	25
		Imports	-22

Structure of employment

	% of total		% of labour force
Agriculture	1	Unemployed 2009	6.3
Industry	24	Av. ann. rate 1995–2009	8.3
Services	75		

Energy

	m TOE		
Total output	15.1	Net energy imports as %	
Total consumption	15.8	of energy use	4
Consumption per head,			
kg oil equivalent	550		

Inflation and finance

Consumer price			av. ann. increase 2005–10
inflation 2011	3.4%	Narrow money (M1)	18.3%
Av. ann. inflation 2006–11	3.1%	Broad money	16.1%
Money market rate, 2011	4.24%		

Exchange rates

	end 2011		2011
New Soles per $	2.70	Effective rates	2005 = 100
New Soles per SDR	4.14	– nominal	...
New Soles per €	3.49	– real	...

Trade

Principal exports		Principal imports	
	$bn fob		$bn fob
Copper	8.9	Intermediate goods	14.0
Gold	7.7	Capital goods	9.1
Fishmeal	1.9	Consumer goods	5.5
Zinc	1.7	Other goods	0.2
Total incl. others	**35.6**	Total	**28.8**

Main export destinations		Main origins of imports	
	% of total		% of total
China	15.6	United States	25.8
United States	13.7	China	13.6
Canada	10.0	Brazil	7.7
Japan	5.6	Chile	6.2

Balance of payments, reserves and debt, $bn

Visible exports fob	35.6	Change in reserves	11.0
Visible imports fob	-28.8	Level of reserves	
Trade balance	6.8	end Dec.	44.2
Invisibles inflows	5.1	No. months of import cover	11.5
Invisibles outflows	-17.1	Official gold holdings, m oz	1.1
Net transfers	3.0	Foreign debt	36.3
Current account balance	-2.3	– as % of GDP	25
– as % of GDP	-1.5	– as % of total exports	89
Capital balance	12.3	Debt service ratio	17
Overall balance	11.0		

Health and education

Health spending, % of GDP	5.1	Education spending, % of GDP	2.6
Doctors per 1,000 pop.	0.9	Enrolment, %: primary	109
Hospital beds per 1,000 pop.	1.5	secondary	92
Improved-water source access,		tertiary	...
% of pop.	85		

Society

No. of households	7.3m	Colour TV households, % with:	
Av. no. per household	4.0	cable	31.6
Marriages per 1,000 pop.	3.0	satellite	0.2
Divorces per 1,000 pop.	0.1	Telephone lines per 100 pop.	10.9
Cost of living, Dec. 2011		Mobile telephone subscribers	
New York = 100	72	per 100 pop.	100.1
Cars per 1,000 pop.	30	Broadband subs per 100 pop.	3.1
		Internet hosts per 1,000 pop.	8.0

PHILIPPINES

Area	300,000 sq km	Capital	Manila
Arable as % of total land	18.1	Currency	Philippine peso (P)

People

Population	93.6m	Life expectancy: men	66.0 yrs
Pop. per sq km	312.0	women	72.6 yrs
Av. ann. growth		Adult literacy	95.4%
in pop. 2010–15	1.68%	Fertility rate (per woman)	3.3
Pop. under 15	33.5%	Urban population	49.8%
Pop. over 60	6.7%		per 1,000 pop.
No. of men per 100 women	100.7	Crude birth rate	24.5
Human Development Index	64.4	Crude death rate	5.7

The economy

GDP	P9,003bn	GDP per head	$2,140
GDP	$200bn	GDP per head in purchasing	
Av. ann. growth in real		power parity (USA=100)	8.4
GDP 2005–10	4.9%	Economic freedom index	57.1

Origins of GDP		Components of GDP	
	% of total		% of total
Agriculture	12	Private consumption	72
Industry, of which:	33	Public consumption	10
manufacturing	21	Investment	21
Services	55	Exports	35
		Imports	-37

Structure of employment

	% of total		% of labour force
Agriculture	35	Unemployed 2010	7.4
Industry	15	Av. ann. rate 1995–2010	8.6
Services	50		

Energy

	m TOE		
Total output	23.5	Net energy imports as %	
Total consumption	38.8	of energy use	40
Consumption per head,			
kg oil equivalent	424		

Inflation and finance

Consumer price		av. ann. increase 2006–10	
inflation 2011	4.4%	Narrow money (M1)	...
Av. ann. inflation 2006–11	4.7%	Broad money	9.8%
Money market rate, 2011	4.54%		

Exchange rates

	end 2011		2011
P per $	43.93	Effective rates	2005 = 100
P per SDR	67.44	– nominal	108.6
P per €	56.84	– real	128.1

Trade

Principal exports		Principal imports	
	$bn fob		$bn fob
Electrical & electronic equip.	31.1	Capital goods	16.4
Clothing	1.7	Mineral fuels	9.5
Coconut oil	1.3	Chemicals	5.2
Petroleum products	0.4	Manufactured goods	4.2
Total incl. others	**51.4**	Total incl. others	**58.2**

Main export destinations		Main origins of imports	
	% of total		% of total
Japan	15.2	Japan	11.6
United States	14.7	United States	10.1
Singapore	14.3	Singapore	8.9
China	11.1	China	7.9
Hong Kong	8.4	Thailand	6.6

Balance of payments, reserves and debt, $bn

Visible exports fob	50.7	Change in reserves	18.1
Visible imports fob	-61.7	Level of reserves	
Trade balance	-11.0	end Dec.	62.3
Invisibles inflows	20.5	No. months of import cover	9.5
Invisibles outflows	-17.2	Official gold holdings, m oz	5.0
Net transfers	16.6	Foreign debt	72.4
Current account balance	8.9	– as % of GDP	35
– as % of GDP	4.5	– as % of total exports	100
Capital balance	9.6	Debt service ratio	18
Overall balance	16.6		

Health and education

Health spending, % of GDP	3.6	Education spending, % of GDP	2.7
Doctors per 1,000 pop.	...	Enrolment, %: primary	107
Hospital beds per 1,000 pop.	0.5	secondary	82
Improved-water source access,		tertiary	29
% of pop.	92		

Society

No. of households	19.5m	Colour TV households, % with:	
Av. no. per household	4.8	cable	51.5
Marriages per 1,000 pop.	6.2	satellite	0.5
Divorces per 1,000 pop.	...	Telephone lines per 100 pop.	7.3
Cost of living, Dec. 2011		Mobile telephone subscribers	
New York = 100	63	per 100 pop.	85.7
Cars per 1,000 pop.	8	Broadband subs per 100 pop.	1.9
		Internet hosts per 1,000 pop.	5.3

POLAND

Area	312,683 sq km	Capital	Warsaw
Arable as % of total land	41.2	Currency	Zloty (Zl)

People

Population	38.0m	Life expectancy: men	72.2 yrs
Pop. per sq km	121.5	women	80.6 yrs
Av. ann. growth		Adult literacy	99.5
in pop. 2010–15	0.04%	Fertility rate (per woman)	1.4
Pop. under 15	14.8%	Urban population	60.7%
Pop. over 60	19.4%		per 1,000 pop.
No. of men per 100 women	93.2	Crude birth rate	10.9
Human Development Index	81.3	Crude death rate	10.5

The economy

GDP	Zl1,415bn	GDP per head	$12,290
GDP	$469bn	GDP per head in purchasing	
Av. ann. growth in real		power parity (USA=100)	42.2
GDP 2005–10	4.7%	Economic freedom index	64.2

Origins of GDP		Components of GDP	
	% of total		% of total
Agriculture	4	Private consumption	61
Industry, of which:	32	Public consumption	19
manufacturing	18	Investment	21
Services	65	Exports	42
		Imports	-43

Structure of employment

	% of total		% of labour force
Agriculture	13	Unemployed 2010	9.6
Industry	30	Av. ann. rate 1995–2010	13.8
Services	57		

Energy

	m TOE		
Total output	67.5	Net energy imports as %	
Total consumption	94.0	of energy use	28
Consumption per head,			
kg oil equivalent	2,464		

Inflation and finance

		av. ann. increase 2005–10	
Consumer price			
inflation 2011	4.2%	Narrow money (M1)	15.3%
Av. ann. inflation 2006–11	3.5%	Broad money	12.9%
Money market rate, 2011	4.10%	Household saving rate, 2011	3.9%

Exchange rates

	end 2011		2011
			2005 = 100
Zl per $	3.42	Effective rates	
Zl per SDR	5.25	– nominal	91.1
Zl per €	4.42	– real	94.4

Trade

Principal exports		**Principal imports**	
	$bn fob		*$bn cif*
Machinery & tranport equip.	64.7	Machinery & transport equip.	59.2
Manufactured goods	31.7	Manufactured goods	30.9
Foodstuffs & live animals	14.5	Chemicals & products	24.8
Total incl. others	**155.7**	Total incl. others	**173.7**

Main export destinations		**Main origins of imports**	
	% of total		*% of total*
Germany	26.8	Germany	28.8
France	6.9	Russia	8.4
United Kingdom	6.5	Netherlands	6.0
Czech Republic	6.1	Italy	5.7
EU27	84.0	EU27	74.9

Balance of payments, reserves and debt, $bn

Visible exports fob	165.7	Change in reserves	14.0
Visible imports fob	-177.5	Level of reserves	
Trade balance	-11.8	end Dec.	93.5
Invisibles inflows	40.0	No. months of import cover	4.8
Invisibles outflows	-53.8	Official gold holdings, m oz	3.3
Net transfers	3.7	Foreign debt	296.0
Current account balance	-21.9	– as % of GDP	63.0
– as % of GDP	-4.7	– as % of total exports	139
Capital balance	46.4	Debt service ratio	25
Overall balance	15.1	Aid given	0.38
		% of GDP	0.08

Health and education

Health spending, % of GDP	7.5	Education spending, % of GDP	5.1
Doctors per 1,000 pop.	2.2	Enrolment, %: primary	97
Hospital beds per 1,000 pop.	6.7	secondary	97
Improved-water source access,		tertiary	71
% of pop.	100		

Society

No. of households	14.6m	Colour TV households, % with:	
Av. no. per household	2.6	cable	31.8
Marriages per 1,000 pop.	6.0	satellite	65.0
Divorces per 1,000 pop.	1.6	Telephone lines per 100 pop.	20.0
Cost of living, Dec. 2011		Mobile telephone subscribers	
New York = 100	81	per 100 pop.	122.7
Cars per 1,000 pop.	452	Broadband subs per 100 pop.	13.0
		Internet hosts per 1,000 pop.	342.9

PORTUGAL

Area	88,940 sq km	Capital	Lisbon
Arable as % of total land	12.3	Currency	Euro (€)

People

Population	10.7m	Life expectancy: men		76.8 yrs
Pop. per sq km	116.1	women		82.8 yrs
Av. ann. growth		Adult literacy		94.9%
in pop. 2010–15	0.05%	Fertility rate (per woman)		1.3
Pop. under 15	15.2%	Urban population		63.2%
Pop. over 60	23.6%			per 1,000 pop.
No. of men per 100 women	94.0	Crude birth rate		8.8
Human Development Index	80.9	Crude death rate		10.1

The economy

GDP	€173bn	GDP per head	$21,490
GDP	$229bn	GDP per head in purchasing	
Av. ann. growth in real		power parity (USA=100)	53.9
GDP 2005–10	0.4%	Economic freedom index	63.0

Origins of GDP		Components of GDP	
	% of total		% of total
Agriculture	2	Private consumption	66
Industry, of which:	23	Public consumption	22
manufacturing	13	Investment	20
Services	74	Exports	31
		Imports	-38

Structure of employment

	% of total		% of labour force
Agriculture	11	Unemployed 2010	10.8
Industry	28	Av. ann. rate 1995–2010	6.7
Services	61		

Energy

	m TOE		
Total output	4.9	Net energy imports as %	
Total consumption	24.1	of energy use	80
Consumption per head,			
kg oil equivalent	2,266		

Inflation and finance

Consumer price		av. ann. increase 2005–10	
inflation 2011	3.7%	Euro area:	
Av. ann. inflation 2006–11	1.9%	Narrow money (M1)	6.3%
Deposit rate, h'holds, 2011	2.82%	Broad money	5.9%
		Household saving rate[a], 2011	9.7%

Exchange rates

	end 2011		2011
€ per $	0.77	Effective rates	2005 = 100
€ per SDR	1.19	– nominal	100.8
		– real	100.2

Trade

Principal exports		Principal imports	
	$bn fob		$bn cif
Machinery & transport equip.	13.0	Machinery & transport equip.	22.6
Food, drink & tobacco	5.0	Mineral fuels & lubricants	10.8
Chemicals & related products	4.0	Chemicals & related products	9.3
Mineral fuels & lubricants	3.2	Food, drink & tobacco	8.9
Total incl. others	**48.8**	Total incl. others	**75.7**

Main export destinations		Main origins of imports	
	% of total		% of total
Spain	26.5	Spain	31.2
Germany	13.0	Germany	13.8
France	11.8	France	7.2
United Kingdom	5.5	Italy	5.7
Angola	5.1	Netherlands	5.2
EU27	75.0	EU27	75.7

Balance of payments, reserves and debt, $bn

Visible exports fob	48.9	Overall balance	1.3
Visible imports fob	-73.0	Change in reserves	5.1
Trade balance	-24.1	Level of reserves	
Invisibles inflows	36.7	end Dec.	20.9
Invisibles outflows	-38.3	No. months of import cover	2.3
Net transfers	2.8	Official gold holdings, m oz	12.3
Current account balance	-22.9	Aid given	0.65
– as % of GDP	-10.0	– as % of GDP	0.29
Capital balance	24.7		

Health and education

Health spending, % of GDP	11.0	Education spending, % of GDP	4.9
Doctors per 1,000 pop.	3.9	Enrolment, %: primary	114
Hospital beds per 1,000 pop.	3.3	secondary[b]	107
Improved-water source access,		tertiary	62
% of pop.	99		

Society

No. of households	4.2m	Colour TV households, % with:	
Av. no. per household	2.6	cable	52.4
Marriages per 1,000 pop.	4.8	satellite	19.0
Divorces per 1,000 pop.	2.5	Telephone lines per 100 pop.	42.0
Cost of living, Dec. 2011		Mobile telephone subscribers	
New York = 100	91	per 100 pop.	142.3
Cars per 1,000 pop.	432	Broadband subs per 100 pop.	19.2
		Internet hosts per 1,000 pop.	343.9

a Gross.
b Includes training for unemployed.

ROMANIA

Area	237,500 sq km	Capital	Bucharest
Arable as % of total land	38.2	Currency	Leu (RON)

People

Population	21.2m	Life expectancy: men	70.6 yrs
Pop. per sq km	89.3	women	78.0 yrs
Av. ann. growth		Adult literacy	97.7%
in pop. 2010–15	-0.23%	Fertility rate (per woman)	1.4
Pop. under 15	15.2%	Urban population	52.9%
Pop. over 60	20.3%		per 1,000 pop.
No. of men per 100 women	94.3	Crude birth rate	10.3
Human Development Index	78.1	Crude death rate	12.1

The economy

GDP	RON514bn	GDP per head	$7,540
GDP	$162bn	GDP per head in purchasing	
Av. ann. growth in real		power parity (USA=100)	30.8
GDP 2005–10	2.5%	Economic freedom index	64.4

Origins of GDP

	% of total
Agriculture	7
Industry, of which:	26
manufacturing	22
Services	67

Components of GDP

	% of total
Private consumption	60
Public consumption	15
Investment	31
Exports	23
Imports	-30

Structure of employment

	% of total		% of labour force
Agriculture	30	Unemployed 2010	7.3
Industry	29	Av. ann. rate 1995–2010	7.0
Services	41		

Energy

	m TOE		
Total output	28.3	Net energy imports as %	
Total consumption	34.4	of energy use	18
Consumption per head,			
kg oil equivalent	1,602		

Inflation and finance

		av. ann. increase 2005–10	
Consumer price			
inflation 2011	5.8%	Narrow money (M1)	27.2%
Av. ann. inflation 2006–11	6.0%	Broad money	15.9%
Money market rate, 2011	4.80%		

Exchange rates

	end 2011		2011
RON per $	3.34	Effective rates	2005 = 100
RON per SDR	5.13	– nominal	85.8
RON per €	4.32	– real	103.8

Trade

Principal exports	$bn fob	Principal imports	$bn cif
Machinery & equipment (incl. transport)	13.4	Machinery & equipment (incl. transport)	17.6
Basic metals & products	5.9	Textiles & products	6.8
Textiles & apparel	4.2	Chemical products	6.2
Minerals, fuels & lubricants	2.7	Minerals, fuels & lubricants	5.5
Total incl. others	**49.4**	Total incl. others	**61.9**

Main export destinations	% of total	Main origins of imports	% of total
Germany	18.1	Germany	16.8
Italy	13.8	Italy	11.6
France	8.3	Hungary	8.7
Turkey	6.9	France	5.9
EU27	72.2	EU27	72.5

Balance of payments, reserves and debt, $bn

Visible exports fob	49.4	Change in reserves	2.3
Visible imports fob	-57.2	Level of reserves	
Trade balance	-7.8	end Dec.	48.0
Invisibles inflows	10.0	No. months of import cover	8.2
Invisibles outflows	-13.2	Official gold holdings, m oz	3.3
Net transfers	4.5	Foreign debt	121.5
Current account balance	-6.5	– as % of GDP	58
– as % of GDP	-4.0	– as % of total exports	171
Capital balance	6.4	Debt service ratio	31
Overall balance	-1.0		

Health and education

Health spending, % of GDP	5.6	Education spending, % of GDP	4.3
Doctors per 1,000 pop.	1.9	Enrolment, %: primary	96
Hospital beds per 1,000 pop.	6.6	secondary	95
Improved-water source access, % of pop.	...	tertiary	64

Society

No. of households	7.5m	Colour TV households, % with:	
Av. no. per household	2.9	cable	49.4
Marriages per 1,000 pop.	5.4	satellite	38.9
Divorces per 1,000 pop.	1.5	Telephone lines per 100 pop.	20.9
Cost of living, Dec. 2011		Mobile telephone subscribers	
New York = 100	65	per 100 pop.	114.7
Cars per 1,000 pop.	149	Broadband subs per 100 pop.	13.9
		Internet hosts per 1,000 pop.	135.4

RUSSIA

Area	17,075,400 sq km	Capital	Moscow
Arable as % of total land	7.4	Currency	Rouble (Rb)

People

Population	140.4m	Life expectancy:	men	63.3 yrs
Pop. per sq km	8.2		women	75.0 yrs
Av. ann. growth		Adult literacy		99.6%
in pop. 2010–15	-0.10%	Fertility rate (per woman)		1.5
Pop. under 15	15.0%	Urban population		74.5%
Pop. over 60	18.1%			per 1,000 pop.
No. of men per 100 women	86.1	Crude birth rate		11.8
Human Development Index	75.5	Crude death rate		14.0

The economy

GDP	Rb44,939bn	GDP per head	$10,440
GDP	$1,480bn	GDP per head in purchasing	
Av. ann. growth in real		power parity (USA=100)	42.2
GDP 2005–10	3.5%	Economic freedom index	50.5

Origins of GDP		Components of GDP	
	% of total		% of total
Agriculture	4	Private consumption	49
Industry, of which:	37	Public consumption	19
manufacturing	16	Investment	23
Services	59	Exports	30
		Imports	-22

Structure of employment

	% of total		% of labour force
Agriculture	10	Unemployed 2010	7.5
Industry	28	Av. ann. rate 1995–2010	9.0
Services	62		

Energy

	m TOE		
Total output	1,181.6	Net energy imports as %	
Total consumption	648.9	of energy use	-83
Consumption per head,			
kg oil equivalent	4,561		

Inflation and finance

			av. ann. increase 2005–10
Consumer price			
inflation 2011	8.4%	Narrow money (M0)	20.3%
Av. ann. inflation 2006–11	10.0%	Broad money	26.9%
Money market rate, 2011	3.93%		

Exchange rates

	end 2011		2011
			2005 = 100
Rb per $	32.20	Effective rates	
Rb per SDR	49.43	– nominal	92.3
Rb per 7	41.66	– real	128.8

Trade

Principal exports

	$bn fob
Fuels	275.4
Metals	42.3
Chemicals	24.4
Machinery & equipment	22.0
Total incl. others	**397.1**

Principal imports

	$bn fob
Machinery & equipment	112.4
Chemicals	40.9
Food & agricultural products	38.4
Metals	17.7
Total incl. others	**273.6**

Main export destinations

	% of total
Germany	8.2
Netherlands	6.5
China	5.9
Italy	3.8

Main origins of imports

	% of total
Germany	14.6
China	13.9
Ukraine	5.5
Japan	3.9

Balance of payments, reserves and debt, $bn

Visible exports fob	400.4	Change in reserves	40.3
Visible imports fob	-248.7	Level of reserves	
Trade balance	151.7	end Dec.	479.2
Invisibles inflows	82.5	No. months of import cover	14.1
Invisibles outflows	-160.3	Official gold holdings, m oz	25.4
Net transfers	-3.6	Foreign debt	384.7
Current account balance	70.3	– as % of GDP	25
– as % of GDP	4.7	– as % of total exports	72
Capital balance	-25.9	Debt service ratio	13
Overall balance	36.7		

Health and education

Health spending, % of GDP	5.1	Education spending, % of GDP	4.1
Doctors per 1,000 pop.	...	Enrolment, %: primary	99
Hospital beds per 1,000 pop.	...	secondary	89
Improved-water source access,		tertiary	76
% of pop.	97		

Society

No. of households	52.7m	Colour TV households, % with:	
Av. no. per household	2.7	cable	37.5
Marriages per 1,000 pop.	8.5	satellite	7.8
Divorces per 1,000 pop.	4.5	Telephone lines per 100 pop.	31.4
Cost of living, Dec. 2011		Mobile telephone subscribers	
New York = 100	102	per 100 pop.	166.3
Cars per 1,000 pop.	188	Broadband subs per 100 pop.	11.0
		Internet hosts per 1,000 pop.	101.2

SAUDI ARABIA

Area	2,200,000 sq km	Capital	Riyadh
Arable as % of total land	1.5	Currency	Riyal (SR)

People

Population	26.2m	Life expectancy: men	73.2 yrs
Pop. per sq km	11.9	women	75.6 yrs
Av. ann. growth		Adult literacy	86.1%
in pop. 2010–15	2.13%	Fertility rate (per woman)	2.6
Pop. under 15	31.9%	Urban population	83.1%
Pop. over 60	4.6%		per 1,000 pop.
No. of men per 100 women	124.0	Crude birth rate	21.4
Human Development Index	77.0	Crude death rate	3.7

The economy

GDP	SR1,630bn	GDP per head	$15,840
GDP	$435bn	GDP per head in purchasing	
Av. ann. growth in real		power parity (USA=100)	48.2
GDP 2005–10	2.8%	Economic freedom index	62.5

Origins of GDP		Components of GDP	
	% of total		% of total
Agriculture	3	Private consumption	34
Industry, of which:	62	Public consumption	23
manufacturing	10	Investment	22
Services	35	Exports	57
		Imports	-35

Structure of employment

	% of total		% of labour force
Agriculture	4	Unemployed 2009	5.4
Industry	20	Av. ann. rate 1995–2009	4.8
Services	76		

Energy

	m TOE		
Total output	528.4	Net energy imports as %	
Total consumption	157.9	of energy use	-235
Consumption per head,			
kg oil equivalent	5,888		

Inflation and finance

		av. ann. increase 2005–10	
Consumer price			
inflation 2011	5.0%	Narrow money (M1)	17.1%
Av. ann. inflation 2006–11	5.9%	Broad money	14.7%
Money market rate, Jun. 2011	0.66%		

Exchange rates

	end 2011		2011
SR per $	3.75	Effective rates	2005 = 100
SR per SDR	5.76	– nominal	92.6
SRE per €	4.85	– real	106.1

Trade

Principal exports		Principal imports	
	$bn fob		$bn cif
Crude oil	177.2	Machinery & transport equip.	49.1
Refined petroleum products	27.6	Foodstuffs	15.0
		Chemicals & metal products	8.8
Total incl. others	**251.1**	Total incl. others	**107.1**

Main export destinations		Main origins of imports	
	% of total		% of total
Japan	14.1	United States	12.3
China	12.9	China	11.0
United States	12.8	France	6.0
South Korea	10.5	South Korea	4.8

Balance of payments, reserves and aid, $bn

Visible exports fob	251.1	Overall balance	35.3
Visible imports fob	-97.4	Change in reserves	55.3
Trade balance	153.7	Level of reserves	
Invisibles inflows	28.9	end Dec.	470.4
Invisibles outflows	-87.9	No. months of import cover	30.5
Net transfers	-27.9	Official gold holdings, m oz	10.4
Current account balance	66.8	Aid given	3.48
– as % of GDP	15.4	– as % of GDP	0.77
Capital balance	-7.2		

Health and education

Health spending, % of GDP	4.3	Education spending, % of GDP	5.6
Doctors per 1,000 pop.	...	Enrolment, %: primary	106
Hospital beds per 1,000 pop.	2.2	secondary	101
Improved-water source access, % of pop.	...	tertiary	37

Society

No. of households	4.9m	Colour TV households, % with:	
Av. no. per household	5.4	cable	0.3
Marriages per 1,000 pop.	4.6	satellite	99.4
Divorces per 1,000 pop.	1.0	Telephone lines per 100 pop.	15.2
Cost of living, Dec. 2011		Mobile telephone subscribers	
New York = 100	64	per 100 pop.	187.9
Cars per 1,000 pop.	472	Broadband subs per 100 pop.	5.5
		Internet hosts per 1,000 pop.	11.0

SINGAPORE

Area	639 sq km	Capital	Singapore
Arable as % of total land	1.0	Currency	Singapore dollar (S$)

People

Population	4.8m	Life expectancy:	men	78.9 yrs
Pop. per sq km	7,511.7		women	83.7 yrs
Av. ann. growth		Adult literacy		94.7%
in pop. 2010–15	1.10%	Fertility rate (per woman)		1.4
Pop. under 15	15.6%	Urban population		100.0%
Pop. over 60	16.0%			per 1,000 pop.
No. of men per 100 women	101.7	Crude birth rate		9.5
Human Development Index	86.6	Crude death rate		5.1

The economy

GDP	S$304bn	GDP per head	$41,120
GDP	$209bn	GDP per head in purchasing	
Av. ann. growth in real		power parity (USA=100)	122.9
GDP 2005–10	6.5%	Economic freedom index	87.5

Origins of GDP		Components of GDP	
	% of total		% of total
Agriculture	0	Private consumption	37
Industry, of which:	28	Public consumption	11
manufacturing	22	Investment	24
Services	72	Exports	211
		Imports	-183

Structure of employment

	% of total		% of labour force
Agriculture	1	Unemployed 2009	5.9
Industry	22	Av. ann. rate 1995–2009	4.1
Services	77		

Energy

	m TOE		
Total output	0.0	Net energy imports as %	
Total consumption	18.5	of energy use	100
Consumption per head,			
kg oil equivalent	3,704		

Inflation and finance

		av. ann. increase 2005–10	
Consumer price			
inflation 2011	5.2%	Narrow money (M1)	19.5%
Av. ann. inflation 2006–11	3.4%	Broad money	12.9%
Money market rate, 2011	0.41%		

Exchange rates

	end 2011		2011
S$ per $	1.30	Effective rates	2005 = 100
S$ per SDR	2.00	– nominal	114.5
S$ per 7	1.68	– real	117.0

Trade

Principal exports	$bn fob	Principal imports	$bn cif
Electronic components & parts	87.5	Machinery & transport equip.	144.3
Mineral fuels	75.9	Mineral fuels	84.8
Chemicals & products	41.6	Misc. manufactured articles	21.8
Manufactured products	24.6	Manufactured products	19.4
Total incl. others	**351.7**	Total incl. others	**311.0**

Main export destinations	% of total	Main origins of imports	% of total
Malaysia	11.9	Malaysia	11.7
Hong Kong	11.7	United States	11.2
China	10.3	China	10.8
United States	7.3	Japan	7.8
Japan	5.3	Taiwan	5.3
Taiwan	4.1	Saudi Arabia	3.1
Thailand	4.1	Thailand	2.9

Balance of payments, reserves and debt, $bn

Visible exports fob	358.5	Change in reserves	37.9
Visible imports fob	-311.7	Level of reserves	
Trade balance	46.8	end Dec.	225.7
Invisibles inflows	162.8	No. months of import cover	5.8
Invisibles outflows	-155.2	Official gold holdings, m oz	...
Net transfers	-4.8	Foreign debt	22.0
Current account balance	49.6	– as % of GDP	10
– as % of GDP	23.7	– as % of total exports	4
Capital balance	-6.9	Debt service ratio	1
Overall balance	42.3		

Health and education

Health spending, % of GDP	4.0	Education spending, % of GDP	3.3
Doctors per 1,000 pop.	1.8	Enrolment, %: primary	...
Hospital beds per 1,000 pop.	3.1	secondary	...
Improved-water source access,		tertiary	...
% of pop.	100		

Society

No. of households	1.5m	Colour TV households, % with:	
Av. no. per household	3.5	cable	54.7
Marriages per 1,000 pop.	4.8	satellite	0.0
Divorces per 1,000 pop.	1.7	Telephone lines per 100 pop.	39.2
Cost of living, Dec. 2011		Mobile telephone subscribers	
New York = 100	142	per 100 pop.	145.2
Cars per 1,000 pop.	105	Broadband subs per 100 pop.	24.9
		Internet hosts per 1,000 pop.	411.2

SLOVAKIA

Area	49,035 sq km	Capital	Bratislava
Arable as % of total land	28.7	Currency	Euro (€)

People

Population	5.4m	Life expectancy: men		71.9 yrs
Pop. per sq km	111.4		women	79.5 yrs
Av. ann. growth		Adult literacy		...
in pop. 2010–15	0.16%	Fertility rate (per woman)		1.4
Pop. under 15	15.2%	Urban population		54.6%
Pop. over 60	17.7%			per 1,000 pop.
No. of men per 100 women	94.6	Crude birth rate		10.7
Human Development Index	83.4	Crude death rate		9.9

The economy

GDP	€65.9bn	GDP per head	$16,070
GDP	$87.2bn	GDP per head in purchasing	
Av. ann. growth in real		power parity (USA=100)	49.4
GDP 2005–10	4.6%	Economic freedom index	67.0

Origins of GDP		Components of GDP	
	% of total		% of total
Agriculture	4	Private consumption	58
Industry, of which:	35	Public consumption	20
Manufacturing	21	Investment	23
Services	61	Exports	81
		Imports	-82

Structure of employment

	% of total		% of labour force
Agriculture	3	Unemployed 2010	14.4
Industry	37	Av. ann. rate 1995–2010	14.6
Services	60		

Energy

	m TOE		
Total output	5.9	Net energy imports as %	
Total consumption	16.7	of energy use	65
Consumption per head,			
kg oil equivalent	3,086		

Inflation and finance

Consumer price		av. ann. increase 2005–10	
inflation 2011	3.9%	Euro area:	
Av. ann. inflation 2006–11	2.8%	Narrow money	6.3%
Deposit rate, h'holds, 2011	1.77%	Broad money	5.9%
		Household saving rate, 2011	5.4%

Exchange rates

	end 2011		2011
€ per $	0.77	Effective rates	2005 = 100
€ per SDR	1.19	– nominal	128.89
		– real	134.06

Trade

Principal exports		Principal imports	
	$bn fob		*$bn fob*
Machinery & transport equip.	35.6	Machinery & transport equip.	27.1
Base metals & articles	8.1	Mineral products	9.1
Mineral products	3.5	Base metals & articles	6.2
Plastics & products	3.4	Chemicals	4.0
Total incl. others	**64.1**	Total incl. others	**63.1**

Main export destinations		Main origins of imports	
	% of total		*% of total*
Germany	18.0	Germany	17.2
Czech Republic	13.1	Czech Republic	16.6
Poland	7.1	Russia	9.0
Hungary	6.5	Hungary	6.6
EU27	84.4	EU27	72.0

Balance of payments, reserves and debt, $bn

Visible exports fob	64.7	Change in reserves	0.4
Visible imports fob	-64.5	Level of reserves	
Trade balance	0.2	end Dec.	2.2
Invisibles inflows	8.9	No. months of import cover	0.3
Invisibles outflows	-11.6	Official gold holdings, m oz	1.0
Net transfers	-0.5	Foreign debt	32.0
Current account balance	-3.0	– as % of GDP	37
– as % of GDP	-3.4	– as % of total exports	42
Capital balance	0.7	Debt service ratio	7
Overall balance	0.0	Aid given	0.07
		% of GDP	0.09

Health and education

Health spending, % of GDP	8.8	Education spending, % of GDP	3.6
Doctors per 1,000 pop.	3.0	Enrolment, %: primary	102
Hospital beds per 1,000 pop.	6.5	secondary	89
Improved-water source access,		tertiary	54
% of pop.	100		

Society

No. of households	2.3m	Colour TV households, % with:	
Av. no. per household	2.4	cable	33.0
Marriages per 1,000 pop.	4.7	satellite	36.0
Divorces per 1,000 pop.	2.2	Telephone lines per 100 pop.	20.1
Cost of living, Dec. 2011		Mobile telephone subscribers	
New York = 100	...	per 100 pop.	108.5
Cars per 1,000 pop.	299	Broadband subs per 100 pop.	12.7
		Internet hosts per 1,000 pop.	258.0

SLOVENIA

Area	20,253 sq km	Capital	Ljubljana
Arable as % of total land	8.7	Currency	Euro (€)

People

Population	2.0m	Life expectancy: men	76.1 yrs
Pop. per sq km	100.2	women	82.8 yrs
Av. ann. growth		Adult literacy	99.7%
in pop. 2010–15	0.23%	Fertility rate (per woman)	1.5
Pop. under 15	13.8%	Urban population	49.8%
Pop. over 60	22.4%		per 1,000 pop.
No. of men per 100 women	95.7	Crude birth rate	9.9
Human Development Index	88.4	Crude death rate	9.8

The economy

GDP	€35.4bn	GDP per head	$22,890
GDP	$46.9bn	GDP per head in purchasing	
Av. ann. growth in real		power parity (USA=100)	57.1
GDP 2005–10	1.8%	Economic freedom index	62.9

Origins of GDP		**Components of GDP**	
	% of total		% of total
Agriculture	2	Private consumption	56
Industry, of which:	32	Public consumption	21
manufacturing	21	Investment	23
Services	66	Exports	65
		Imports	-65

Structure of employment

	% of total		% of labour force
Agriculture	9	Unemployed 2010	7.2
Industry	33	Av. ann. rate 1995–2010	6.4
Services	58		

Energy

	m TOE		
Total output	3.5	Net energy imports as %	
Total consumption	7.0	of energy use	49
Consumption per head,			
kg oil equivalent	3,417		

Inflation and finance

Consumer price		av. ann. increase 2005–10	
inflation 2011	1.8%	Euro area:	
Av. ann. inflation 2006–11	2.7%	Narrow money (M1)	6.3%
Money market rate, 2011	1.18%	Broad money	5.9%
		Household saving rate, 2011	9.0%

Exchange rates

	end 2011		2011
€ per $	0.77	Effective rates	2005 = 100
€ per SDR	1.19	– nominal	...
		– real	...

Trade

Principal exports		Principal imports	
	$bn fob		*$bn fob*
Machinery & transport equip.	9.4	Machinery & transport equip.	7.7
Manufactures	5.4	Manufactures	5.1
Chemicals	3.9	Chemicals	3.6
Miscellaneous manufactures	2.6	Miscellaneous manufactures	2.6
Total incl. others	**24.2**	**Total incl. others**	**26.4**

Main export destinations		Main origins of imports	
	% of total		*% of total*
Germany	23.3	Germany	18.4
Italy	14.6	Italy	17.9
Austria	9.0	Austria	12.1
France	8.3	France	5.5
Croatia	7.8	Croatia	5.3
Hungary	5.0	China	4.7
EU27	71.1	EU27	67.9

Balance of payments, reserves and debt, $bn

Visible exports fob	24.4	Change in reserves	0.0
Visible imports fob	-26.0	Level of reserves	
Trade balance	-1.6	end Dec.	1.1
Invisibles inflows	7.0	No. months of import cover	0.4
Invisibles outflows	-6.0	Official gold holdings, m oz	0.1
Net transfers	0.1	Foreign debt	...
Current account balance	-0.4	– as % of GDP	...
– as % of GDP	-0.8	– as % of total exports	...
Capital balance	0.4	Debt service ratio	...
Overall balance	0.0		

Health and education

Health spending, % of GDP	9.4	Education spending, % of GDP	5.2
Doctors per 1,000 pop.	2.5	Enrolment, %: primary	98
Hospital beds per 1,000 pop.	4.6	secondary	97
Improved-water source access,		tertiary	87
% of pop.	99		

Society

No. of households	0.7m	Colour TV households, % with:	
Av. no. per household	2.8	cable	68.6
Marriages per 1,000 pop.	3.1	satellite	13.1
Divorces per 1,000 pop.	1.2	Telephone lines per 100 pop.	44.9
Cost of living, Dec. 2011		Mobile telephone subscribers	
New York = 100	...	per 100 pop.	104.6
Cars per 1,000 pop.	529	Broadband subs per 100 pop.	24.3
		Internet hosts per 1,000 pop.	210.6

SOUTH AFRICA

Area	1,225,815 sq km	Capital	Pretoria
Arable as % of total land	11.8	Currency	Rand (R)

People

Population	50.5m	Life expectancy: men		53.1 yrs
Pop. per sq km	41.2		women	54.1 yrs
Av. ann. growth		Adult literacy		88.7%
in pop. 2010–15	0.51%	Fertility rate (per woman)		2.4
Pop. under 15	30.3%	Urban population		63.8%
Pop. over 60	7.3%			per 1,000 pop.
No. of men per 100 women	98.1	Crude birth rate		20.5
Human Development Index	61.9	Crude death rate		14.3

The economy

GDP	R2,664bn	GDP per head	$7,280
GDP	$364bn	GDP per head in purchasing	
Av. ann. growth in real		power parity (USA=100)	22.4
GDP 2005–10	3.2%	Economic freedom index	62.7

Origins of GDP		**Components of GDP**	
	% of total		% of total
Agriculture	3	Private consumption	57
Industry, of which:	31	Public consumption	20
manufacturing	15	Investment	25
Services	66	Exports	26
		Imports	-27

Structure of employment

	% of total		% of labour force
Agriculture	5	Unemployed 2009	23.8
Industry	25	Av. ann. rate 1995–2009	24.9
Services	70		

Energy

	m TOE		
Total output	160.6	Net energy imports as %	
Total consumption	144.0	of energy use	-12
Consumption per head,			
kg oil equivalent	2,921		

Inflation and finance

Consumer price		av. ann. increase 2005–10	
inflation 2011	5.0%	Narrow money (M1)	11.4%
Av. ann. inflation 2006–11	7.0%	Broad money	13.7%
Money market rate, 2011	5.29%		

Exchange rates

	end 2011		2011
R per $	8.14	Effective rates	2005 = 100
R per SDR	12.50	– nominal	71.6
R per €	10.53	– real	92.0

Trade

Principal exports		Principal imports	
	$bn fob		*$bn cif*
Platinum	9.4	Petrochemicals	11.2
Gold	8.5	Motor vehicle components	5.2
Coal	5.5	Cars & other vehicles	4.1
Ferro-alloys	4.7	Petroleum oils & other	3.3
Car & other components	4.2	Telecoms components	0.3
Total incl. others	**81.8**	Total incl. others	**80.2**

Main export destinations		Main origins of imports	
	% of total		*% of total*
China	12.7	China	14.8
United States	9.3	Germany	12.4
Japan	8.1	United States	7.7
India	7.7	Saudi Arabia	5.9

Balance of payments, reserves and debt, $bn

Visible exports fob	85.7	Change in reserves	4.2
Visible imports fob	-81.9	Level of reserves	
Trade balance	3.8	end Dec.	43.8
Invisibles inflows	18.7	No. months of import cover	4.7
Invisibles outflows	-30.3	Official gold holdings, m oz	4.0
Net transfers	-2.3	Foreign debt	45.2
Current account balance	-10.1	– as % of GDP	15
– as % of GDP	-2.8	– as % of total exports	45
Capital balance	10.4	Debt service ratio	5
Overall balance	3.8		

Health and education

Health spending, % of GDP	8.9	Education spending, % of GDP	6.0
Doctors per 1,000 pop.	...	Enrolment, %: primary	102
Hospital beds per 1,000 pop.	...	secondary	94
Improved-water source access,		tertiary	...
% of pop.	91		

Society

No. of households	13.9m	Colour TV households, % with:	
Av. no. per household	3.6	cable	0.0
Marriages per 1,000 pop.	3.9	satellite	8.9
Divorces per 1,000 pop.	1.0	Telephone lines per 100 pop.	8.4
Cost of living, Dec. 2011		Mobile telephone subscribers	
New York = 100	86	per 100 pop.	100.5
Cars per 1,000 pop.	103	Broadband subs per 100 pop.	1.5
		Internet hosts per 1,000 pop.	98.4

SOUTH KOREA

Area	99,274 sq km	Capital	Seoul
Arable as % of total land	16.4	Currency	Won (W)

People

Population	48.5m	Life expectancy:	men	77.3 yrs
Pop. per sq km	488.5		women	84.0 yrs
Av. ann. growth		Adult literacy		...
in pop. 2010–15	0.38%	Fertility rate (per woman)		1.4
Pop. under 15	16.2%	Urban population		84.3%
Pop. over 60	15.6%			per 1,000 pop.
No. of men per 100 women	99.4	Crude birth rate		9.9
Human Development Index	89.7	Crude death rate		5.9

The economy

GDP	W1,173trn	GDP per head	$20,760
GDP	$1,014bn	GDP per head in purchasing	
Av. ann. growth in real		power parity (USA=100)	61.7
GDP 2005–10	3.8%	Economic freedom index	69.9

Origins of GDP

	% of total
Agriculture	3
Industry, of which:	39
manufacturing	31
Services	58

Components of GDP

	% of total
Private consumption	53
Public consumption	15
Investment	29
Exports	52
Imports	-50

Structure of employment

	% of total		% of labour force
Agriculture	7	Unemployed 2010	3.7
Industry	17	Av. ann. rate 1995–2010	3.7
Services	76		

Energy

	m TOE		
Total output	44.3	Net energy imports as %	
Total consumption	229.2	of energy use	81
Consumption per head,			
kg oil equivalent	4,701		

Inflation and finance

Consumer price		av. ann. increase 2005–10	
inflation 2011	4.0%	Narrow money (M1)	8.1%
Av. ann. inflation 2006–11	3.4%	Broad money	9.4%
Money market rate, 2011	3.09%	Household saving rate, 2011	3.1%

Exchange rates

	end 2011		2011
W per $	1,152	Effective rates	2005 = 100
W per SDR	1,768	– nominal	...
W per €	1,490	– real	68.6

Trade

Principal exports		Principal imports	
	$bn fob		*$bn cif*
Machinery & transport equip.	263.9	Machinery & transport equip.	123.3
Manufactured goods	60.4	Mineral fuels & lubricants	122.6
Chemicals & related products	49.0	Manufactured goods	56.1
Mineral fuels & lubricants	32.6	Chemicals & related products	41.1
Total incl. others	**466.4**	Total incl. others	**425.2**

Main export destinations		Main origins of imports	
	% of total		*% of total*
China	25.1	China	16.8
United States	10.7	Japan	15.1
Japan	6.0	United States	9.5
Hong Kong	5.4	Saudi Arabia	6.3

Balance of payments, reserves and debt, $bn

Visible exports fob	464.3	Change in reserves	21.7
Visible imports fob	-422.4	Level of reserves	
Trade balance	41.9	end Dec.	292.1
Invisibles inflows	98.6	No. months of import cover	6.6
Invisibles outflows	-109.0	Official gold holdings, m oz	0.5
Net transfers	-3.2	Foreign debt	362.0
Current account balance	28.2	– as % of GDP	34
– as % of GDP	2.8	– as % of total exports	64
Capital balance	1.8	Debt service ratio	7
Overall balance	27.2	Aid given	1.17
		% of GDP	0.12

Health and education

Health spending, % of GDP	6.9	Education spending, % of GDP	4.8
Doctors per 1,000 pop.	2.0	Enrolment, %: primary	104
Hospital beds per 1,000 pop.	10.3	secondary	97
Improved-water source access,		tertiary	104
% of pop.	98		

Society

No. of households	18.1m	Colour TV households, % with:	
Av. no. per household	2.7	cable	85.3
Marriages per 1,000 pop.	6.2	satellite	14.1
Divorces per 1,000 pop.	4.6	Telephone lines per 100 pop.	59.2
Cost of living, Dec. 2011		Mobile telephone subscribers	
New York = 100	113	per 100 pop.	105.4
Cars per 1,000 pop.	268	Broadband subs per 100 pop.	35.7
		Internet hosts per 1,000 pop.	6.1

SPAIN

Area	504,782 sq km	Capital	Madrid
Arable as % of total land	25.1	Currency	Euro (€)

People

Population	45.3m	Life expectancy: men	78.8 yrs
Pop. per sq km	89.7	women	84.8 yrs
Av. ann. growth		Adult literacy	97.7%
in pop. 2010–15	0.62%	Fertility rate (per woman)	1.5
Pop. under 15	14.9%	Urban population	78.0%
Pop. over 60	22.4%		per 1,000 pop.
No. of men per 100 women	97.5	Crude birth rate	10.6
Human Development Index	87.8	Crude death rate	8.7

The economy

GDP	€1,063bn	GDP per head	$30,550
GDP	$1,407bn	GDP per head in purchasing	
Av. ann. growth in real		power parity (USA=100)	68.4
GDP 2005–10	0.9%	Economic freedom index	69.1

Origins of GDP		Components of GDP	
	% of total		% of total
Agriculture	3	Private consumption	58
Industry, of which:	26	Public consumption	21
manufacturing	13	Investment	23
Services	72	Exports	26
		Imports	-28

Structure of employment

	% of total		% of labour force
Agriculture	4	Unemployed 2010	20.1
Industry	23	Av. ann. rate 1995–2010	14.8
Services	73		

Energy

	m TOE		
Total output	29.7	Net energy imports as %	
Total consumption	126.5	of energy use	78
Consumption per head,			
kg oil equivalent	2,756		

Inflation and finance

			av. ann. increase 2005–10
Consumer price			
inflation 2011	3.2%	Euro area:	
Av. ann. inflation 2006–11	2.3%	Narrow money (M1)	6.3%
Money market rate, 2011	1.02%	Broad money	5.9%
		Household saving rate[a], 2011	12.0%

Exchange rates

	end 2011		2011
€ per $	0.77	Effective rates	2005 = 100
€ per SDR	1.19	– nominal	102.9
		– real	107.6

Trade

Principal exports		Principal imports	
	$bn fob		*$bn cif*
Machinery & transport equip.	81.6	Machinery & transport equip.	89.2
Chemicals & related products	35.0	Mineral fuels & lubricants	57.0
Food, drink & tobacco	33.3	Chemicals & related products	44.0
Mineral fuels & lubricants	15.6	Food, drink & tobacco	29.0
Total incl. others	**246.4**	Total incl. others	**315.7**

Main export destinations		Main origins of imports	
	% of total		*% of total*
France	19.1	Germany	13.2
Germany	11.0	France	12.1
Italy	9.3	Italy	7.7
Portugal	9.2	China	6.7
EU27	68.7	EU27	59.0

Balance of payments, reserves and aid, $bn

Visible exports fob	253.0	Overall balance	1.1
Visible imports fob	-315.3	Change in reserves	3.8
Trade balance	-62.4	Level of reserves	
Invisibles inflows	178.4	end Dec.	31.9
Invisibles outflows	-170.9	No. months of import cover	0.8
Net transfers	-9.5	Official gold holdings, m oz	9.1
Current account balance	-64.3	Aid given	5.95
– as % of GDP	-4.6	– as % of GDP	0.43
Capital balance	68.6		

Health and education

Health spending, % of GDP	9.5	Education spending, % of GDP	4.6
Doctors per 1,000 pop.	4.0	Enrolment, %: primary	107
Hospital beds per 1,000 pop.	3.2	secondary	119
Improved-water source access,		tertiary	73
% of pop.	100		

Society

No. of households	17.6m	Colour TV households, % with:	
Av. no. per household	2.6	cable	14.2
Marriages per 1,000 pop.	4.6	satellite	16.3
Divorces per 1,000 pop.	2.2	Telephone lines per 100 pop.	43.9
Cost of living, Dec. 2011		Mobile telephone subscribers	
New York = 100	116	per 100 pop.	112.0
Cars per 1,000 pop.	505	Broadband subs per 100 pop.	22.9
		Internet hosts per 1,000 pop.	94.2

a Gross.

SWEDEN

Area	449,964 sq km	Capital	Stockholm
Arable as % of total land	6.4	Currency	Swedish krona (Skr)

People

Population	9.3m	Life expectancy: men		79.7 yrs
Pop. per sq km	20.7	women		83.7 yrs
Av. ann. growth		Adult literacy		...
in pop. 2010–15	0.56%	Fertility rate (per woman)		1.9
Pop. under 15	16.5%	Urban population		85.8%
Pop. over 60	25.0%			per 1,000 pop.
No. of men per 100 women	99.2	Crude birth rate		12.0
Human Development Index	90.4	Crude death rate		9.6

The economy

GDP	Skr3,305bn	GDP per head	$48,900
GDP	$459bn	GDP per head in purchasing	
Av. ann. growth in real		power parity (USA=100)	82.8
GDP 2005–10	1.6%	Economic freedom index	71.7

Origins of GDP		**Components of GDP**	
	% of total		% of total
Agriculture	2	Private consumption	49
Industry, of which:	27	Public consumption	27
manufacturing	16	Investment	18
Services	71	Exports	50
		Imports	-44

Structure of employment

	% of total		% of labour force
Agriculture	2	Unemployed 2010	8.4
Industry	20	Av. ann. rate 1995–2010	6.5
Services	78		

Energy

	m TOE		
Total output	30.3	Net energy imports as %	
Total consumption	45.4	of energy use	33
Consumption per head,			
kg oil equivalent	4,663		

Inflation and finance

		av. ann. increase 2005–10	
Consumer price			
inflation 2011	3.0%	Narrow money (M1)	7.8%
Av. ann. inflation 2006–11	1.8%	Broad money	7.7%
Repurchase rate, end 2011	2.00%	Household saving rate, 2011	9.7%

Exchange rates

	end 2011		2011
Skr per $	6.89	Effective rates	2005 = 100
Skr per SDR	10.57	– nominal	103.5
Skr per €	8.91	– real	99.8

Trade

Principal exports	$bn fob	Principal imports	$bn cif
Machinery & transport equip.	60.5	Machinery & transport equip.	54.6
Chemicals & related products	18.4	Fuels & lubricants	19.7
Mineral fuels & lubricants	11.7	Chemicals & related products	16.5
Raw materials	10.7	Food, drink & tobacco	12.4
Total incl. others	**158.4**	Total incl. others	**148.8**

Main export destinations	% of total	Main origins of imports	% of total
Germany	9.9	Germany	17.9
Norway	9.3	Norway	8.5
United Kingdom	7.4	Denmark	8.3
Denmark	6.6	Netherlands	6.2
Finland	6.2	United Kingdom	5.6
EU27	57.1	EU27	67.0

Balance of payments, reserves and aid, $bn

Visible exports fob	160.4	Overall balance	-1.1
Visible imports fob	-149.5	Change in reserves	1.0
Trade balance	10.9	Level of reserves	
Invisibles inflows	119.8	end Dec.	48.2
Invisibles outflows	-94.1	No. months of import cover	2.4
Net transfers	-6.2	Official gold holdings, m oz	4.0
Current account balance	30.4	Aid given	4.53
– as % of GDP	6.6	– as % of GDP	0.97
Capital balance	-43.5		

Health and education

Health spending, % of GDP	9.6	Education spending, % of GDP	6.8
Doctors per 1,000 pop.	3.8	Enrolment, %: primary	100
Hospital beds per 1,000 pop.	...	secondary	100
Improved-water source access,		tertiary	71
% of pop.	100		

Society

No. of households	4.6m	Colour TV households, % with:	
Av. no. per household	2.0	cable	60.9
Marriages per 1,000 pop.	5.4	satellite	37.8
Divorces per 1,000 pop.	2.5	Telephone lines per 100 pop.	52.5
Cost of living, Dec. 2011		Mobile telephone subscribers	
New York = 100	115	per 100 pop.	116.1
Cars per 1,000 pop.	466	Broadband subs per 100 pop.	31.9
		Internet hosts per 1,000 pop.	626.6

SWITZERLAND

| Area | 41,293 sq km | Capital | Berne |
| Arable as % of total land | 10.2 | Currency | Swiss franc (SFr) |

People

Population	7.6m	Life expectancy: men	80.2 yrs
Pop. per sq km	185.6	women	84.7 yrs
Av. ann. growth		Adult literacy	...
in pop. 2010–15	0.39%	Fertility rate (per woman)	1.5
Pop. under 15	15.2%	Urban population	74.0%
Pop. over 60	23.3%		per 1,000 pop.
No. of men per 100 women	96.7	Crude birth rate	10.0
Human Development Index	90.3	Crude death rate	8.3

The economy

GDP	SFr551bn	GDP per head	$67,460
GDP	$528bn	GDP per head in purchasing	
Av. ann. growth in real		power parity (USA=100)	98.4
GDP 2005–10	2.0%	Economic freedom index	81.1

Origins of GDP		**Components of GDP**	
	% of total		% of total
Agriculture	1	Private consumption	58
Industry, of which:	27	Public consumption	11
manufacturing	19	Investment	19
Services	72	Exports	54
		Imports	-42

Structure of employment

	% of total		% of labour force
Agriculture	3	Unemployed 2010	4.2
Industry	21	Av. ann. rate 1995–2010	3.6
Services	76		

Energy

	m TOE		
Total output	12.8	Net energy imports as %	
Total consumption	27.0	of energy use	53
Consumption per head,			
kg oil equivalent	3,480		

Inflation and finance

Consumer price		av. ann. increase 2005–10	
inflation 2011	0.2%	Narrow money (M1)	10.4%
Av. ann. inflation 2006–11	0.7%	Broad money	5.0%
Money market rate, 2011	0.07%	Household saving rate, 2011	11.4%

Exchange rates

	end 2011		2011
SFr per $	0.94	Effective rates	2005 = 100
SFr per SDR	1.44	– nominal	125.9
SFr per €	1.22	– real	114.5

Trade

Principal exports	$bn	Principal imports	$bn
Chemicals	72.8	Chemicals	36.2
Precision instruments, watches & jewellery	35.4	Machinery, equipment & electronics	30.1
Machinery, equipment & electronics	34.9	Precision instruments, watches & jewellery	17.6
Metals & metal manufactures	12.2	Motor vehicles	15.9
Total incl. others	**186.1**	Total incl. others	**167.3**

Main export destinations	% of total	Main origins of imports	% of total
Germany	20.3	Germany	33.7
United States	10.7	Italy	10.7
Italy	8.2	France	9.0
France	8.0	United States	5.6
United Kingdom	6.2	Netherlands	4.8
China	3.9	Austria	4.6
Japan	3.5	United Kingdom	4.1
EU27	58.6	EU27	77.5

Balance of payments, reserves and aid, $bn

Visible exports fob	258.5	Overall balance	125.4
Visible imports fob	-246.2	Change in reserves	135.9
Trade balance	12.3	Level of reserves	
Invisibles inflows	198.1	end Dec.	270.3
Invisibles outflows	-121.3	No. months of import cover	8.8
Net transfers	-12.3	Official gold holdings, m oz	33.4
Current account balance	76.9	Aid given	2.30
– as % of GDP	14.6	– as % of GDP	0.40
Capital balance	39.7		

Health and education

Health spending, % of GDP	11.5	Education spending, % of GDP	5.4
Doctors per 1,000 pop.	4.1	Enrolment, %: primary	102
Hospital beds per 1,000 pop.	5.2	secondary	95
Improved-water source access, % of pop.	100	tertiary	51

Society

No. of households	3.4m	Colour TV households, % with:	
Av. no. per household	2.3	cable	93.8
Marriages per 1,000 pop.	5.5	satellite	17.7
Divorces per 1,000 pop.	2.7	Telephone lines per 100 pop.	57.1
Cost of living, Dec. 2011		Mobile telephone subscribers	
New York = 100	157	per 100 pop.	124.3
Cars per 1,000 pop.	518	Broadband subs per 100 pop.	37.9
		Internet hosts per 1,000 pop.	706.5

TAIWAN

Area	36,179 sq km	Capital	Taipei
Arable as % of total land	...	Currency	Taiwan dollar (T$)

People

Population	23.0m	Life expectancy:[a] men	75.7 yrs
Pop. per sq km	635.7	women	81.5 yrs
Av. ann. growth		Adult literacy	96.1%
in pop. 2010–15	0.15%	Fertility rate (per woman)	1.1
Pop. under 15	16.7%	Urban population	...
Pop. over 60	14.5%		per 1,000 pop.
No. of men per 100 women	101	Crude birth rate	9.0
Human Development Index	...	Crude death rate[a]	7.1

The economy

GDP	T$13,603bn	GDP per head	$18,570
GDP	$430bn	GDP per head in purchasing	
Av. ann. growth in real		power parity (USA=100)	75.5
GDP 2005–10	4.1%	Economic freedom index	71.9

Origins of GDP		Components of GDP	
	% of total		% of total
Agriculture	2	Private consumption	58
Industry, of which:	32	Public consumption	12
manufacturing	27	Investment	23
Services	66	Exports	74
		Imports	-67

Structure of employment

	% of total		% of labour force
Agriculture	5	Unemployed 2010	5.9
Industry	37	Av. ann. rate 1995–2010	3.7
Services	59		

Energy

	m TOE		
Total output	...	Net energy imports as %	
Total consumption	...	of energy use	...
Consumption per head,			
kg oil equivalent	...		

Inflation and finance

Consumer price		av. ann. increase 2005–10	
inflation 2011	1.4%	Narrow money (M1)	7.8%
Av. ann. inflation 2006–11	1.4%	Broad money (M2)	4.8%
Interbank rate, end 2011	0.41%		

Exchange rates

	end 2011		2011
T$ per $	30.31	Effective rates	2005 = 100
T$ per SDR	46.69	– nominal	...
T$ per €	39.26	– real	...

Trade

Principal exports		**Principal imports**	
	$bn fob		*$bn cif*
Electronic products	131.3	Intermediate goods	189.7
Basic metals	25.9	Capital goods	41.8
Precision instruments,		Consumer goods	19.9
clocks & watches	23.6		
Plastics & plastic articles	22.3		
Total incl. others	**274.6**	Total	**251.4**

Main export destinations		**Main origins of imports**	
	% of total		*% of total*
China	29.4	Japan	20.7
Hong Kong	14.5	China	14.3
United States	12.0	United States	10.1
Japan	6.9	South Korea	6.4

Balance of payments, reserves and debt, $bn

Visible exports fob	274.3	Change in reserves	33.8
Visible imports fob	-243.4	Level of reserves	
Trade balance	26.9	end Dec.	382.0
Invisibles inflows	63.3	No. months of import cover	16.1
Invisibles outflows	47.5	Official gold holdings, m oz	0.0
Net transfers	-2.7	Foreign debt	102.0
Current account balance	39.9	– as % of GDP	24
– as % of GDP	9.3	– as % of total exports	30
Capital balance	0.1	Debt service ratio	4
Overall balance	40.2	Aid given	0.38
		% of GDP	0.10

Health and education

Health spending, % of GDP	...	Education spending, % of GDP	...
Doctors per 1,000 pop.	...	Enrolment, %: primary	...
Hospital beds per 1,000 pop.	...	secondary	...
Improved-water source access,		tertiary	...
% of pop.	...		

Society

No. of households	7.7m	Colour TV households, % with:	
Av. no. per household	3.0	cable	82.6
Marriages per 1,000 pop.	7.3	satellite	0.4
Divorces per 1,000 pop.	3.7	Telephone lines per 100 pop.	70.1
Cost of living, Dec. 2011		Mobile telephone subscribers	
New York = 100	90	per 100 pop.	119.9
Cars per 1,000 pop.	249	Broadband subs per 100 pop.	22.7
		Internet hosts per 1,000 pop.	270.7

a 2012 estimate.

THAILAND

Area	513,115 sq km	Capital	Bangkok
Arable as % of total land	29.9	Currency	Baht (Bt)

People

Population	68.1m	Life expectancy: men	71.1 yrs
Pop. per sq km	132.7	women	78.8 yrs
Av. ann. growth		Adult literacy	93.5%
in pop. 2010–15	0.50%	Fertility rate (per woman)	1.5
Pop. under 15	21.5%	Urban population	35.6%
Pop. over 60	11.7%		per 1,000 pop.
No. of men per 100 women	96.7	Crude birth rate	11.5
Human Development Index	68.2	Crude death rate	9.5

The economy

GDP	Bt10,105bn	GDP per head	$4,610
GDP	$319bn	GDP per head in purchasing	
Av. ann. growth in real		power parity (USA=100)	18.1
GDP 2005–10	3.6%	Economic freedom index	64.9

Origins of GDP		**Components of GDP**	
	% of total		% of total
Agriculture	12	Private consumption	54
Industry, of which:	45	Public consumption	13
manufacturing	36	Investment	26
Services	43	Exports	71
		Imports	-64

Structure of employment

	% of total		% of labour force
Agriculture	42	Unemployed 2009	1.2
Industry	20	Av. ann. rate 1995–2009	1.7
Services	38		

Energy

	m TOE		
Total output	61.7	Net energy imports as %	
Total consumption	103.3	of energy use	40
Consumption per head,			
kg oil equivalent	1,504		

Inflation and finance

Consumer price		av. ann. increase 2005–10	
inflation 2011	3.8%	Narrow money	7.9%
Av. ann. inflation 2006–11	2.8%	Broad money	8.2%
Money market rate, 2011	2.80%		

Exchange rates

	end 2011		2011
Bt per $	31.69	Effective rates	2005 = 100
Bt per SDR	48.66	– nominal	...
Bt per €	41.00	– real	...

Trade

Principal exports		Principal imports	
	$bn fob		*$bn cif*
Electronics	33.6	Machinery, equip. & supplies	32.9
Vehicles, parts & accessories	22.4	Fuel & lubricants	31.9
Agri-manufacturing products	21.6	Electrical & electronic parts	26.7
Machinery & equipment	14.9	Minerals & base metals	20.6
Total incl. others	**195.3**	Total incl. others	**182.9**

Main export destinations		Main origins of imports	
	% of total		*% of total*
China	11.0	Japan	20.8
Japan	10.5	China	13.3
United States	10.4	United States	5.9
Hong Kong	6.7	United Arab Emirates	5.9

Balance of payments, reserves and debt, $bn

Visible exports fob	193.6	Change in reserves	33.6
Visible imports fob	-161.3	Level of reserves	
Trade balance	32.3	end Dec.	172.0
Invisibles inflows	40.1	No. months of import cover	9.2
Invisibles outflows	-62.5	Official gold holdings, m oz	3.2
Net transfers	4.8	Foreign debt	71.3
Current account balance	14.8	– as % of GDP	24
– as % of GDP	4.6	– as % of total exports	31
Capital balance	17.2	Debt service ratio	5
Overall balance	31.2	Aid given	0.01
		– as % of GDP	0.00

Health and education

Health spending, % of GDP	3.9	Education spending, % of GDP	3.8
Doctors per 1,000 pop.	0.3	Enrolment, %: primary	91
Hospital beds per 1,000 pop.	2.1	secondary	79
Improved-water source access,		tertiary	48
% of pop.	96		

Society

No. of households	18.5m	Colour TV households, % with:	
Av. no. per household	3.5	cable	9.2
Marriages per 1,000 pop.	4.3	satellite	4.6
Divorces per 1,000 pop.	1.1	Telephone lines per 100 pop.	10.0
Cost of living, Dec. 2011		Mobile telephone subscribers	
New York = 100	89	per 100 pop.	103.6
Cars per 1,000 pop.	53	Broadband subs per 100 pop.	4.6
		Internet hosts per 1,000 pop.	48.3

TURKEY

Area	779,452 sq km	Capital	Ankara
Arable as % of total land	27.7	Currency	Turkish Lira (YTL)

People

Population	75.7m	Life expectancy: men		72.0 yrs
Pop. per sq km	97.1		women	76.6 yrs
Av. ann. growth		Adult literacy		90.8%
in pop. 2010–15	1.41%	Fertility rate (per woman)		2.0
Pop. under 15	26.4%	Urban population		75.1%
Pop. over 60	9.0%			per 1,000 pop.
No. of men per 100 women	99.5	Crude birth rate		16.9
Human Development Index	69.9	Crude death rate		5.5

The economy

GDP	YTL1,104bn	GDP per head	$10,090
GDP	$734bn	GDP per head in purchasing	
Av. ann. growth in real		power parity (USA=100)	33.3
GDP 2005–10	3.2%	Economic freedom index	62.5

Origins of GDP

Components of GDP

	% of total		% of total
Agriculture	10	Private consumption	71
Industry, of which:	27	Public consumption	14
manufacturing	18	Investment	20
Services	64	Exports	21
		Imports	-27

Structure of employment

	% of total		% of labour force
Agriculture	24	Unemployed 2010	11.9
Industry	26	Av. ann. rate 1995–2010	9.3
Services	50		

Energy

	m TOE		
Total output	30.3	Net energy imports as %	
Total consumption	97.7	of energy use	69
Consumption per head,			
kg oil equivalent	1,359		

Inflation and finance

			av. ann. increase 2005–10
Consumer price			
inflation 2011	6.5%	Narrow money (M1)	16.9%
Av. ann. inflation 2006–11	8.1%	Broad money	18.6%
Money market rate, 2011	2.99%		

Exchange rates

	end 2011		2011
YTL per $	1.89	Effective rates	2005 = 100
YTL per SDR	2.91	– nominal	...
YTL per €	2.45	– real	...

Trade

Principal exports		Principal imports	
	$bn fob		*$bn cif*
Agricultural products	21.6	Chemicals	27.0
Transport equipment	14.9	Fuels	21.4
Iron & steel	14.5	Transport equipment	15.8
Textiles & clothing	11.8	Mechanical machinery	15.5
Total incl. others	**113.9**	Total incl. others	**185.5**

Main export destinations		Main origins of imports	
	% of total		*% of total*
Germany	10.1	Russia	11.6
Italy	5.7	Germany	9.5
France	5.7	China	9.3
United Kingdom	5.3	United States	6.6
Iraq	5.3	Italy	5.5
EU27	46.3	EU27	39.3

Balance of payments, reserves and debt, $bn

Visible exports fob	120.9	Change in reserves	11.0
Visible imports fob	-177.3	Level of reserves	
Trade balance	-56.4	end Dec.	86.0
Invisibles inflows	39.2	No. months of import cover	4.9
Invisibles outflows	-31.3	Official gold holdings, m oz	3.7
Net transfers	1.4	Foreign debt	293.9
Current account balance	-47.1	– as % of GDP	39
– as % of GDP	-6.4	– as % of total exports	165
Capital balance	57.9	Debt service ratio	37
Overall balance	15.0	Aid given	0.97
		% of GDP	0.13

Health and education

Health spending, % of GDP	6.7	Education spending, % of GDP	...
Doctors per 1,000 pop.	1.5	Enrolment, %: primary	102
Hospital beds per 1,000 pop.	2.5	secondary	78
Improved-water source access,		tertiary	46
% of pop.	100		

Society

No. of households	18.6m	Colour TV households, % with:	
Av. no. per household	3.9	cable	13.6
Marriages per 1,000 pop.	6.2	satellite	45.1
Divorces per 1,000 pop.	1.6	Telephone lines per 100 pop.	22.3
Cost of living, Dec. 2011		Mobile telephone subscribers	
New York = 100	92	per 100 pop.	84.9
Cars per 1,000 pop.	103	Broadband subs per 100 pop.	9.7
		Internet hosts per 1,000 pop.	51.5

UKRAINE

Area	603,700 sq km	Capital	Kiev
Arable as % of total land	56.1	Currency	Hryvnya (UAH)

People

Population	45.4m	Life expectancy: men		63.5 yrs
Pop. per sq km	75.2		women	74.6 yrs
Av. ann. growth		Adult literacy		99.7%
in pop. 2010–15	-0.55%	Fertility rate (per woman)		1.5
Pop. under 15	13.9%	Urban population		69.7%
Pop. over 60	20.9%			per 1,000 pop.
No. of men per 100 women	85.2	Crude birth rate		10.9
Human Development Index	72.9	Crude death rate		16.2

The economy

GDP	UAH1,095bn	GDP per head	$3,010
GDP	$138bn	GDP per head in purchasing	
Av. ann. growth in real		power parity (USA=100)	14.3
GDP 2005–10	1.0%	Economic freedom index	46.1

Origins of GDP		Components of GDP	
	% of total		% of total
Agriculture	8	Private consumption	63
Industry, of which:	31	Public consumption	20
manufacturing	17	Investment	19
Services	61	Exports	50
		Imports	-53

Structure of employment

	% of total		% of labour force
Agriculture	16	Unemployed 2009	8.8
Industry	23	Av. ann. rate 1995–2009	8.8
Services	61		

Energy

	m TOE		
Total output	76.9	Net energy imports as %	
Total consumption	115.5	of energy use	33
Consumption per head,			
kg oil equivalent	2,507		

Inflation and finance

		av. ann. increase 2005–10	
Consumer price			
inflation 2011	8.0%	Narrow money (M1)	24.1%
Av. ann. inflation 2006–11	14.1%	Broad money	25.2%
Money market rate, 2011	7.11%		

Exchange rates

	end 2011		2011
UAH per $	7.99	Effective rates	2005 = 100
UAH per SDR	12.27	– nominal	66.5
UAH per €	10.34	– real	104.0

Trade

Principal exports		Principal imports	
	$bn fob		$bn cif
Non-precious metals	17.3	Fuels and mineral products	19.6
Food & agricultural produce	9.9	Machinery & equipment	12.7
Machinery & equipment	9.2	Chemicals	6.4
Fuels & mineral products	6.7	Food & agricultural produce	5.8
Chemicals	3.5		
Total incl. others	**51.5**	Total incl. others	**60.9**

Main export destinations		Main origins of imports	
	% of total		% of total
Russia	26.1	Russia	36.6
Turkey	5.9	China	7.8
Italy	4.7	Germany	7.6
Belarus	3.7	Poland	4.6
Poland	3.5	Belarus	4.2

Balance of payments, reserves and debt, $bn

Visible exports fob	52.2	Change in reserves	8.1
Visible imports fob	-60.6	Level of reserves	
Trade balance	-8.4	end Dec.	34.6
Invisibles inflows	21.8	No. months of import cover	5.2
Invisibles outflows	-19.4	Official gold holdings, m oz	0.9
Net transfers	3.0	Foreign debt	116.8
Current account balance	-3.0	– as % of GDP	75
– as % of GDP	-2.2	– as % of total exports	144
Capital balance	6.3	Debt service ratio	41
Overall balance	5.0		

Health and education

Health spending, % of GDP	7.7	Education spending, % of GDP	5.3
Doctors per 1,000 pop.	3.2	Enrolment, %: primary	99
Hospital beds per 1,000 pop.	8.7	secondary	96
Improved-water source access,		tertiary	79
% of pop.	98		

Society

No. of households	20.0m	Colour TV households, % with:	
Av. no. per household	2.3	cable	21.6
Marriages per 1,000 pop.	6.7	satellite	13.1
Divorces per 1,000 pop.	2.7	Telephone lines per 100 pop.	28.5
Cost of living, Dec. 2011		Mobile telephone subscribers	
New York = 100	72	per 100 pop.	118.6
Cars per 1,000 pop.	118	Broadband subs per 100 pop.	6.5
		Internet hosts per 1,000 pop.	44.0

UNITED ARAB EMIRATES

Area	83,600 sq km	Capital	Abu Dhabi
Arable as % of total land	1.9	Currency	Dirham (AED)

People

Population	4.7m	Life expectancy: men		76.0 yrs
Pop. per sq km	56.2		women	78.0 yrs
Av. ann. growth		Adult literacy		90.0%
in pop. 2010–15	2.17%	Fertility rate (per woman)		1.7
Pop. under 15	19.1%	Urban population		85.5%
Pop. over 60	2.0%			per 1,000 pop.
No. of men per 100 women	228.3	Crude birth rate		12.3
Human Development Index	84.6	Crude death rate		1.4

The economy

GDP	AED1,093bn	GDP per head	$39,620
GDP	$298bn	GDP per head in purchasing	
Av. ann. growth in real		power parity (USA=100)	100.1
GDP 2005–10	3.6%	Economic freedom index	69.3

Origins of GDP		**Components of GDP**	
	% of total		% of total
Agriculture	1	Private consumption	57
Industry, of which:	54	Public consumption	8
manufacturing	10	Investment	25
Services	46	Exports	78
		Imports	-69

Structure of employment

	% of total		% of labour force
Agriculture	8	Unemployed 2008	4.0
Industry	22	Av. ann. rate 1995–2008	2.6
Services	70		

Energy

			m TOE
Total output	168.8	Net energy imports as %	
Total consumption	59.6	of energy use	-183
Consumption per head,			
kg oil equivalent	8,588		

Inflation and finance

Consumer price		av. ann. increase 2005–10	
inflation 2011	0.9%	Narrow money (M1)	17.4%
Av. ann. inflation 2006–11	5.2%	Broad money	19.4%
Interbank rate, end 2011	1.52%		

Exchange rates

	end 2011		2011
AED per $	3.67	Effective rates	2005 = 100
AED per SDR	5.64	– nominal	97.0
AED per €	4.75	– real	...

Trade

Principal exports		Principal imports	
	$bn fob		*$bn cif*
Re-exports	86.2	Precious stones & metals	37.9
Crude oil	60.0	Machinery & electrical equip.	25.7
Gas	11.6	Vehicles & other transport equipment	16.4
		Base metals & related products	11.4
Total incl. others	**212.3**	Total incl. others	**183.4**

Main export destinations		Main origins of imports	
	% of total		*% of total*
India	16.0	India	18.9
Japan	15.1	China	13.6
Iran	11.6	United States	7.5
South Korea	6.3	Germany	5.5

Balance of payments, reserves and debt, $bn

Visible exports fob	212.3	Change in reserves	6.7
Visible imports fob	-161.4	Level of reserves	
Trade balance	50.9	end Dec.	42.8
Invisibles, net	-28.4	No. months of import cover	2.5
Net transfers	-11.3	Official gold holdings, m oz	0.0
Current account balance	11.3	Foreign debt	152.0
– as % of GDP	3.8	– as % of GDP	51.0
Capital balance	2.0	– as % of total exports	63.0
Overall balance	7.3	Debt service ratio	6
		Aid given	0.41
		% of GDP	0.16

Health and education

Health spending, % of GDP	3.7	Education spending, % of GDP	1.0
Doctors per 1,000 pop.	2.0	Enrolment, %: primary	...
Hospital beds per 1,000 pop.	1.9	secondary	...
Improved-water source access,		tertiary	...
% of pop.	100		

Society

No. of households	0.7m	Colour TV households, % with:	
Av. no. per household	6.3	cable	51.3
Marriages per 1,000 pop.	3.7	satellite	98.1
Divorces per 1,000 pop.	1.1	Telephone lines per 100 pop.	19.7
Cost of living, Dec. 2011		Mobile telephone subscribers	
New York = 100	76	per 100 pop.	145.5
Cars per 1,000 pop.	228	Broadband subs per 100 pop.	10.5
		Internet hosts per 1,000 pop.	79.1

UNITED KINGDOM

Area	242,534 sq km	Capital	London
Arable as % of total land	25.0	Currency	Pound (£)

People

Population	61.9m	Life expectancy:	men	78.3 yrs
Pop. per sq km	255.2		women	82.4 yrs
Av. ann. growth		Adult literacy		...
in pop. 2010–15	0.60%	Fertility rate (per woman)		1.9
Pop. under 15	17.4%	Urban population		80.1%
Pop. over 60	22.7%			per 1,000 pop.
No. of men per 100 women	96.8	Crude birth rate		12.1
Human Development Index	86.3	Crude death rate		9.4

The economy

GDP	£1,464bn	GDP per head	$36,340
GDP	$2,262bn	GDP per head in purchasing	
Av. ann. growth in real		power parity (USA=100)	75.7
GDP 2005–10	0.5%	Economic freedom index	74.1

Origins of GDP		**Components of GDP**	
	% of total		% of total
Agriculture	1	Private consumption	64
Industry, of which:	22	Public consumption	23
manufacturing	11	Investment	15
Services	78	Exports	30
		Imports	-33

Structure of employment

	% of total		% of labour force
Agriculture	1	Unemployed 2010	7.8
Industry	19	Av. ann. rate 1995–2010	6.1
Services	80		

Energy

	m TOE		
Total output	158.9	Net energy imports as %	
Total consumption	196.8	of energy use	19
Consumption per head,			
kg oil equivalent	3,183		

Inflation and finance

Consumer price		av. ann. increase 2005–10	
inflation 2011	4.5%	Narrow money	...
Av. ann. inflation 2006–11	3.2%	Broad money	10.1%
Money market rate, 2011	0.52%	Household saving rate[a], 2011	7.4%

Exchange rates

	end 2011		2011
£ per $	0.65	Effective rates	2005 = 100
£ per SDR	0.99	– nominal	79.7
£ per €	0.84	– real	86.6

Trade

Principal exports

	$bn fob
Machinery & transport equip.	139.2
Chemicals & related products	77.0
Mineral fuels & lubricants	51.3
Food, drink & tobacco	24.3
Total incl. others	**410.6**

Principal imports

	$bn fob
Machinery & transport equip.	198.1
Chemicals & related products	69.7
Mineral fuels & lubricants	62.1
Food, drink & tobacco	51.0
Total incl. others	**562.8**

Main export destinations

	% of total
United States	10.4
Germany	10.1
Netherlands	7.7
France	7.0
Ireland	6.2
EU27	53.9

Main origins of imports

	% of total
Germany	12.6
China	8.7
Netherlands	7.2
France	5.8
United States	5.6
EU27	51.5

Balance of payments, reserves and aid, $bn

Visible exports fob	410.2	Overall balance	10.0
Visible imports fob	-563.2	Change in reserves	15.8
Trade balance	-152.9	Level of reserves	
Invisibles inflows	494.2	end Dec.	82.4
Invisibles outflows	-382.1	No. months of import cover	1.0
Net transfers	-30.8	Official gold holdings, m oz	10.0
Current account balance	-71.6	Aid given	13.05
– as % of GDP	-3.2	– as % of GDP	0.57
Capital balance	68.6		

Health and education

Health spending, % of GDP	9.6	Education spending, % of GDP	5.4
Doctors per 1,000 pop.	2.7	Enrolment, %: primary	106
Hospital beds per 1,000 pop.	3.3	secondary	102
Improved-water source access,		tertiary	59
% of pop.	100		

Society

No. of households	27.4m	Colour TV households, % with:	
Av. no. per household	2.3	cable	13.9
Marriages per 1,000 pop.	5.1	satellite	38.8
Divorces per 1,000 pop.	3.0	Telephone lines per 100 pop.	53.8
Cost of living, Dec. 2011		Mobile telephone subscribers	
New York = 100	117	per 100 pop.	130.8
Cars per 1,000 pop.	500	Broadband subs per 100 pop.	31.6
		Internet hosts per 1,000 pop.	153.9

a Gross.

UNITED STATES

Area	9,372,610 sq km	Capital	Washington DC
Arable as % of total land	17.8	Currency	US dollar ($)

People

Population	317.6m	Life expectancy: men	76.2 yrs
Pop. per sq km	33.9	women	81.3 yrs
Av. ann. growth		Adult literacy	...
in pop. 2010–15	0.85%	Fertility rate (per woman)	2.1
Pop. under 15	20.2%	Urban population	83.3%
Pop. over 60	18.2%		per 1,000 pop.
No. of men per 100 women	97.4	Crude birth rate	13.7
Human Development Index	91.0	Crude death rate	8.3

The economy

GDP	$14,587bn	GDP per head	$47,150
Av. ann. growth in real		GDP per head in purchasing	
GDP 2005–10	0.7%	power parity (USA=100)	100
		Economic freedom index	76.3

Origins of GDP		Components of GDP	
	% of total		% of total
Agriculture	1	Private consumption	71
Industry, of which:	20	Public consumption	17
manufacturing	13	Non-government investment	15
Services[a]	79	Exports	13
		Imports	-16

Structure of employment

	% of total		% of labour force
Agriculture	2	Unemployed 2010	9.6
Industry	17	Av. ann. rate 1995–2010	5.6
Services	81		

Energy

	m TOE		
Total output	1,686	Net energy imports as %	
Total consumption	2,163	of energy use	23
Consumption per head,			
kg oil equivalent	7,051		

Inflation and finance

Consumer price		av. ann. increase 2005–10	
inflation 2011	3.2%	Narrow money (M1)	6.0%
Av. ann. inflation 2006–11	2.2%	Broad money	5.1%
Fed funds rate, 2011	0.10%	Household saving rate, 2011	4.7%

Exchange rates

	end 2011		2011
$ per SDR	1.54	Effective rates	2005 = 100
$ per €	1.29	– nominal	90.3
		– real	89.9

Trade

Principal exports		Principal imports	
	$bn fob		*$bn fob*
Capital goods, excl. vehicles	446.6	Industrial supplies	602.7
Industrial supplies	391.8	Consumer goods, excl. vehicles	483.3
Consumer goods, excl. vehicles	165.9	Capital goods, excl. vehicles	449.2
Vehicles & products	112.0	Vehicles & products	225.1
Total incl. others	**1,278.3**	**Total incl. others**	**1,913.2**

Main export destinations		Main origins of imports	
	% of total		*% of total*
Canada	19.4	China	20.0
Mexico	12.8	Canada	14.7
China	7.2	Mexico	12.1
Japan	4.7	Japan	6.5
United Kingdom	3.8	Germany	4.4
Germany	3.8	United Kingdom	2.6
EU27	19.2	EU27	16.9

Balance of payments, reserves and aid, $bn

Visible exports fob	1,293	Overall balance	2
Visible imports fob	-1,936	Change in reserves	84.8
Trade balance	-642	Level of reserves	
Invisibles inflows	1,208	end Dec.	488.9
Invisibles outflows	-900	No. months of import cover	2.1
Net transfers	-136	Official gold holdings, m oz	261.5
Current account balance	-471	Aid given	30.35
– as % of GDP	-3.2	– as % of GDP	0.21
Capital balance	256		

Health and education

Health spending, % of GDP	17.9	Education spending, % of GDP	5.5
Doctors per 1,000 pop.	2.4	Enrolment, %: primary	102
Hospital beds per 1,000 pop.	3.0	secondary	96
Improved-water source access,		tertiary	95
% of pop.	99		

Society

No. of households	119.9m	Colour TV households, % with:	
Av. no. per household	2.6	cable	58.7
Marriages per 1,000 pop.	6.8	satellite	28.1
Divorces per 1,000 pop.	3.2	Telephone lines per 100 pop.	48.7
Cost of living, Dec. 2011		Mobile telephone subscribers	
New York = 100	100	per 100 pop.	89.9
Cars per 1,000 pop.	447	Broadband subs per 100 pop.	27.6
		Internet hosts per 1,000 pop.[b]	1,709.4

a Including utilities.
b Includes all hosts ending ".com", ".net" and ".org" which exaggerates the numbers.

VENEZUELA

Area	912,050 sq km	Capital	Caracas
Arable as % of total land	3.1	Currency	Bolivar (Bs)

People

Population	29.0m	Life expectancy:	men	71.8 yrs
Pop. per sq km	31.8		women	77.7 yrs
Av. ann. growth		Adult literacy		95.2%
in pop. 2010–15	1.49%	Fertility rate (per woman)		2.4
Pop. under 15	29.5%	Urban population		94.3%
Pop. over 60	8.6%			per 1,000 pop.
No. of men per 100 women	100.7	Crude birth rate		19.8
Human Development Index	73.5	Crude death rate		5.2

The economy

GDP	Bs1,102bn	GDP per head	$13,590
GDP	$392bn	GDP per head in purchasing	
Av. ann. growth in real		power parity (USA=100)	25.9
GDP 2005–10	3.7%	Economic freedom index	38.1

Origins of GDP		**Components of GDP**	
	% of total		% of total
Agriculture	4	Private consumption	57
Industry, of which:	36	Public consumption	11
manufacturing	...	Investment	21
Services	60	Exports	29
		Imports	-17

Structure of employment

	% of total		% of labour force
Agriculture	9	Unemployed 2009	7.6
Industry	23	Av. ann. rate 1995–2009	12.1
Services	68		

Energy

	m TOE		
Total output	263.5	Net energy imports as %	
Total consumption	66.9	of energy use	-204
Consumption per head,			
kg oil equivalent	2,357		

Inflation and finance

Consumer price		av. ann. increase 2005–10	
inflation 2011	27.1%	Narrow money	48.0%
Av. ann. inflation 2006–11	26.9%	Broad money	36.2%
Money market rate, 2011	4.93%		

Exchange rates

	end 2011		2011
Bs per $	4.29	Effective rates	2005 = 100
Bs per SDR	9.59	– nominal	46.1
Bs per €	5.55	– real	159.5

Trade

Principal exports		Principal imports	
	$bn fob		$bn fob
Oil	63.5	Intermediate goods	17.8
Non-oil	2.3	Capital goods	8.3
		Consumer goods	7.6
Total	**65.7**	**Total**	**33.8**

Main export destinations		Main origins of imports	
	% of total		% of total
United States	40.2	United States	28.8
China	7.9	Colombia	8.6
Netherlands Antilles	7.7	Brazil	8.6
Colombia	5.4	Mexico	4.3

Balance of payments, reserves and debt, $bn

Visible exports fob	65.8	Change in reserves	-4.7
Visible imports fob	-38.6	Level of reserves	
Trade balance	27.2	end Dec.	29.7
Invisibles inflows	3.7	No. months of import cover	6.5
Invisibles outflows	-15.9	Official gold holdings, m oz	11.8
Net transfers	-0.6	Foreign debt	55.6
Current account balance	14.4	– as % of GDP	...
– as % of GDP	3.7	– as % of total exports	...
Capital balance	-18.7	Debt service ratio	...
Overall balance	-7.9		

Health and education

Health spending, % of GDP	4.9	Education spending, % of GDP	3.7
Doctors per 1,000 pop.	...	Enrolment, %: primary	103
Hospital beds per 1,000 pop.	1.3	secondary	83
Improved-water source access, % of pop.	...	tertiary	78

Society

No. of households	6.5m	Colour TV households, % with:	
Av. no. per household	4.5	cable	27.7
Marriages per 1,000 pop.	2.5	satellite	5.4
Divorces per 1,000 pop.	0.9	Telephone lines per 100 pop.	24.4
Cost of living, Dec. 2011		Mobile telephone subscribers	
New York = 100	109	per 100 pop.	96.2
Cars per 1,000 pop.	94	Broadband subs per 100 pop.	5.4
		Internet hosts per 1,000 pop.	14.1

VIETNAM

Area	331,114 sq km	Capital	Hanoi
Arable as % of total land	20.3	Currency	Dong (D)

People

Population	89.0m	Life expectancy: men		73.4 yrs
Pop. per sq km	268.8		women	77.4 yrs
Av. ann. growth		Adult literacy		92.8%
in pop. 2010–15	1.49%	Fertility rate (per woman)		1.8
Pop. under 15	25.1%	Urban population		33.6%
Pop. over 60	6.7%			per 1,000 pop.
No. of men per 100 women	97.7	Crude birth rate		15.9
Human Development Index	59.3	Crude death rate		5.2

The economy

GDP	D1,981trn	GDP per head	$1,220
GDP	$106bn	GDP per head in purchasing	
Av. ann. growth in real		power parity (USA=100)	6.8
GDP 2005–10	7.0%	Economic freedom index	51.3

Origins of GDP		**Components of GDP**	
	% of total		% of total
Agriculture	21	Private consumption	65
Industry, of which:	41	Public consumption	7
manufacturing	20	Investment	39
Services	38	Exports	78
		Imports	-88

Structure of employment

	% of total		% of labour force
Agriculture	...	Unemployed 2004	2.1
Industry	...	Av. ann. rate 2003–04	2.2
Services	...		

Energy

	m TOE		
Total output	76.6	Net energy imports as %	
Total consumption	64.0	of energy use	-20
Consumption per head,			
kg oil equivalent	745		

Inflation and finance

Consumer price		av. ann. increase 2005–10	
inflation 2010	8.9%	Narrow money (M1)	20.9
Av. ann. inflation 2006–10	11.7%	Broad money	30.7
Refinancing rate, end 2011	15.0%		

Exchange rates

	end 2011		2011
D per $	16,977	Effective rates	2005 = 100
D per SDR	26,149	– nominal	...
D per €	21,966	– real	...

Trade

Principal exports		Principal imports	
	$bn fob		*$bn cif*
Textiles & garments	11.2	Machinery & equipment	13.5
Footwear	5.1	Steel	6.2
Fisheries products	5.0	Petroleum products	5.7
Crude oil	4.9	Textiles	5.4
Total incl. others	**71.7**	Total incl. others	**83.8**

Main export destinations		Main origins of imports	
	% of total		*% of total*
United States	19.9	China	23.9
Japan	10.8	South Korea	11.7
China	10.2	Japan	10.8
South Korea	4.3	Thailand	6.7
Australia	3.8	Singapore	4.9
Switzerland	3.7	United States	4.5
Germany	3.3	Malaysia	4.1

Balance of payments, reserves and debt, $bn

Visible exports fob	72.2	Change in reserves	-3.9
Visible imports fob	-77.3	Level of reserves	
Trade balance	-5.1	end Dec.	12.9
Invisibles inflows	7.9	No. months of import cover	1.7
Invisibles outflows	-14.9	Official gold holdings, m oz	...
Net transfers	7.9	Foreign debt	35.1
Current account balance	-4.3	– as % of GDP	30
– as % of GDP	-4.0	– as % of total exports	37
Capital balance	6.2	Debt service ratio	2
Overall balance	-1.8		

Health and education

Health spending, % of GDP	6.8	Education spending, % of GDP	5.3
Doctors per 1,000 pop.	1.2	Enrolment, %: primary	...
Hospital beds per 1,000 pop.	3.1	secondary	...
Improved-water source access,		tertiary	...
% of pop.	95		

Society

No. of households	20.1m	Colour TV households, % with:	
Av. no. per household	4.3	cable	0.8
Marriages per 1,000 pop.	5.7	satellite	1.4
Divorces per 1,000 pop.	0.2	Telephone lines per 100 pop.	18.7
Cost of living, Dec. 2011		Mobile telephone subscribers	
New York = 100	67	per 100 pop.	175.3
Cars per 1,000 pop.	...	Broadband subs per 100 pop.	4.1
		Internet hosts per 1,000 pop.	2.0

ZIMBABWE

Area	390,759 sq km	Capital	Harare
Arable as % of total land	10.8	Currency	Zimbabwe dollar (Z$)

People

Population	12.6m	Life expectancy: men	54.0 yrs
Pop. per sq km	32.2	women	52.7 yrs
Av. ann. growth		Adult literacy	91.9%
in pop. 2010–15	2.15%	Fertility rate (per woman)	3.1
Pop. under 15	39.5%	Urban population	40.6%
Pop. over 60	5.8%		per 1,000 pop.
No. of men per 100 women	97.2	Crude birth rate	28.7
Human Development Index	37.6	Crude death rate	11.7

The economy

GDP[a]	$7.5bn	GDP per head[a]	$590
Av. ann. growth in real		GDP per head in purchasing	
GDP 2005–10	-2.6%	power parity (USA=100)[a]	0.9
		Economic freedom index	26.3

Origins of GDP		**Components of GDP**	
	% of total		% of total
Agriculture	17	Private consumption	101
Industry, of which:	29	Public consumption	17
manufacturing	15	Investment	1
Services	53	Exports	37
		Imports	-56

Structure of employment

	% of total		% of labour force
Agriculture	...	Unemployed 2004	4.2
Industry	...	Av. ann. rate 1997–2004	6.4
Services	...		

Energy

	m TOE		
Total output	8.5	Net energy imports as %	
Total consumption	9.5	of energy use	10
Consumption per head,			
kg oil equivalent	763		

Inflation[a] and finance

Consumer price		av. ann. increase 2005–10	
inflation 2011	6.5%	Narrow money (M1)	...
Av. ann. inflation 2006–11	212%	Broad money	...
Treasury bill rate, Dec. 2010	7.5%		

Exchange rates

	end 2011		2011
Z$ per $	...	Effective rates	2005 = 100
Z$ per SDR	...	– nominal	...
Z$ per €	...	– real	...

Trade

Principal exports		**Principal imports**	
	$bn fob		*$bn cif*
Gold	0.5	Machinery & transportation	
Ferro-alloys	0.4	equipment	0.5
Tobacco	0.4	Fuels & energy	0.4
Platinum	0.3	Manufactures	0.3
		Chemicals	0.2
Total incl. others	**2.1**	Total incl. others	**3.8**

Main export destinations		**Main origins of imports**	
	% of total		*% of total*
Congo-Kinshasa	14.8	South Africa	56.1
South Africa	13.4	China	8.4
Botswana	13.2	Botswana	3.4
China	12.7	Zambia	3.2
Netherlands	5.9	Malawi	2.2

Balance of payments[a], reserves[a] and debt, $bn

Visible exports fob	3.4	Change in reserves	-0.1
Visible imports fob	-5.2	Level of reserves	
Trade balance	-1.8	end Dec.	0.3
Invisibles, net	-0.9	No. months of import cover	0.5
Net transfers	1.2	Official gold holdings, m oz	0.0
Current account balance	-1.5	Foreign debt	5.0
– as % of GDP	-26.3	– as % of GDP[b]	110
Capital balance	0.5	– as % of total exports	275
Overall balance	-0.6	Debt service ratio[ab]	...

Health and education

Health spending, % of GDP	...	Education spending, % of GDP	2.5
Doctors per 1,000 pop.	...	Enrolment, %: primary	...
Hospital beds per 1,000 pop.	...	secondary	...
Improved-water source access,		tertiary	6
% of pop.	80		

Society

No. of households	3.5m	Colour TV households, % with:	
Av. no. per household	3.6	cable	...
Marriages per 1,000 pop.	...	satellite	...
Divorces per 1,000 pop.	...	Telephone lines per 100 pop.	3.0
Cost of living, Dec. 2011		Mobile telephone subscribers	
New York = 100	...	per 100 pop.	61.3
Cars per 1,000 pop.	45	Broadband subs per 100 pop.	0.3
		Internet hosts per 1,000 pop.	2.4

a Estimates.
b 2008

EURO AREA[a]

Area	2,573,704 sq km	Capital	–
Arable as % of total land	24.4	Currency	Euro (€)

People

Population	328.2m	Life expectancy: men		79.5 yrs
Pop. per sq km	127.5	women		85.1 yrs
Av. ann. growth		Adult literacy		...
in pop. 2010–15	0.24%	Fertility rate (per woman)		1.6
Pop. under 15	15.4%	Urban population		76.4%
Pop. over 60	23.8%			per 1,000 pop.
No. of men per 100 women	96.1	Crude birth rate		10.2
Human Development Index	88.4	Crude death rate		9.9

The economy

GDP	€9,385bn	GDP per head	$36,620
GDP	$12,149bn	GDP per head in purchasing	
Av. ann. growth in real		power parity (USA=100)	72.8
GDP 2005–10	0.8%	Economic freedom index	66.3

Origins of GDP		**Components of GDP**	
	% of total		% of total
Agriculture	2	Private consumption	58
Industry, of which:	26	Public consumption	22
manufacturing	16	Investment	19
Services	72	Exports	41
		Imports	-39

Structure of employment

	% of total		% of labour force
Agriculture	4	Unemployed 2010	9.3
Industry	25	Av. ann. rate 1995–2010	9.1
Services	71		

Energy

	m TOE		
Total output	473.3	Net energy imports as %	
Total consumption	1,205.7	of energy use	62
Consumption per head,			
kg oil equivalent	3,641		

Inflation and finance

		av. ann. increase 2005–10	
Consumer price			
inflation 2011	2.7%	Narrow money (M1)	6.3%
Av. ann. inflation 2006–11	2.0%	Broad money	5.9%
Interbank rate, 2011	0.87%	Household saving rate, 2011	10.5%

Exchange rates

	end 2011		2011
€ per $	0.77	Effective rates	2005 = 100
€ per SDR	1.19	– nominal	100.6
		– real	94.3

Trade[b]

Principal exports	$bn fob	Principal imports	$bn cif
Machinery & transport equip.	758.4	Machinery & transport equip.	586.5
Manufactures	411.5	Mineral fuels & lubricants	506.0
Chemicals	312.6	Manufactures	477.5
Mineral fuels & lubricants	101.2	Chemicals	182.2
Food, drink & tobacco	100.2	Food, drink & tobacco	107.0
Raw materials	50.2	Raw materials	93.3
Total incl. others	**1,788.1**	Total incl. others	**1,990.9**

Main export destinations	% of total	Main origins of imports	% of total
United States	18.0	China	18.7
China	8.4	United States	11.3
Switzerland	7.8	Russia	10.6
Russia	6.4	Switzerland	5.5
Turkey	4.5	Norway	5.3
Norway	3.1	Japan	4.4

Balance of payments, reserves and aid, $bn

Visible exports fob	2,064	Overall balance	14
Visible imports fob	2,046	Change in reserves	126.9
Trade balance	18	Level of reserves	
Invisibles inflows	1,283	end Dec.	788.0
Invisibles outflows	-1,219	No. months of import cover	2.9
Net transfers	-138	Official gold holdings, m oz	347.0
Current account balance	-56	Aid given[c]	49.6
– as % of GDP	-0.5	– as % of GDP[c]	0.41
Capital balance	81		

Health and education

Health spending, % of GDP	10.8	Education spending, % of GDP	5.5
Doctors per 1,000 pop.	3.6	Enrolment, %: primary	105
Hospital beds per 1,000 pop.	5.8	secondary	107
Improved-water source access,		tertiary	60
% of pop.	100		

Society

No. of households	130.5	Colour TV households, % with:	
Av. no. per household	2.39	cable	43.2
Marriages per 1,000 pop.	4.6	satellite	27.0
Divorces per 1,000 pop.	2.1	Telephone lines per 100 pop.	42.7
Cost of living, Dec. 2011		Mobile telephone subscribers	
New York = 100	...	per 100 pop.	121.1
Cars per 1,000 pop.	496	Broadband subs per 100 pop.	25.5
		Internet hosts per 1,000 pop.	405.9

a Data generally refer to the 16 EU members that had adopted the euro before
   December 31 2010: Austria, Belgium, Cyprus, Finland, France, Germany, Greece,
   Ireland, Italy, Luxembourg, Malta, Netherlands, Portugal, Slovakia, Slovenia and
   Spain. Estonia joined on January 1 2011.
b EU27, excluding intra-trade.   c Excluding Cyprus and Malta.

WORLD

| Area | 148,698,382 sq km | Capital | ... |
| Arable as % of total land | 10.7 | Currency | ... |

People

Population	6,908.7m	Life expectancy: men	67.1 yrs
Pop. per sq km	46.5	women	71.6 yrs
Av. ann. growth		Adult literacy	83.7%
in pop. 2010–15	1.16%	Fertility rate (per woman)	2.5
Pop. under 15	26.9%	Urban population	53.9%
Pop. over 60	11.0%		per 1,000 pop.
No. of men per 100 women	101.7	Crude birth rate	20.0
Human Development Index	68.2	Crude death rate	8.2

The economy

GDP	$63.3trn	GDP per head	$9,170
Av. ann. growth in real		GDP per head in purchasing	
GDP 2005–10	3.6%	power parity (USA=100)	23.2
		Economic freedom index	56.8

Origins of GDP		**Components of GDP**	
	% of total		% of total
Agriculture	3	Private consumption	62
Industry, of which:	25	Public consumption	19
manufacturing	16	Investment	20
Services	72	Exports	28
		Imports	-28

Structure of employment[a]

	% of total		% of labour force
Agriculture	...	Unemployed 2010	8.6
Industry	...	Av. ann. rate 1995–2010	7.1
Services	...		

Energy

	m TOE		
Total output	12,241	Net energy imports as %	
Total consumption	11,787	of energy use	-4
Consumption per head,			
kg oil equivalent	1,788		

Inflation and finance

Consumer price		av. ann. increase 2005–10	
inflation 2011	4.4%	Narrow money (M1)[a]	6.7%
Av. ann. inflation 2006–11	3.9%	Broad money[a]	6.9%
LIBOR $ rate, 3-month, 2011	0.34%	Household saving rate, 2011[a]	6.5%

Trade

World exports

	$bn fob		$bn fob
Manufactures	10,496	Ores & minerals	761
Fuels	1,825	Agricultural raw materials	304
Food	1,217	Total incl. others	**15,211**

Main export destinations

	% of total
United States	11.9
China	8.3
Germany	6.8
France	4.2
Japan	4.1
United Kingdom	3.8

Main origins of imports

	% of total
China	12.0
Germany	8.1
United States	7.9
Japan	5.2
France	3.5
Netherlands	3.4

Balance of payments, reserves and aid, $bn

Visible exports fob	14,971	Overall balance	0
Visible imports fob	-14,696	Change in reserves	1,430
Trade balance	275	Level of reserves	
Invisibles inflows	6,725	end Dec.	11,038
Invisibles outflows	-6,546	No. months of import cover	6
Net transfers	-138	Official gold holdings, m oz	982
Current account balance	316	Aid given[b]	135.7
– as % of GDP	0.5	– as % of GDP[b]	0.32
Capital balance	-249		

Health and education

Health spending, % of GDP	10.4	Education spending, % of GDP	4.6
Doctors per 1,000 pop.	1.4	Enrolment, %: primary	107
Hospital beds per 1,000 pop.	...	secondary	68
Improved-water source access, % of pop.	88	tertiary	27

Society

No. of households	...	Colour TV households, % with:	
Av. no. per household	...	cable	...
Marriages per 1,000 pop.	...	satellite	...
Divorces per 1,000 pop.	...	Telephone lines per 100 pop.	22.4
Cost of living, Dec. 2011		Mobile telephone subscribers	
New York = 100	...	per 100 pop.	91
Cars per 1,000 pop.	...	Broadband subs per 100 pop.	19.8
		Internet hosts per 1,000 pop.	105.9

a OECD countries.
b OECD, non-OECD Europe and Middle East countries.

Glossary

Balance of payments The record of a country's transactions with the rest of the world. The **current account** of the balance of payments consists of: visible trade (goods); "invisible" trade (services and income); private transfer payments (eg, remittances from those working abroad); official transfers (eg, payments to international organisations, famine relief). Visible imports and exports are normally compiled on rather different definitions to those used in the trade statistics (shown in principal imports and exports) and therefore the statistics do not match. The **capital account** consists of long- and short-term transactions relating to a country's assets and liabilities (eg, loans and borrowings). The **current and capital accounts**, plus an errors and omissions item, make up the **overall balance**. **Changes in reserves** include gold at market prices and are shown without the practice often followed in balance of payments presentations of reversing the sign.

Big Mac index A light-hearted way of looking at exchange rates. If the dollar price of a burger at McDonald's in any country is higher than the price in the United States, converting at market exchange rates, then that country's currency could be thought to be over-valued against the dollar and vice versa.

Body-mass index A measure for assessing obesity – weight in kilograms divided by height in metres squared. An index of 30 or more is regarded as an indicator of obesity; 25 to 29.9 as over-weight. Guidelines vary for men and for women and may be adjusted for age.

CFA Communauté Financière Africaine. Its members, most of the francophone African nations, share a common currency, the CFA franc, pegged to the euro.

Cif/fob Measures of the value of merchandise trade. Imports include the cost of "carriage, insurance and freight" (cif) from the exporting country to the importing. The value of exports does not include these elements and is recorded

"free on board" (fob). Balance of payments statistics are generally adjusted so that both exports and imports are shown fob; the cif elements are included in invisibles.

Crude birth rate The number of live births in a year per 1,000 population. The crude rate will automatically be relatively high if a large proportion of the population is of childbearing age.

Crude death rate The number of deaths in a year per 1,000 population. Also affected by the population's age structure.

Debt, foreign Financial obligations owed by a country to the rest of the world and repayable in foreign currency. The **debt service ratio** is debt service (principal repayments plus interest payments) expressed as a percentage of the country's earnings from exports of goods and services.

Economic Freedom Index The ranking includes data on labour and business freedom as well as trade policy, taxation, monetary policy, the banking system, foreign-investment rules, property rights, the amount of economic output consumed by the government, regulation policy, the size of the black market and the extent of wage and price controls.

Effective exchange rate The nominal index measures a currency's depreciation (figures below 100) or appreciation (figures over 100) from a base date against a trade-weighted basket of the currencies of the country's main trading partners. The real effective exchange rate reflects adjustments for relative movements in prices or costs.

EU European Union. Members are: Austria, Belgium, Bulgaria, Cyprus, Czech Republic, Denmark, Estonia, Finland, France, Germany, Greece, Hungary, Ireland, Italy, Latvia, Lithuania, Luxembourg, Malta, Netherlands, Poland, Portugal, Romania, Slovakia, Slovenia, Spain, Sweden and the United Kingdom.

Euro area The 17 euro area members of the EU are Austria, Belgium, Cyprus, Finland, France, Germany, Greece, Ireland, Italy, Luxembourg, Malta, Netherlands, Portugal, Slovakia, Slovenia and Spain. Estonia joined on January 1 2011. Their common currency is the euro, which came into circulation on January 1 2002.

Fertility rate The average number of children born to a woman who completes her childbearing years.

G7 Group of seven countries: United States, Japan, Germany, United Kingdom, France, Italy and Canada.

GDP Gross domestic product. The sum of all output produced by economic activity within a country. GNP (gross national product) and GNI (gross national income) include net income from abroad eg, rent, profits.

Household saving rate Household savings as % of disposable household income.

Import cover The number of months of imports covered by reserves ie, reserves ÷ $\frac{1}{12}$ annual imports (visibles and invisibles).

Inflation The annual rate at which prices are increasing. The most common measure and the one shown here is the increase in the consumer price index.

Internet hosts Websites and other computers that sit permanently on the internet.

Life expectancy The average length of time a baby born today can expect to live.

Literacy is defined by UNESCO as the ability to read and write a simple sentence, but definitions can vary from country to country.

Median age Divides the age distribution into two halves. Half of the population is above and half below the median age.

Money supply A measure of the "money" available to buy goods and services.

Various definitions exist. The measures shown here are based on definitions used by the IMF and may differ from measures used nationally. Narrow money (M1) consists of cash in circulation and demand deposits (bank deposits that can be withdrawn on demand). "Quasi-money" (time, savings and foreign currency deposits) is added to this to create broad money.

OECD Organisation for Economic Co-operation and Development. The "rich countries" club was established in 1961 to promote economic growth and the expansion of world trade. It is based in Paris and now has 34 members.

Official reserves The stock of gold and foreign currency held by a country to finance any calls that may be made for the settlement of foreign debt.

Opec Organisation of Petroleum Exporting Countries. Set up in 1960 and based in Vienna, Opec is mainly concerned with oil pricing and production issues. Members are: Algeria, Angola, Ecuador, Iran, Iraq, Kuwait, Libya, Nigeria, Qatar, Saudi Arabia, United Arab Emirates and Venezuela.

PPP Purchasing power parity. PPP statistics adjust for cost of living differences by replacing normal exchange rates with rates designed to equalise the prices of a standard "basket"of goods and services. These are used to obtain PPP estimates of GDP per head. PPP estimates are shown on an index, taking the United States as 100.

Real terms Figures adjusted to exclude the effect of inflation.

SDR Special drawing right. The reserve currency, introduced by the IMF in 1970, was intended to replace gold and national currencies in settling international transactions. The IMF uses SDRs for book-keeping purposes and issues them to member countries. Their value is based on a basket of the US dollar (with a weight of 44%), the euro (34%), the Japanese yen (11%) and the pound sterling (11%).

List of countries

Wherever data is available, the world rankings consider 195 countries: all those which had (in 2010) or have recently had a population of at least 1m or a GDP of at least $1bn. Here is a list of them.

	Population	GDP	GDP per head	Area '000 sq	Median age
	m, 2010	$bn, 2010	$PPP, 2010	km	yrs, 2010
Afghanistan	29.10	17.2	1,210	652	16.6
Albania	3.20	11.8	8,590	29	30.0
Algeria	35.40	162.0	8,430	2,382	26.2
Andorra	0.09	3.5	41,750[ab]	0.4	40.0
Angola	19.00	84.9	6,190	1,247	16.6
Antigua & Barbuda	0.09	1.2	20,950	0.4	30.0
Argentina	40.70	368.7	16,010	2,767	30.4
Armenia	3.10	9.4	5,460	30	32.1
Aruba	0.11	2.5	21,800[ab]	0.2	38.3
Australia	21.50	1,131.6	38,160	7,682	36.9
Austria	8.40	379.1	40,010	84	41.8
Azerbaijan	8.90	51.8	9,940	87	29.5
Bahamas	0.30	7.7	31,750	14	30.9
Bahrain	0.80	22.9	27,040	0.7	30.1
Bangladesh	164.40	100.4	1,660	144	24.2
Barbados	0.30	4.1	19,420[a]	0.4	37.5
Belarus	9.60	54.7	13,930	208	38.3
Belgium	10.70	469.4	37,630	31	41.2
Belize	0.30	1.4	6,670	23	21.8
Benin	9.20	6.6	1,590	113	17.9
Bermuda	0.07	5.8	89,240[b]	0.1	42.4
Bhutan	0.70	1.5	5,330	47	24.6
Bolivia	10.00	19.7	4,850	1,099	21.7
Bosnia	3.80	16.6	8,690	51	39.4
Botswana	2.00	14.9	13,890	581	22.9
Brazil	195.40	2,087.9	11,210	8,512	29.1
British Virgin Islands	0.03	0.9	39,110[b]	0.2	29.5
Brunei	0.40	13.0	49,940[a]	6	28.9
Bulgaria	7.50	47.7	13,930	111	41.6
Burkina Faso	16.30	8.8	1,260	274	17.1
Burundi	8.50	1.6	410	28	20.2
Cambodia	15.10	11.2	2,190	181	22.9
Cameroon	20.00	22.5	2,290	475	19.3
Canada	33.90	1,577.0	39,050	9,971	39.9
Cape Verde	0.50	1.6	3,880	4	22.8
Cayman Islands	0.05	3.2	57,050[b]	0.3	38.7
Central African Republic	4.50	2.0	790	622	19.4
Chad	11.50	7.6	1,370	1,284	17.1
Channel Islands	0.15	11.5[a]	51,930[ab]	0.2	42.6
Chile	17.10	212.7	15,780	757	32.1
China	1,354.10	5,926.6	7,600	9,561	34.5
Colombia	46.30	288.9	9,450	1,142	26.8

	Population	GDP	GDP per head	Area '000 sq	Median age
	m, 2010	$bn, 2010	$PPP, 2010	km	yrs, 2010
Congo-Brazzaville	3.80	12.0	4,250	342	19.6
Congo-Kinshasa	67.80	13.1	350	2,345	16.7
Costa Rica	4.60	35.8	11,570	51	28.4
Côte d'Ivoire	21.60	22.8	1,900	322	19.2
Croatia	4.40	60.9	19,540	57	41.5
Cuba	11.20	64.2	9,900[b]	111	38.4
Cyprus	0.90	23.1	31,090	9	34.2
Czech Republic	10.40	192.0	24,520	79	39.4
Denmark	5.50	312.0	40,160	43	40.6
Djibouti	0.90	1.0[a]	2,310[a]	23	21.4
Dominican Republic	10.20	51.8	9,350	48	25.1
Ecuador	13.80	58.0	8,030	272	25.5
Egypt	84.50	218.9	6,180	1,000	24.4
El Salvador	6.20	21.2	6,670	21	23.2
Equatorial Guinea	0.70	14.0	34,750	28	20.3
Eritrea	5.20	2.1	550	117	19.0
Estonia	1.30	19.2	20,660	45	39.7
Ethiopia	85.00	29.7	1,040	1,134	18.7
Faroe Islands	0.05	2.2[a]	30,500[ab]	1	35.6
Fiji	0.90	3.2	4,660	18	26.4
Finland	5.30	238.0	36,470	338	42.0
France	62.60	2,560.0[c]	34,120	544	39.9
French Guiana	0.23	4.5[a]	16,660[a]	90	24.3
French Polynesia	0.30	6.7	18,000[b]	3	29.1
Gabon	1.50	13.1	15,050	268	21.6
Gambia, The	1.80	0.8	1,410	11	17.8
Georgia	4.20	11.7	5,070	70	37.3
Germany	82.10	3,280.5	37,400	358	44.3
Ghana	24.30	32.3	1,640	239	20.5
Greece	11.20	301.1	28,410	132	41.4
Greenland	0.06	2.0	26,020[ab]	2,176	29.6
Guadeloupe	0.50	11.2[a]	20820[a]	2	36.8
Guam	0.20	2.8[ab]	15,000[ab]	0.5	29.2
Guatemala	14.40	41.2	4,790	109	18.9
Guinea	10.30	4.5	1,090	246	18.3
Guinea-Bissau	1.60	0.9	1,190	36	19.0
Guyana	0.80	2.2	3,430	215	23.8
Haiti	10.20	6.7	1,110	28	21.5
Honduras	7.60	15.4	3,920	112	21.0
Hong Kong	7.10	224.5	46,500	1	41.8
Hungary	10.00	128.6	20,550	93	39.8
Iceland	0.30	12.6	35,640	103	34.8
India	1,214.50	1,727.1	3,430	3,287	25.1
Indonesia	232.50	706.6	4,330	1,904	27.8
Iran	75.10	386.7	12,720	1,648	27.1
Iraq	31.50	82.2	3,560	438	18.3
Ireland	4.60	206.6	40,460	70	34.7

	Population	GDP	GDP per head	Area '000 sq	Median age
	m, 2010	$bn, 2010	$PPP, 2010	km	yrs, 2010
Israel	7.30	217.3	28,570	21	30.1
Italy	60.10	2,061.0	31,950	301	43.2
Jamaica	2.70	14.3	7,670	11	27.0
Japan	127.00	5,458.8	33,730	378	44.7
Jordan	6.50	27.6	5,750	89	20.7
Kazakhstan	15.80	149.1	12,170	2,717	29.0
Kenya	40.90	32.2	1,650	583	18.5
Kosovo	1.80	5.6	3,290[b]	11	28.7
Kuwait	3.10	124.3	38,780	18	28.2
Kyrgyzstan	5.60	4.6	2,240	199	23.8
Laos	6.40	7.3	2,550	237	21.5
Latvia	2.20	24.0	16,340	64	40.2
Lebanon	4.30	39.0	14,070	10	29.1
Lesotho	2.10	2.2	1,600	30	20.3
Liberia	4.10	1.0	420	111	18.2
Libya	6.50	71.9	16,990[a]	1,760	25.9
Lithuania	3.30	36.3	18,370	65	39.3
Luxembourg	0.50	53.3	86,120	3	38.9
Macau	0.54	28.0	63,680	0.02	37.6
Macedonia	2.00	9.2	11,160	26	35.9
Madagascar	20.10	8.7	970	587	18.2
Malawi	15.70	5.1	880	118	16.9
Malaysia	27.90	237.8	14,730	333	26.0
Maldives	0.30	1.9	8,520	0.3	24.6
Mali	13.30	9.3	1,070	1,240	16.3
Malta	0.40	8.3	26,450	0.3	39.5
Martinique	0.40	10.8[a]	22,700[a]	1	39.4
Mauritania	3.40	3.6	2,460	1,031	19.8
Mauritius	1.30	9.7	13,700	2	32.4
Mexico	110.60	1,035.9	14,560	1,973	26.6
Moldova	3.60	5.8	3,110	34	35.2
Mongolia	2.70	6.2	4,040	1,565	25.4
Montenegro	0.60	4.1	12,860	14	35.9
Morocco	32.40	90.8	4,710	447	26.3
Mozambique	23.40	9.6	940	799	17.8
Myanmar	50.50	42.0	1,950	677	28.2
Namibia	2.20	12.2	6,480	824	21.2
Nepal	29.90	15.7	1,200	147	21.4
Netherlands	16.70	779.4	42,170	42	40.7
Netherlands Antilles	0.20	4.1	20,320[b]	1	37.9
New Caledonia	0.30	8.9	35,320[b]	19	30.3
New Zealand	4.30	141.4	29,540	271	36.6
Nicaragua	5.80	6.6	2,910	130	22.1
Niger	15.90	5.5	730	1,267	15.5
Nigeria	158.30	202.5	2,400	924	18.5
North Korea	24.00	12.3	1,800[b]	121	32.9
Norway	4.90	417.5	57,230	324	38.7

	Population	GDP	GDP per head	Area '000 sq	Median age
	m, 2010	$bn, 2010	$PPP, 2010	km	yrs, 2010
Oman	2.90	57.8	26,790[a]	310	25.3
Pakistan	184.80	176.9	2,690	804	21.7
Panama	3.50	26.7	13,610	77	27.3
Papua New Guinea	6.90	9.5	2,470	463	20.4
Paraguay	6.50	18.3	5,180	407	23.1
Peru	29.50	157.1	9,540	1,285	25.6
Philippines	93.60	199.6	3,970	300	22.2
Poland	38.00	469.4	19,890	313	38.0
Portugal	10.70	228.6	25,420	89	41.0
Puerto Rico	4.00	96.3	16,300[b]	9	34.4
Qatar	1.50	127.3	88,220	11	31.6
Réunion	0.80	20.8[a]	21,090[a]	3	29.9
Romania	21.20	161.6	14,520	238	38.5
Russia	140.40	1,479.8	19,890	17,075	37.9
Rwanda	10.30	5.6	1,160	26	18.7
St Lucia	0.16	1.2	6,560[b]	0.6	27.4
Saudi Arabia	26.20	434.7	22,710	2,200	25.9
Senegal	12.90	12.9	1,940	197	17.8
Serbia	9.90	38.4	11,350	88	37.6
Sierra Leone	5.80	1.9	830	72	18.4
Singapore	4.80	208.8	57,930	0.6	37.6
Slovakia	5.40	87.3	23,300	49	36.9
Slovenia	2.00	46.9	26,930	20	41.7
Somalia	9.40	1.1	600[b]	638	17.5
South Africa	50.50	363.9	10,570	1,226	24.9
South Korea	48.50	1,014.5	29,100	99	37.9
South Sudan[d]	8.30[a]	13.2	...	644	...
Spain	45.30	1,407.4	32,230	505	40.1
Sri Lanka	20.40	49.6	5,080	66	30.7
Sudan[e]	43.20	62.0	2,260	2,506	19.7
Suriname	0.50	3.7	7,660[a]	164	27.6
Swaziland	1.20	3.7	5,950	17	19.5
Sweden	9.30	458.6	39,020	450	40.7
Switzerland	7.60	527.9	46,380	41	41.4
Syria	22.50	59.1	5,290	185	21.1
Taiwan	23.00	430.2	35,600	36	38.0
Tajikistan	7.10	5.6	2,160	143	20.4
Tanzania	45.00	22.9	1,430	945	17.5
Thailand	68.10	318.5	8,550	513	34.2
Timor-Leste	1.20	0.7	930	15	16.6
Togo	6.80	3.2	1,000	57	19.7
Trinidad & Tobago	1.30	20.6	25,740	5	30.8
Tunisia	10.40	44.3	9,550	164	28.9
Turkey	75.70	734.4	15,690	779	28.3
Turkmenistan	5.20	20.0	8,270	488	24.5
Uganda	33.80	17.0	1,270	241	15.7
Ukraine	45.40	137.9	6,720	604	39.3

	Population	GDP	GDP per head	Area	Median age
	m, 2010	$bn, 2010	$PPP, 2010	'000 sq km	yrs, 2010
United Arab Emirates	4.70	297.6	47,210	84	30.1
United Kingdom	61.90	2,261.7	35,690	243	39.8
United States	317.60	14,586.7	47,150	9,373	36.9
Uruguay	3.40	39.1	14,110	176	33.7
Uzbekistan	27.80	39.0	3,110	447	24.2
Venezuela	29.00	391.8	12,230	912	26.1
Vietnam	89.00	106.4	3,210	331	28.2
Virgin Islands (US)	0.11	1.6[ab]	14,500[ab]	0.4	38.8
West Bank and Gaza	4.40	7.3	2,900[ab]	6	18.1
Yemen	24.30	31.3	2,650	528	17.4
Zambia	13.30	16.2	1,560	753	16.7
Zimbabwe	12.60	7.5	440[b]	391	19.3
	-				
Euro area (16)	328.20	12,149.1	34,350	2,497	41.8
World	6,908.70	63,257.0	11,130	148,698	29.2

a Latest available year.
b Estimate.
c Including French Guiana, Guadeloupe, Martinique and Réunion.
d South Sudan became an independent state in July 2011.
e Data include South Sudan.

Sources

AFM Research
Airports Council International, *Worldwide Airport Traffic Report*
Art Newspaper, *The*

Bloomberg
BP, *Statistical Review of World Energy*
Business Software Alliance

CAF, *The World Giving Index*
Central Banking Publications
Central Bank Directory
Central banks
Central Intelligence Agency, *The World Factbook*
CIRFS, *International Rayon and Synthetic Fibres Committee*
Corporate Resources Group, *Quality of Living Report*

The Economist
  www.economist.com
Economist Intelligence Unit, *Cost of Living Survey; Country Forecasts; Country Reports; Democracy index; Global Outlook – Business Environment Rankings*
ERC Statistics International, *World Cigarette Report*
Euromonitor, *International Marketing Data and Statistics; European Marketing Data and Statistics*
Eurostat, *Statistics in Focus*

Facebook
Finance ministries
Food and Agriculture Organisation

The Heritage Foundation, *Index of Economic Freedom*

IFPI
IMD, *World Competitiveness Yearbook*

IMF, *International Financial Statistics; World Economic Outlook*
International Centre for Prison Studies, *World Prison Brief*
International Cocoa Organisation, *Quarterly Bulletin of Cocoa Statistics*
International Coffee Organisation
International Cotton Advisory Committee, *March Bulletin*
International Diabetes Federation, *Diabetes Atlas*
International Grains Council
International Institute for Strategic Studies, *Military Balance*
International Labour Organisation
International Rubber Study Group, *Rubber Statistical Bulletin*
International Sugar Organisation, *Statistical Bulletin*
International Telecommunication Union, *ITU Indicators*
International Union of Railways
International Wool Trade Organisation
Internet Systems Consortium
Inter-Parliamentary Union

Johnson Matthey

Knight Frank

McDonald's

National statistics offices
Nobel Foundation

OECD, *Development Assistance Committee Report; Economic Outlook; Environmental Data; Government at a Glance; Revenue Statistics*
www.olympic.org

Reporters Without Borders, *Press Freedom Index*
Reuters Thomson

Standard & Poor's *Emerging Stock Markets Factbook*
Schneider, Dr Friedrich, University of Linz
Stockholm International Peace Research Institute

Taiwan Statistical Data Book
The Times, *Atlas of the World*
Transparency International

UN, *Demographic Yearbook; Global Refugee Trends; National Accounts; State of World Population Report; Survey on Crime Trends; World Contraceptive Use; World Population Database; World Population Prospects; World Urbanisation Prospects*
UNAIDS, *Report on the Global AIDS Epidemic*

UNCTAD, *Review of Maritime Transport; World Investment Report*
UNCTAD/WTO International Trade Centre
UN Development Programme, *Human Development Report*
UNESCO, Institute for Statistics
US Census Bureau
US Department of Agriculture

Visionofhumanity.org

WHO, *Global Immunisation Data; World Health Statistics Annual*
World Bank, *Doing Business; Global Development Finance; Migration and Remittances Factbook; World Development Indicators; World Development Report*
World Bureau of Metal Statistics, *World Metal Statistics*
World Economic Forum/Harvard University, *Global Competitiveness Report*
World Resources Institute, *World Resources*
World Tourism Organisation, *Yearbook of Tourism Statistics*
World Trade Organisation, *Annual Report*